International Acclaim for *Driving Brand Value*

"If your company is ready to break down functional silos and get serious about integrating marketing and building brand equity, this book is a must read. It is packed with hands-on examples, tools and checklists. It charts the course from transactional to relationship marketing, from customer to stakeholder focus, from schizophrenic to consistent positioning, from mass to interactive media, and from full service to an integrated communication agency."

> Peje Emilsson, CEO
> *The Kreab Group of Companies*
> Stockholm, Sweden

"Tom Duncan and Sandra Moriarty have written the perfect book for the times ahead. *Driving Brand Value* is an outstanding blend of strategic insight and practical guidelines that will make us all better practitioners of integrated marketing."

> Lynn Upshaw, author
> *Building Brand Identify—A Strategy*
> *For Success In A Hostile Marketplace*

"What makes *Driving Brand Value* so good is that it works internationally. Duncan and Moriarty's 10 drivers of integrated marketing are just as applicable to multinational as to our national clients when it comes to helping them manage their brand relationships and build brand equity."

> Richard Zammit, Managing Director
> Communiqué, Brisbane, Australia

"Duncan and Moriarty's *Driving Brand Value* is a valuable asset to anyone seeking to build brands effectively and efficiently. It is based on good insights and recommends a process that makes it easy to practice the concepts presented in the book. Highly recommended!"

> R. Sridhar, Director IMC
> Ogilvy & Mather, Bombay, India

DRIVING BRAND VALUE

Using Integrated Marketing to Manage Profitable Stakeholder Relationships

TOM DUNCAN
SANDRA MORIARTY

McGraw-Hill

New York San Francisco Washington, D.C. Auckland Bogotá
Caracas Lisbon London Madrid Mexico City Milan
Montreal New Delhi San Juan Singapore
Sydney Tokyo Toronto

Library of Congress Cataloging-in-Publication Data

Author:	Duncan, Tom (Thomas R.)
Title:	Driving brand value using integrated marketing to manage profitable stakeholder relationships / Thomas R. Duncan, Sandra E. Moriarty.
Published:	New York : McGraw-Hill, 1997
Description:	p. cm.
LC Call No.:	HF5415.13.D845 1997
Dewey No.:	658.8/2721
ISBN:	0786308222
Notes:	Includes bibliographical references.
Subjects:	Brand name products—Marketing—Management.
	Brand name products—Marketing—Management—Case studies.
	Corporate image—Case studies.
Other authors:	Moriarty, Sandra E. (Sandra Ernst)
Control No.:	97001667

McGraw-Hill

A Division of The McGraw-Hill Companies

2 3 4 5 6 7 8 9 0   DOC/DOC   9 0 2 1 0 9 8 7

ISBN 0-7863-0822-2

The sponsoring editor for this book was Jeffrey Krames, the managing editor was Kevin Thornton, and the production supervisor was Suzanne W. B. Rapcavage. It was set in Times Roman by Jana Fisher through the services of Barry E. Brown (Broker—Editing, Design, and Production).

Printed and bound by R. R. Donnelley & Sons Company.

McGraw-Hill books are available at special quantity discounts to use as premiums and sales promotions, or for use in corporate training programs. For more information, please write to the Director of Special Sales, McGraw-Hill, 11 West 19th Street, New York, NY 10011. Or contact your local bookstore.

 This book is printed on recycled, acid-free paper containing a minimum of 50% recycled de-inked fiber.

*To my schoolteacher mother and to my father whose
entrepreneurial spirit made it possible for me at an
early age to learn the risks, workings, and rewards of
business.*

TD

*To my mother whose perseverance and love of
learning taught me to be curious, ask questions, and
seek new and better ways of doing things.*

SM

CONTENTS

Introduction xi

Acknowledgments xix

PART 1

OVERVIEW OF INTEGRATED MARKETING

Chapter 1

Managing the Intangible Side of Business 3

Integrated marketing: a new business model 4

A tale of two companies 6

The re-integration of marketing 8

Replacing the value chain with the value field 11

The 10 strategic drivers of brand equity 15

Chapter 2

Overcoming Barriers to Integrated Marketing 23

What needs to be integrated? 24

How integrated is your company? 26

The IM mini-audit 26

Barriers to IM 29

Companies that don't get it 29

Areas of dis-integrating relationships that IM can address 30

PART 2

IMPLEMENTING INTEGRATED MARKETING

Chapter 3

Focus on Brand Relationships 41

Leveraging brand relationships 43

The added value of relationships   45
Relationship links, ties, and bonds   46
Tracking brand relationships   48
Factors affecting lifetime customer value   50
Reminding customers of relationship benefits   52

Chapter 4

Manage Stakeholder Impact and Overlap   55

How stakeholders impact the bottom line   57
Don't overlook stakeholder overlap   60
Relationship building plan needed for each stakeholder group   62
Integrating the stakeholder value field   63
Understanding stakeholder perceptions   64

PART 3

IM PROCESSES

Chapter 5

Develop Strategic Consistency   69

Maintaining strategic consistency   70
The consistency factors   70
Managing message chaos   75
The four sources of brand messages   77
The integration triangle   90
Message impact varies by source of message   91

Chapter 6

Make Interactivity Purposeful   95

Created and intrinsic brand contact points   96
Managing brand contacts   97
Maximizing value-added interactivity   99
Leveraging interactive media   104
Leveraging addressable media   110
Role of databases in interactivity   111
Mass customization of brand messages   112

The "5 Rs" of purposeful dialogue   114
Using interactivity to create a learning organization   120
Making interactivity purposeful   123

Chapter 7

Market the Mission   126

Benefits of mission marketing   128
The corporate mission's role in IM   130
Missions with direct social responsibility   133
Importance of consolidating philanthropic activities   135
Limitations of cause marketing   137
Differences between cause and mission marketing   139
The five criteria of mission marketing   140
How to establish and manage mission marketing   145

Chapter 8

Use Zero-Based Planning Strategy   148

SWOT analysis and prioritization   149
Relationship analysis   152
Using prioritized SWOTs to determine MC mix   155
Integrating messages   158
Integrating media   161
Managing complexity   165

PART 4

IM INFRASTRUCTURE

Chapter 9

Use Cross-Functional Planning and Monitoring   169

The cross-functional brand equity team   170
Responsibilities of the cross-functional brand equity team   174

Supporting the cross-function team   180
The organizational dimensions of IM   189

Chapter 10

Create Core Competencies   192

How to create core competencies   194
Benefits of a core competency   206

Chapter 11

Make Integrated Marketing Data-Driven   208

Setting up databases   210
IM database applications   214
Database application checklist   226
Privacy issues   228
The data future   229

Chapter 12

Create a Partnership with an Integrated Communication Agency   231

Few agencies understand and practice integration   233
20 questions for doing an ICA agency search and review   234
Working with agency networks   242
The integrated communication agency (ICA) model   243
Compensating the ICA   253
Benefits and concerns of using an ICA   255

PART 5

IM EVALUATION AND AUDIT

Chapter 13

Evaluate Using Relationship Metrics and the IM Audit   261

Output and process controls   261
Relationship metrics—output controls   262
The IM Audit—a process control   264

Focus of an IM Audit   265
How to conduct an IM Audit   268
Benefits of doing an IM Audit   277
Integrating the Audit   278

INDEX   280

INTRODUCTION

Traditional marketing can no longer justify its existence. No longer can a company just make a product, price it, place it, promote it and expect to survive unless it has a cure for cancer. That's linear, inside-out thinking. As products, pricing and distribution increasingly become commodities, the new competitive arena is brand value which creates long-term, profitable brand relationships.

Technology has enabled us to move from a one-way to a two-way, interactive marketing relationship environment. (More than 50% of all capital equipment expenditures of U.S. companies is now for information technology.[1]) How companies manage their two-way interactivity (read: brand relationships) is becoming more important than products themselves. This means brand value will be determined by how well companies not only create, but retain and grow their brand relationships.

The old traditional production-based value chain needs to be replaced by the non-linear, interactive *value field*—a brand relationship environment containing many *stakeholder* groups (e.g., employees, shareholders, suppliers, the media, as well as customers), extensive brand contact points, aftermarket support, the reputation of the company, customer recourse and many other relationship-sensitive factors. And because traditional marketing departments are still focused on managing transactions, they don't know how to manage brand relationships. The result is, the marketing function has become marginalized.

After studying 100 blue chip organizations, Cooper & Lybrand recently concluded: "They [marketing departments] appear out of place in the more demanding business environment of the 1990s. There is a gap between what marketing should be and what is being done in marketing departments."

According to a recent McKinsey report: "Some marketing practices are certain to need reform. One approach is to treat marketing as a process, rather than as a department. Here the organization is not divided by function—into marketing, sales and production—but by its core processes, such as brand development and delivery system fulfillment. In the last two decades, marketing departments have generated few new ideas. True, they have helped to execute the necessary structural changes arising from developments in globalization, information and communication technology, strategic planning and organizational design. But when we look for new marketing frameworks, or for fresh approaches that will help build the long-term relationships that manufacturers most need today, the examples are few." [2]

This book presents an integrated marketing (IM) business model for developing brand value for both companies and their customers and other stakeholders. The model is both a concept and an interactive process for not only acquiring, but more importantly, for retaining and maximizing the lifetime value of brand relationships. IM is basically about how to reengineer the intangible side of business—the management of brand value and brand equity, which in many companies has a market value greater than the physical assets.

IM is based on the fact that everything a company does, and sometimes what it doesn't do, sends a message. It recognizes and responds to the fact that increasingly everyone in the organization has the potential to "touch" the customer. Every brand message, to some extent, has one of three effects: strengthens relationships by adding value, reconfirms current relationships, or weakens brand relationships by reducing brand value. The primary differences between integrated marketing and the traditional marketing concepts are

- ◆ shifting the emphasis from *acquiring* customers to *retaining* and *growing* them
- ◆ communicating *with* rather than just *to* customers and other stakeholders, and
- ◆ expanding the "marketing" responsibility beyond the marketing department (e.g., making marketing less a function and more a philosophy of doing business).

Because IM is designed to increase brand value by strengthening relationships, it can be applied to any type of business—packaged goods, services, business-to-business, retail, industrial, and nonprofits. It is a process that can also be used to manage relationships with other stakeholders besides customers—employees, shareholders, government regulators, the media, suppliers, community.

Having a process for managing brand relationships is critical because relationships are the components of brand equity. Sales and brand share are important, but they are historical measures. Although brand equity is influenced by how a brand has performed, investors are more interested in the brand's future performance—the collective net-sum support of customers and other stakeholders. In essence, brand equity is determined by the quality of a brand's relationships with its customers and other key stakeholders.

But because brand equity and brand relationships are seen as the soft or intangible side of business, companies have found it easier and more comfortable to focus on cutting costs in the tangible areas (e.g., production, distribution, sourcing, pricing), by reengineering, downsizing, and right-sizing. Although these cost cutting efforts have increased shareholder value and profitability, the questions now are: How sustainable are the results? What will be the affect on long-term relationships with customers and other stakeholders? In what ways have and will these changes affect brand value?

It is astonishing that although brand equity now accounts for the majority of many companies' market value, little is being done to strategically manage it. A major reason is that brand equity is still considered an intangible and something most people find difficult to grasp and understand.

Brand equity no longer needs to be such a mystery, however. Relationships can be measured. Lifetime customer value can be measured. We know current customers are five-to-ten times less expensive to sell to than new customers. We have the ability to economically track customers, learn their behavior, and more accurately predict how they will respond.

Also, because the cost of acquiring stakeholders, whether new customers, new employees, new distributors, or new investors has never been higher, companies need a new model for leveraging these expensive acquisitions and maximizing their relationship productivity.

As companies have gotten bigger and more departmentalized and their marketing communication agencies have gotten more specialized and more expert in what they do, customers and other stakeholders have increasingly received mixed messages about brands and companies and felt increasingly disenfranchised. Over the last decade companies and agencies thought they could end all these mixed messages and build better relationships by merely making sure their marketing communications had "one voice, one look." Unfortunately, building long-term profitable brand relationships requires much more.

One-voice, one-look integration alone has generally failed because it focuses on tactics and continues to talk to, rather than with, customers. Creating one voice, one look is a logistical challenge; creating and nourishing brand relationships is a strategic challenge, starting with how a company is organized. The responsibility for creating, retaining and growing profitable brand relationships can no longer be assigned to a single department. It is not a function. That is why IM is and must be a cross-functional process that involves all key business activities and takes into consideration all stakeholders.

Since 1990 there have been several major studies done on integrated marketing communications (IMC) which is a part of integrated marketing:

1. University of Colorado in cooperation with Advertising Age surveyed a broad range of 240 U.S. businesses

2. Northwestern University in cooperation with the American Association of Advertising Agencies surveyed a small sample of mega companies based in the U.S.

3. Helen Mitchel (now at Cranfield's School of Management) surveyed United Kingdom companies, and

4. R. Sridhar, Ogilvy & Mather Direct in Bombay, surveyed Indian companies.

All four studies came up with two consistent findings: IMC is a great idea, but only a small percent of companies are really doing it.

In analyzing these studies and working with marketing communication agencies and clients, we soon realized the reason so few companies were practicing IMC was that it could not really work unless companies made significant changes in how they were organized and what their corporate priorities were. This is because marketing communications (e.g., advertising, sales promotion, product publicity, direct marketing, packaging) play only a part—and often only a small part—in determining the quantity and quality of brand relationships. In other words, increasing the number of long-term profitable brand relationships requires more than IMC. It requires a cross-functional process that has a corporate focus, a new type of compensation system, core competencies, a database management system that tracks customer interactions, strategic consistency in all brand messages, marketing of the company's mission, and zero-based marketing planning.

Having practiced, researched, taught and consulted on this topic for years, we have learned that IMC is only the tip of the integration iceberg and what is needed is a total re-integration of marketing in order to have a cost-effective relationship building process.

The difference between IMC and IM is like the difference between cosmetics and character building. Cosmetics can make most people look better and more attractive, however, if their behavior and character are not consistent, those who have been attracted will soon end the relationships. In other words, integrating the marketing communications is futile if *contrary, more powerful messages are being sent by other actions of a company*.

IM is also broader and more encompassing than database marketing which focuses primarily on how to efficiently generate repeat business from current customers. Like IMC, however, database marketing is an essential element of IM. Because IM is more macro and inclusive than IMC, direct marketing, and even relationship marketing, IM requires top management's endorsement and commitment, an organizational structure that is truly integrated, and communication that places as much emphasis on listening to customers and other stakeholders as it does on sending messages to these groups.

In *Driving Brand Value* we present and explain ten basic drivers successful companies are using to build brand value by better managing their brand relationships. These 10 drivers, each explained in separate chapters with examples of how they can be executed, are the core of integrated marketing.

Two of the drivers relate to the corporate focus which must be on relationships and stakeholders. We explain why relationships are more important than transactions; why it's necessary to take into consideration all stakeholders rather than just focusing on customers when planning and executing marketing programs; why and how you must be strategically consistent when communicating with different stakeholder groups; and why managers must have a thorough understanding of commercial relationships. We show how to determine what customers want and do not want in a commercial relationship; how to know when your commercial relationship becomes too close and smothering; and how to measure the strength of brand relationships.

Four drivers are IM process strategies. In these chapters the four sources of brand messages are identified as a first step in controlling or influencing the information delivered at all brand contact points. The process strategies explain how to have strategic consistency that creates trust in all brand messages. These strategies also show how to develop purposeful and cost effective dialogue with customers, how to leverage the universal customer need for recognition; how to facilitate and encourage dissatisfied customers to identify themselves and express themselves to you (rather than other customers); how to create the most effective mix of mass, interactive and addressable media (IM is not about replacing mass media with one-to-one media, but rather adding one-to-one media to the media mix); and how to mass customize brand messages in order to support the mass-customization of products.

Although many companies have a mission, it is seldom used as a platform for their integrated marketing effort. Likewise, most companies are involved in many philanthropic activities but are getting little return on these efforts (most companies don't even bother to systematically evaluate these programs), a missed opportunity for increasing brand value for little or no additional investment. The mission marketing strategy shows how to turn these situations around.

The last process strategy shows how to use prioritized SWOTs to do zero-based planning which becomes the basis for profitable resource allocation. Zero-based communication planning assumes all media and marketing communication functions are of equal value. The marketing communication mix is then based on this objective analysis rather than on precedent.

The final four IM drivers are infrastructure strategies. If a company is not internally integrated, it will never be externally integrated. IM starts internally to eliminate the knowledge gaps and lost opportunities that result from functional or silo organization. The four infrastructure strategies show how to do cross-functional planning and monitoring, create core competencies in those responsible for managing IM programs, and set up and use integrated databases to ensure universal customer information and create a learning organization.

Another of the infrastructure drivers is how to find, and then work with, an integrated communication agency which will be the full service agency in the 21st century. This discussion includes 20 questions you can use when doing an agency review or searching for a new agency that really understands and really does do integrated marketing (they all say they do, but few actually deliver).

In the last part we present a list of relationship metrics—output controls— that can be used to determine the strength of your brand relationships and how they are developing over time. This chapter also explains and provides a step-by-step discussion of how to do an IM Audit which is a process control.

IM is a continuum, and the far right side is the perfectly integrated company. To our knowledge, that company doesn't exist. The point is, you can benefit from IM in stages, the more integrated your company becomes, the more benefit you will see.

To practice what we preach in this book, we look forward to your reactions and comments on the ideas we have presented. Please let us hear from you. Both of us can be reached using the following address and fax number:

Tom Duncan/Sandra Moriarty
University of Colorado
Campus Box 287
Boulder, CO 80309
Fax 303/492-0969

email: tduncan@spot.colorado.edu
           Sandra.Moriarty@Colorado.edu

ENDNOTES

1. John F. Rockart, Michael Earl, and Jeanne Ross, "Eight Imperatives for the New IT Organization," Sloan Management Review, Fall, 1996, p. 47
2. John Brady and Ian Davis, "Marketing's Mid-life Crisis," The McKinsey Quarterly, 1993, No. 2. p. 27

ACKNOWLEDGMENTS

As with most new ideas and books of this nature, many people contributed thoughts, ideas, criticisms, and suggestions. Without them, the book would never have been. We are extremely grateful to Bill Arens and Suzanne Lainson who helped research and brainstorm during the early stages of the book's development. We are also especially indebted to those who took time to read early drafts and provide extensive feedback: David Miln of Cordiant-London provided extensive feedback that often made us rethink and revise, Mark Goldstein of Fallon McElligott provided excellent examples and helped ensure we were being real-world in our ideas, Richard Zammit of Communiqué-Australia shared ideas from down under with a true Aussie sense of humor that helped keep us going, and Anders Gronstedt of University of Colorado provided many good ideas from his work and research in TQM and IMC.

We are equally indebted to John Tammaro of Texas Instruments, John Deighton of Harvard University, R. Sridhar of Ogilvy & Mather-Bombay, Joe Plummer of Audit & Surveys, Steve Howard, consultant - Singapore, Bill Foley formerly with Y&R, Peje Emilsson of Kreab-Stockholm, and Bruce Kolter of Market Vision. They generously shared rich case histories and insights.

We also appreciate the feedback and ideas from George Schweitzer of CBS, Don Schultz and Clarke Caywood of Northwestern University, Kevin Clarke of IBM, Pat Murphy of Notre Dame, Lynn Upshaw formerly EVP of Ketchum Advertising, Brett Robbs and Larry Weisberg of the University of Colorado, Loren Lindeke, consultant, and Ken Giffin of Gage Integrated Marketing. For their cooperation and enthusiasm in providing financial interpretations and encouragement along the way, we thank Cheryl Meese, Sam Kuczun, and Joe Parker.

Finally, we must thank Steve Patterson of Irwin who put the whole book deal together and to Kevin Thornton, our editor, who patiently turned final copy into what you are holding in your hand.

PART ONE

OVERVIEW OF INTEGRATED MARKETING

1

CHAPTER

Managing the Intangible Side of Business

When trains pull into some of London's tube stations, passengers hear the warning, "Mind the gap!" This is to alert them to the treacherous space between the train and the platform. This warning is also appropriate for most companies where there is a widening gap between themselves and their customers and other key stakeholders—employees, suppliers, journalists, government regulators, special interest groups, and even competitors. Similar to the London tube stops, these gaps can be killers, but in this case killers of brand relationships and eventually, brand equity.

The widening of these relationship gaps has never been greater due to the increase in mergers and acquisitions, expansion of the global marketplace, the growing competition among the various internal departments and external suppliers, the increase in more critical and demanding customers and other stakeholders, and the changing nature of what now constitutes a "product" (e.g., more service sensitive). As Alvin Toffler has written, physical assets are no longer what matters, but rather intangibles such as relationships and communication: "No one buys a share of Apple Computer or IBM stock because of the firm's material assets. What counts are not the company's buildings or machines, but the contacts [relationships] and power of its marketing and sales force, the organizational capacity of its management. . . ."[1]

INTEGRATED MARKETING: A NEW BUSINESS MODEL

How a company makes its goods or performs its primary services will not be its number one priority in the future, but rather, how it manages its stakeholder relationships that determine its brand equity. This is because brand equity—which is the value of a company beyond its physical assets used to manufacture and deliver services[2]—is often of greater value than physical assets.

In 1989 Philip Morris paid $12.9 billion for Kraft, six times its net asset value. According to then Philip Morris CEO Hamish Maxwell, his company needed a portfolio of brands that had strong brand loyalty [customer relationships] that could be leveraged to enable the tobacco company to diversify [i.e., investor, financial relationships], especially in the retail food industry [i.e., trade relationships].[3] In other words, Philip Morris was willing to pay billions for a set of relationships and the anticipated support such relationships would provide.

Another example of brand equity's value was the initial public offering in June 1996 of a 50 percent stake in Donna Karan International, popular designer of women's and men's upscale clothing and accessories. Karan is not a manufacturer (so has few physical assets) but rather, as *Barron's* magazine has explained, "an originator and purveyor of image." The 10.8 million shares opened at $24 and immediately rose to $28, generating over $250 million dollars. However, not only do shareholders own few physical assets other than inventories, they don't even own the brand name or trademark (which was retained by Karan) but merely a licensing agreement to use her name and trademark. In this case, shareholders basically paid over $250 million to rent Karan's brand equity.

In 1995 the average market value (determined by the number of outstanding shares times the share price) of all American-based publicly held companies was 70 percent greater than their replacement cost (e.g., their tangible net asset value).[4] As companies continue to outsource and downsize, and as technology increases production efficiencies, brand equity will continue to account for a larger and larger portion of market value.

Another way market value of a company is determined is by using a multiple of earnings rule-of-thumb. But the value of brand relationships can significantly alter this estimate. For example, in 1994 AT&T paid $11.5 billion for McCaw Cellular Communications even though the company had yet to show a profit. The investment was justified, however, based on future prospects of McCaw's number of subscribers, i.e., its relationships with its cable providers and customers.

Although brand equity accounts for an ever higher proportion of companies' market value, surprisingly, most companies do little to manage the stakeholder relationships that are primarily responsible for brand equity. In recent years companies have focused almost exclusively on increasing production efficiencies, decreasing time to market, adopting just-in-time delivery, decreasing their level of product defects, streamlining their accounting procedures, and increasing their distribution logistics. Many of these logistical and physical improvements have been driven by reengineering and TQM applications.

What is needed now is a management tool similar in scope and efficacy to reengineering and TQM that can be used to make improvements on the "intangible" side of business by managing the brand relationships with customers and other key stakeholders driving brand equity. That new tool is integrated marketing.

Merely placing more emphasis on traditional marketing practices is no longer the efficient way to build brands. These practices are simply too inefficient. Marketing's traditional 4-Ps, for example, have become a millstone around the necks of companies. Marketing was never meant to be just about product, pricing, place, and promotion but, rather, about creating brand relationships—long-lasting, profitable relationships. Unfortunately somewhere in the 1960s and 70s marketing was functionalized and the 4-Ps became commodities.

> **Merely placing more emphasis on traditional marketing practices is no longer the efficient way to build brands.**

It is no wonder that more and more CEOs are having doubts about the effectiveness and value of today's marketing practices. In a Cooper & Lybrand study of 100 large British companies, respondents were asked about the productivity of their three major divisions—manufacturing, administration, and marketing. It was found that the relative costs of operating the manufacturing and administration divisions had decreased over the last several decades, while those of marketing had more than doubled. And yet most respondents felt they were getting less, rather than more, from their marketing investment. There was a feeling that marketing had become "ill-focused and overindulged," and compared to the other divisions, the marketing function was "critically ill."[5]

A TALE OF TWO COMPANIES

The difference between using integrated marketing and doing business in the traditional way, where decisions are made in isolation with little regard for consequences in other areas, is illustrated in the following examples of how two companies, US West and Ukrop's, have managed their brand relationships.

Beginning in 1993, at a projected cost of $880 million, US West's reengineering initiative called for reducing costs by, among other things, consolidating 530 customer service offices in 14 states into 26 customer service, maintenance, and repair "megacenters" in 10 cities. US West was determined to cut the fat out of its operations and optimize its internal productivity. The goal was to do more with less. But by the fall of 1994, bad things were happening.[6]

When customers and prospective customers tried to call the phone company's business offices to order service or complain, they were frequently greeted with busy signals or put on hold for lengthy periods. Due to understaffing its customer service lines, US West essentially prevented many of its customers from interacting with the company. Meanwhile, the company was spending approximately $50 million a year in mass media advertising, some of which explained how several of its products could help businesses improve their customer service.[7]

As more and more customers became frustrated that they couldn't talk to their own phone company, they began calling people who would answer their phones and listen—government regulators. One state regulatory commission after another found fault with US West's customer service. In Colorado, its home state, some 2,000 people complained that they had been forced to wait for over 30 days for new telephone service. In Iowa, people accused the company of missing appointments for installation and service and complained that new orders were incorrectly provisioned and that repairs took too long.

Following an investigation by the Colorado Public Utilities Commission in 1995, US West agreed to pay what was in essence $4 million in fines as restitution for customer service problems. And following that, Arizona, like Colorado, set service standards that US West had to meet or face fines of up to $5,000 per occurrence. But months after it paid its first fine in Colorado, the company continued to miss the performance standards set by regulators and thus continued to be fined, which in turn produced more and more negative media coverage.

And US West's communication problems have not been limited to customers; other important stakeholders have been affected as well. Following the announcement in early 1996 of its $10.8 billion buyout of Continental Cablevision to form the country's largest network of cable subscribers, US West held a phone press conference. When a reporter from *Advertising Age* called in to join the press conference, he got a recorded message saying the lines were overloaded and to call back later to hear a replay of the press conference. When he called back later he still failed to get the story—what he got was another recorded message: "Due to technical difficulties . . ."[8]

Is it any wonder that analysts scoffed when the media trumpeted the news in the summer of 1996 that US West was seeking a 20 percent rate hike? Furthermore, preparing for the competitive entry of AT&T and MCI, the president of US West admitted his company would have to change in the way it was conducting its business if it was to successfully meet this new competition.[9]

How could a company, especially one that specializes in communication, find itself sending such negative brand messages? Ironically, a primary reason for wanting to streamline its business was to offer better customer service. In the end, it paid dearly. In fact, if we consider the amount of marketing dollars it wasted selling customers and potential customers on new services who couldn't even reach the company to order them, and then add up the resulting negative impact on the company's reputation and brand relationships, the total cost to US West was probably considerably greater than the $5 million plus it eventually paid in fines. It's no wonder that several top executives were fired over this affair.

In contrast, another company in the retail business, Ukrop's Food Stores, an independent grocery chain of 23 stores in Virginia, intuitively understands the importance of managing brand relationships and takes whatever steps are necessary to strengthen them.

Several years ago, the chain did a study to determine what brand messages it was sending and which of them had the greatest impact on attracting and keeping customers. It learned that one of the most critical customer contact points was the check-out counter, where customers interacted with the check-out clerks and baggers (employees sacked all the purchases). It also learned the messages being sent by these people were not as positive as they should and could be.

Like most companies, however, Ukrop's training budget was too small to really change the situation. After much discussion, it finally decided to move money from advertising into training in an effort to leverage this and other employee-customer contact points.

Ukrop's employees (referred to as "associates") were taught how to interact with customers in a more pleasant manner. They learned how to respond sincerely and accurately to frequently asked questions and how to avoid controversial subjects. When customers asked for help, the associates were instructed to respond promptly, taking personal responsibility for making sure the customers' requests were satisfied. Ukrop's has gone to great effort to ensure that employee responses are consistent, reliable, and predictable. Competing against powerful food chains such as Food Lion, Ukrop's has demonstrated an intuitive understanding of the basic principles of integrated marketing.

This training program and other customer-focused programs have produced phenomenal results for the chain. Not only does Ukrop's have a 34 percent share of its market, but even more impressive is its per-store volume, which is 50 percent higher than its nearest competitor (Ukrop's stores are similar in size to its competitors' stores).[10] Also, several competing chains spend more in advertising, stay open longer hours, and in some cases offer lower prices than Ukrop's. Moreover, the chain sells no alcoholic beverages or state lottery tickets, and is not open on Sundays so employees can spend the day with their families.

Ukrop's effort to identify the sources of brand messages that had the most impact on customer relationships and its willingness to change historical budget allocations to act on these findings is rare.

THE RE-INTEGRATION OF MARKETING

In his early writings, Peter Drucker explained that marketing involves much more than selling and should not be considered a function or specialized activity. As he pointed out, true marketing should be a companywide endeavor, a "whole business" as seen from the customer's point of view. Ukrop's success is a result of employing this integrated philosophy of marketing.

As traditional marketing has become departmentalized, it has become marginalized. Consequently it has lost sight of the company's whole business and its relationship with customers and other key stakeholders. Marketing has become a function fixated on persuading customers to buy. This transactional strategy is primarily a unilateral process that produces mass market products and distribution, supported by a broadside of brag-and-boast brand messages. The original marketing philosophy has disintegrated under the pressure for short-term results.

Simply put, marketing needs to be re-integrated—which is what integrated marketing (IM) is designed to do. Just as importantly, IM is designed for the 21st century commercial environment, taking advantage of the technologies and addressing the problems. **Integrated marketing is a cross-functional process for managing profitable brand relationships by bringing people and corporate learning together in order to maintain strategic consistency in brand communications, facilitate purposeful dialogue with customers and other stakeholders, and market a corporate mission that increases brand trust.**

The fuel that drives any relationship—personal or commercial—is communication. There is no way to have a relationship without some form of communication. For this reason, communication is the lifeblood of integrated marketing. And real communication means listening as well as speaking. The creative frontier of the 21st century will be in defining and refining purposeful two-way communication in commercial relationships.

> **Companies often forget that brands exist in stakeholders' heads and hearts, not on the sides of packages, those are simply brand names and logos.**

Companies often forget that brands exist in stakeholders' heads and hearts, not on the sides of packages, those are simply brand names and logos. In other words, although a company may own a brand name and logo, its stakeholders "own" the brand (as the old adage regarding ownership declares, "possession is nine-tenths of the law"). And these brands that live in stakeholder's heads are formed and reformed based on a "bundle" of brand messages that stakeholders automatically integrate. Therefore, companies that fail to integrate their brand messages are abdicating the message integration process to their stakeholders, a risky situation.

Inherent in the IM concept is the recognition that every department and function within a company has a communication dimension. The fact that everything a company does (and sometimes doesn't do) can send a brand message is critical to understanding the value of IM. If the product isn't conveniently available, if the price is perceived as too high, if the service is perceived as too slow or rude, the ads insulting, the promotional offer too complex or misleading, if the product fails to live up to expectations, or if the company is contacted and it doesn't respond, the result is a negative message and a diminished brand relationship. All of these situations send brand messages, each having a different impact depending on the situation. Those practicing IM also recognize that messages originating in each of these areas influence not only customers, but all stakeholders.

Because most companies are internally focused on reducing costs and operating more efficiently, they forget that their actions (as well as inactions) make statements to customers as well as to employees, investors, the media, and potential customers. As Stanford University professor Paul Watzlawick once explained, "One cannot not communicate."[11] Recognizing and respecting these communication dimensions and making an effort to manage them is the core of the IM process. This is because communication is the driver of brand relationships, as shown in the brand equity equation (Figure 1–1). The stakeholders' automatically integrated bundle of brand messages (e.g., communication) defines their relationships with the brand and that, in turn, determines to what extent they support a brand. The accumulated support of all stakeholders is what produces brand equity.

Although this book focuses on managing customer relationships, the system for doing so—integrated marketing—can and should also be used to manage relationships with other key stakeholders. IM recognizes that other key stakeholder groups can often impact profits and brand equity as much if not more than customers.

F I G U R E 1–1

The Brand Equity Equation

Communication ⟶ Brand relationships ⟶ Brand support = Brand equity

REPLACING THE VALUE CHAIN WITH THE VALUE FIELD

Because we live in a more connected world where there is greater interaction and interdependence of brand stakeholders than in the past, a *value field* metaphor is more helpful than the traditional value chain metaphor in understanding how brand relationships and brand equity are created and how best to manage them. The value chain concept is linear, describing a series of value-added, sequential steps. It shows how the supply side is linked to the demand side, moving raw materials through a series of value-added production steps, through marketing and sales, then to channel members who provide the final added-value elements for the end user. (Figure 1–2)

Because the value chain is based on an industrial economic model and takes an inside-out perspective, it literally ends when the final sale is made. It also fails to include the value-adding role of relationships and two-way communication with customers. Its linear approach works for explaining transaction-based, traditional marketing that focuses on products. It does little, however, to explain the ongoing interactions of all the important stakeholder groups that can both add and remove value.

FIGURE 1–2

Value Chain

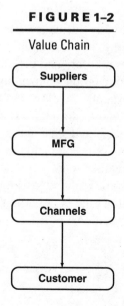

Think of what happens to a field of corn during its growth, or "production." Although the plowing and seeding are done sequentially, the cross-pollination, rain, sunshine, and release of nutrients in the ground are ongoing, with their interactivity greatly affecting the yield per acre and the quality of the corn. At the same time there are weeds and pests that can take value away if not properly controlled. Once the corn is harvested, its value is impacted by the grain warehouses, brokers, mills, processors and channel members. All of these stakeholders have ongoing, interactive relationships, the quality of which affects to what extent value is added to the end products. For example, if the relationship between a manufacturer and a major chain is weak, retail distribution and or pricing of Corn Flakes will likely suffer.

The value chain metaphor overlooks the interactive nature of all the various relationships that make up a brand's environment or what James Moore calls the ecosystem. The value field model, however, shows how brand equity is a result of a field of relationships and that adding value is a nonlinear, dynamic process with continuous, overlapping interactions, transactions, and feedback. Evert Gummesson, the Swedish guru of relationship marketing, calls this an imaginary organization.[12] In a *Harvard Business Review* article in 1993, Richard Normann and Refael Ramirez described this concept as a "value constellation." [13]

As shown in the value field illustration (Figure 1–3), a typical brand exists within a *field* of stakeholder interactions. The company may or may not be directly involved in all the interactions, and yet these interactions can greatly influence its brand relationships and brand equity. Retailers, for example, not only interact with a manufacturer's suppliers but also end users and the media (which may or may not be used to carry ads for a product depending on the relationship between the retailer and particular media vehicles). Companies communicate directly with consumers and retailers, at the same time retailers are talking with customers, and customers are discussing a brand among themselves. If a major retailer and the local media do not agree on advertising costs, a retailer may cut back on the advertising and cause certain brands not to be featured. Meanwhile suppliers as well as competitors are talking about the brand. Finally, journalists are reporting on the company and brand. All of these events happen sporadically and spontaneously.

FIGURE 1–3

Value Field

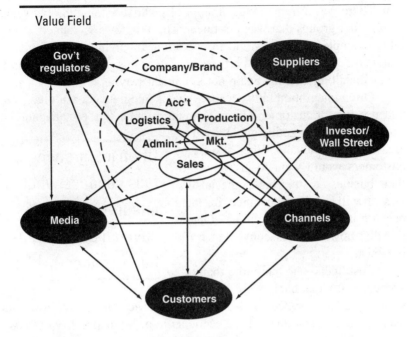

This value field model shows that the customer is receiving brand inputs from many other sources than the company. Therefore, in order to maintain customer focus, it is necessary to manage relationships with all the key stakeholders because they impact customer attitudes and behavior. The field metaphor illustrates this: It takes cross-pollination to make corn grow and flowers bloom.

An example of a well-managed value field is Saturn's. Because Saturn understands the existence and value that is generated beyond the traditional value chain, it has become a successful brand in an extremely competitive category. By managing its relationship field, Saturn has been able to do things such as its 1995 Homecoming, which attracted over 40,000 people to isolated Spring Hill, Tennessee. This was done by integrating employees, the media, its dealers, and its customers. The employees staffed the event and interacted with the customers who attended as well as the media who covered it. Dealers interacted with their customers and their local media and sponsored tie-in events. Journalists gave the event fantastic coverage. None of these stakeholder groups had to cooperate. It was almost a grass-roots operation. There was a tremendous amount of positive interaction between stakeholder groups that was not linear. The Windows 95 launch is another example of a value-field in operation, involving a global effort that included suppliers and partners as well as customers, dealers, and the media all interacting, again not in a linear way.

Often integration fails because what is integrated doesn't have an added value for customers. In an IM audit of a bank, top management said the bank's marketing goal was to increase customer loyalty. When asked why customers would want to give more of their business to this bank, the answer was, "It will be more convenient for them because it's one-stop shopping." Operationally, however, this convenience did not exist.

> **Often integration fails because what is integrated doesn't have an added value for customers.**

Customers who had more than one account with the bank were receiving separate monthly statements for each of their accounts. No effort had been made to consolidate these accounts in order to simplify the customers' ability to manage their overall finances. Bank tellers were not able to tell how many different accounts a particular customer had with the bank but only if they had a savings and/or checking account. And because the bank was organized into individual profit centers—mortgage department, investor department, trust department, regular checking account and savings department—when a customer went to one department to invest money, he or she was not informed about options in other departments, even when higher rates of return were available in these other areas.

One reason integration had not taken place at this bank was because of a corporate strategy of having service areas compete against each other. This often results because compensation is based on sales results rather than on customer satisfaction and retention. Although brand loyalty was a priority to the executives of this bank (e.g., how loyal customers were to the bank), *customer loyalty* (e.g., how loyal the bank was to customers) was not.

What makes this example interesting is that the bank was producing record profits. In other words, the weaknesses we found had not yet had a negative effect, primarily because the bank's service was no worse than its competitors'. To successfully compete in the future and sustain profits, a company must create its own future. It does this by reinventing its business and business processes to provide greater value. In the case of this bank, by integrating its operations to focus on the customer rather than using a traditional organizational structure and reward system, it could carve out a sustainable competitive advantage in a service category that has become a commodity.

THE 10 STRATEGIC DRIVERS OF BRAND VALUE

The most frequently asked questions about IM are: "How do we do it? What do we need to change? How do we overcome the many barriers to be more integrated?" Because businesses differ so much by product category and basic operations, it is impossible to have one IM formula or model that fits all. Through our research and IM audits, however, we have identified 10 strategies, or as we like to call them brand relationship drivers, that companies benefiting from IM are using. It is not necessary for all 10 drivers to be fully in place before a company can begin benefiting from IM because integration is a continuum. We have found that IM works best when it starts at the top, supported by the proper infrastructure that makes it possible to apply the IM processes. To date we have not found any one company fully using all 10 drivers although many are benefiting from being more integrated. The point is, a company can gradually move into IM. Naturally, the more drivers that are applied, the greater the benefit.

As shown in Figure 1–4, the 10 drivers divide into three categories. Two of them—creating and nourishing relationships and focusing on stakeholders—relate to corporate focus. IM must be driven from the top. This means top management must be convinced that focusing on relationships is more important than focusing on transactions; also, they must realize that stakeholders overlap and their management must be integrated. The second category includes the four process drivers—strategic consistency, purposeful interactivity, mission marketing, and zero-based planning. These operational processes run IM. The third category consists of the four organizational drivers—cross-functional management, core competencies, data-driven marketing, and working with an integrated agency. These are the organizational strategies needed to create the corporate infrastructure that must be in place to support the process drivers. When most people think about IM they

FIGURE 1–4

Drivers of Brand Relationships

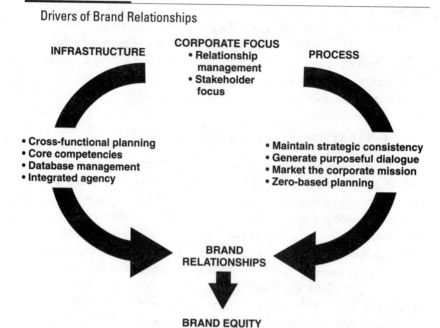

think just about processes or applications. As shown, however, only four of the 10 drivers are processes. IM is mainly about organization!

Following are brief explanations of the 10 drivers, each of which are discussed in much greater detail in Chapters 3 through 12.

- ◆ **Creating and nourishing relationships rather than just making transactions.** Because of the increasing cost of acquiring a new customer, companies are finding that putting more investment into growing current customers is a smarter way to spend marketing dollars. This assumes companies know their customers. The more companies know about their current customers, and the more they can use this information when communicating with these customers, the more credibility their communications will have and the stronger the relationships will become.

- ◆ **Focusing on stakeholders rather than just customers or shareholders.** Brand equity is determined by the number and quality of relationships that a company has, not only with customers, but with all its stakeholders. Although return on shareholder equity must always be a fundamental objective of business, there is flexibility in its timetable. As companies return to building brands and brand relationships, they are finding that gaining the support of key stakeholders in the short term generates greater long-term profits for investors.

◆ **Maintaining strategic consistency rather than independent brand messages.** Recognizing the communication dimensions of *all* brand contacts and the sources of these messages is critical because they impact positively or negatively on customers' and other stakeholders' behavior. The more the brand's position is strategically integrated into all the brand messages, the more consistent and distinct will be the company's identity and reputation. The more a big idea is emphasized, the more likely all the marketing communication efforts will have integrity.

◆ **Generating purposeful interactivity rather than just a mass media monologue:** Interactivity is itself a form of integration. A balance between mass, personalized, and interactive media is used to enrich feedback from customers, as well as reach them. The more customer feedback and dialogue is facilitated, the more integrated the customers can be into the company's planning and operations. This means doing more listening and learning and less telling and selling.

◆ **Marketing a corporate mission rather than just product claims.** The only way a genuine mission will make a positive contribution to the company is when it is integrated into everything that the company does, from planning to execution, regardless of department or program. Furthermore, even more impact is derived by integrating all philanthropic efforts into a single, major program that develops an association with the mission and energizes stakeholder commitment. In a focused mission program, a company can develop a distinct presence rather than the fragmented image that results from sponsoring a wide variety of social causes.

◆ **Using zero-based planning rather than tweaking last year's plan.** In the planning of integrated marketing communications (IMC) campaigns, the process starts with a

SWOT analysis, which takes into consideration all of the brand-relevant internal strengths and weaknesses as well as the external opportunities and threats. Once the SWOT findings are prioritized, they are leveraged or addressed by the MC functions that can do the job required most cost-effectively. Zero-based communication planning means that all communication objectives and strategies must be justified in terms of what needs to be done to better manage relationships, as opposed to simply adjusting last year's allocations and programs.

◆ **Using cross-functional rather than departmental planning and monitoring.** Organizationally, integration is about linking expertise and sharing information. Internal groups, especially sales, marketing, and customer service, must interact more frequently and more quickly, sharing their respective expertise and creating universal customer information that helps ensure customers will be treated consistently. As explained earlier, a cross-functional management process for planning and monitoring relationships provides a way to link (rather than merge) specialty departments and functions, allowing them to maintain their specialization but eliminating their isolation.

◆ **Creating core competencies rather than just communication specialization and expertise.** Marketing managers must have a basic understanding of the strengths and weaknesses of major marketing communications (MC) functions. They must objectively evaluate and respect these strengths and weaknesses and apply them in a mix that maximizes the cost-effectiveness of each function. Experts are needed to produce materials, but communication generalists are needed to plan and manage an integrated communications program.

◆ **Using an integrated agency rather than a traditional, full-service agency.** A communication management agency takes the responsibility for coordinating a brand's total communication program. Besides planning, it also handles routine executions internally, but when communication expertise is needed it has relationships with other specialist agencies who can provide it. It continues to stay in the loop and monitor the work of the specialist agencies to see that they stay focused on strategy and execute at the appropriate level of quality.

◆ **Building and managing databases to retain customers rather than just acquiring new customers.** Information is the bloodstream of integration. How customer (and other stakeholder) data are collected, organized, and shared determines whether or not an organization has a memory of its stakeholders' transactions and interactions. Without a program of building and using databases, it is difficult, if not impossible, to create personalized communication.

On occasion the comment is made that there is really nothing new about integrated marketing. Conceptually, this is correct if the origin of marketing is seen as focusing on customers. But there can be no argument about the differences in the focus of traditional marketing practices versus integrated marketing, as shown in Figure 1–5.

When companies and brands are integrated, all the pieces work together to reinforce one another. Companies that have been on the

FIGURE 1–5

Differences Between Traditional Marketing and Integrated Marketing

Focus of Traditional Marketing	*Focus of Integrated Marketing*
Transactions	Relationships
Customers	Stakeholders
Mix of MC tools	Strategic consistency in brand messages
Mass media (monologue)	Interactivity (dialogue)
Cause marketing	Mission marketing
Adjust prior year's plan	Zero-based campaign planning
Functional organization	Cross-functional organization
Specializations	Core competencies
Mass marketing	Data-driven marketing
Stable of agencies	Communication management agency

skids in the 1980s and 1990s but have turned around—Sears, IBM, GM, Jaguar, Tandy—have re-integrated their marketing efforts to a much higher level than before, moving from traditional marketing practices to IM strategies. These companies are pulling their marketing activities back together, aligning their words and deeds with their mission, and closing the gap between company and customer. A company must be willing to make such significant changes if it is to build brand relationships efficiently and effectively.

When consumers have a commercial relationship, that relationship can be with a specific brand, a company, or in many cases a combination of both. In this book, we use the term brand and company interchangeably. If your company uses a different brand name for your products than your company, then you must determine through research and listening to your customers and other stakeholders how *they* identify your products (e.g., what roles the product brand and corporate brand play in their relationships and buying decisions).

With multi-tiered branding you also want to determine how each brand is perceived and then strategically determine what the proportion of emphasis should be. Customers can have a commercial relationship with the same product, for example, on two or three levels. Take a car. The relationship with the corporate brand is primarily psychological (e.g., "I feel confident because it's a General Motors product"); with the nameplate also psychological (e.g., "My friends think I'm pretty cool driving a Pontiac Grand Prix"); while social and financial with the local dealer (e.g., "I've really gotten to know the guy that sold me my Grand Prix and as soon as the lease is up I will probably buy another from him.") The point is, what can and should each brand bring to the overall relationship and are they complementary?

Relationship building is a companywide responsibility, not just the responsibility of marketing, sales, or customer service.

Relationship building is a companywide responsibility, not just the responsibility of marketing, sales, or customer service. Integrating and coordinating efforts to build more long-lasting, profitable relationships is difficult, however, when managers and their departments are totally focused on quotas, quarterly goals, bonuses, sales, share of market, and this year's campaign. What delivers immediate sales may harm the brand image; what delivers short-term investor value may hurt employee relations and reduce customer value; and a campaign that promotes sales to "switchers" may significantly reduce the profitability of heavy brand users. This does not mean sales and share gains are not important, but rather that programs designed to make increases in these areas should first be evaluated and used with a broader perspective; e.g., their effect on long-term brand relationships.

Success in the 21st century requires a new business model built around a brand relationship-building process. This process will be revolutionary for most organizations, requiring them to walk away from some of the practices that made them successful and buy into a new way of thinking and acting. The new business environment created by the information revolution, the fragmentation of mass markets, social change, deregulation, blurring of industry lines, international competition, and technological advances have played to the strengths of small companies while wreaking havoc on rigid, large businesses that are slow to change. The lesson is that many of the old formulas no longer work—the future belongs to companies that are willing to change.

Marketing dis-integration occurs when companies fail to integrate their relationship goals with sales and share objectives. Sales and share tell how you *have* performed; the number and strength of your brand relationships indicate how you *will* perform.

E N D N O T E S

1. Alvin Toffler, *Power Shift* (New York: Bentan Books, 1990), p. 59.
2. Alexander Biel, "Converting Image into Equity," chapter in Brand *Equity and Advertising*, edited by David A. Aaker and Alexander Biel, (Hillsday, NJ: Lawrence Erlbaum Associates, 1993), p.69
3. David A. Aaker and Alexander Biel, *Brand Equity & Advertising* (Hillsday, NJ: Lawrence Erlbaum Associates, 1993), p.1.
4. Floyd Norris, "According to the Q Ration, the End is Near," *International Herald Tribune*, May 29, 1996, p. 19.
5. Jagdish Seth and Rajendra Sisodia, "Feeling the Heat," *Marketing Management* 4: 2 (Fall, 1995), p. 10.
6. Tom Williams, "US West Revamps Customer Service," *Telephony* (February 12, 1995), p. 7: Julia King, "US West's Failed

Restructuring Spells IS Overhaul," *Computerworld* (February 17, 1995), p. 6.

7. Bonn-Oh Kim, "Business Process Reengineering: Building a Cross-functional Information Architecture," *Journal of Systems Management* (December, 1994): 30-35; Tim Greene, "Service Suffers as RBOC's Retool for Deregulation," *Network World* (August 7, 1995), p. 1, 58; "US West to Pay $4 Million Fine," *Daily Camera* (February 3, 1995), p. 4C; Paula Bernier, "US West Addresses Re-engineering Snafu," *Telephony* (October 24, 1995), p. 13.

8. Bradley Johnson, "Adages," *Advertising Age*, March 4, 1996, p. 8.

9. "US West prepares for local-service competition," *The Daily Camera*, March 5, 1996, p. 7A.

10. Deborah L. Cowles, "Relationship Marketing for Transaction Marketing Firms: Viable Strategy Via 'Command Performance'," in *1994 Relationship Marketing Conference* proceedings, Jagdish Seth and ATul Parvatiyar, editors, Emory University, Atlanta, June, 1994, p. 5.

11. Paul Watzlawick, Janet Beavin Bavelas, and Don D. Jackson, *Pragmatics of Human Communication*, Norton, 1967, New York, p. 2.24.

12. Evert Gummesson, *Relationsmarknadsforing*: Fran 4P till 30 R, Malmo; Liber-Hermods, Sweden, 1995.

13. Richard Normann and Rafael Ramirez, "From Value Chain to Value Constellation: Designing Interactive Strategy, *Harvard Business Review*, July-August, 1993, p. 66.

2

CHAPTER

Overcoming Barriers to Integrated Marketing

As Bill Murphy, president of Meredith Direct, has observed, "I don't get what the 'mystery' of integration is all about. To me it's the most basic and straightforward approach you could ever take. It's a very logical thing. Somehow, somewhere in the 60s and 70s everything got separated. Now, someone has to bring it back together." Bringing things back together—departments, stakeholders, and the company's mission—is what we mean by re-integration.

Integration means unity of effort—unity of purpose, unity of process, unity of goal, and unity of action. Integration means interacting with active and potential customers, consumers, investors, and other important stakeholders in a consistent manner regardless of venue. When an organization becomes more integrated, its interactions become more consistent, its reputation more distinct, and its stakeholders more trustful. In essence, it has greater integrity. Integration produces integrity because an organization that is seen as a whole rather than as a collection of disparate, autonomous functions is perceived as being more sound and trustworthy, and these are important prerequisites for sustainable relationships. Re-integration is how companies get back on track after finding themselves going off in all directions.

TQM and reengineering are two other business practices that bring things together. Integration is a constant theme in TQM because quality programs depend upon a unity of effort. One of the basic steps in TQM is breaking down barriers between departments. Another key practice is to integrate the quality-improvement processes through team efforts at all levels.[1]

Reengineering creates integrated systems and processes to reduce red tape and redundant procedures. Although reengineering authors seldom mention marketing or integrated marketing, they do say that the only way a cross-functional program (which is what integrated marketing is) can work efficiently is to look beyond functional departments to processes. Likewise, TQM only works when it is approached as a cross-functional process. The point is, IM uses some of the same basic concepts that have been successfully used in reengineering and TQM.

Like quality, integration is a continuum as well as a process. Just as every product has some level of quality, every company is integrated to some degree. But most are only partway there, not fully benefiting from IM's impact on creating and nourishing relationships. The secret is to understand not only the processes of integration, but the areas to be integrated.

WHAT NEEDS TO BE INTEGRATED?

The original concept of marketing was integration—all efforts were focused on meeting the customer's needs. In a sense, integrated marketing merely means returning to marketing's roots, but in an entirely new marketplace situation. In this complex environment, there are six areas in most companies that can be better integrated:

1. **Employees.** Integration links the expertise within the organization's various departments. People whose activities impact on each other should be in contact. Some take this to mean that all departments must become one, or that all experts must become generalists. This, of course, is ridiculous. These areas of expertise need to be preserved but also linked. Areas of expertise should not be allowed to function in isolation and compete against each other. This can be accomplished by involving them in the brand-building/ growing/planning process and monitoring the brand relationships. Once relationship objectives, strategies and programs have been agreed upon (e.g., the planning stage), they can be taken back to every department and integrated

into the individual department's operations and programs. Through ongoing monitoring, the corporate cross-functional team charged with managing brand relationships must determine what changes in brand messages need to be executed by each department.

2. **Customers and other stakeholders.** Customers and other key stakeholders need to be integrated into the total operations of the company. As speed and flexibility increase in manufacturing, so too must communication between a company and its stakeholders. One way to achieve this is to have frequent, in-depth interactions with customers and stakeholders in order to detect more quickly their changing wants, needs, and concerns. The more feedback and dialogue that is facilitated, the more integrated the customers and stakeholders will be in the company's planning and operations. As a company moves to more customized marketing, it needs the support of more customized communication.

3. **Corporate learning.** As companies expand their databases, buy more outside data enhancement services, and become more sophisticated in tracking interactions, transactions, and the behavior of customers, this information needs to be integrated into a meaningful form—knowledge—and made available to everyone who can use it to increase customer service or add value to the brand in some way.

4. **Brand positioning.** Because customers and potential customers form their opinions of a brand based on a variety of brand messages (not just marketing communication messages), the brand position must be integrated in all brand contact points where it is reasonable to do so. The more a brand's position is integrated into all the messages originating from all message sources, the more consistent and distinct will be the company's identity and reputation.

5. **Big creative idea.** As companies have become larger and able to afford more marketing communication expertise, both internally and externally, IMC brand messages have become diffused as each MC specialty group comes up with its own great ideas. A brand needs to have one big creative idea and then ensure that it is integrated into all IMC messages. This

requires working with marketing communication agencies that understand integrated marketing and value a good idea above their own egos.

6. **Corporate mission.** A company that has a real mission based on a set of corporate values can maximize the impact of the mission by integrating it into everything it does. Stakeholders are impressed with corporate integrity, but only if they are convinced it exists. An easy first step in this direction is to combine all philanthropic efforts into a single, major program that reinforces the company's mission and creates greater awareness of the company's social investment.

HOW INTEGRATED IS YOUR COMPANY? THE IM MINI-AUDIT

Because all companies are integrated to some extent, we have developed an IM audit that helps determine which areas companies need to focus on to become more integrated. Because the complete audit is quite complex and takes a research team anywhere from six to eight weeks to complete, we have developed an IM mini-audit which we use in workshops and seminars.[2] (The full audit is explained in Chapter 13.) Although greatly simplified, the 20 questions in the IM mini-audit provide executives with a rough idea where their organizations stand on the integration scale.

One of the most helpful applications of this IM mini-audit is when a group of executives from the same company complete it and then compare their answers. Seldom is there a consensus, which prompts some interesting and useful discussions. To get a quick idea to what extent your own company is practicing IM, circle the number in the mini-audit (next page) that best describes how your organization operates for each of the statements (one is "Never do" and five is "Always do"). If a question does not apply to your organization, leave it blank. When you are done, add up your scores and divide by the number of questions you answered.

If your company scored 4.0 or higher, it is well above average. We have administered this IM mini-audit to over 1,500 marketing and business executives around the world. The average score is 2.8, with little variation relative to the type of business, whether it is located in North America, Europe, or Asia. The only variations have been in time. In the early 1990s, the average was 2.6, and it has moved over the years to 2.8.

INTEGRATED MARKETING MINI-AUDIT

ORGANIZATIONAL INFRASTRUCTURE   NEVER   ALWAYS

1. In our company, the process of managing brand/company reputation and building stakeholder relationships is a cross-functional responsibility which includes departments besides marketing, such as production, operations, finance, human resources, etc.

   1   2   3   4   5

2. The people managing our communication programs have a good understanding of the strengths and weaknesses of *all* major marketing communication tools, such as direct response, PR, sales promotion, advertising, and packaging.   1   2   3   4   5

3. We do a good job of internal marketing, informing all areas of the organization about our objectives and marketing programs.

   1   2   3   4   5

4. Our major communication agencies have at least monthly contact with each other regarding our communication programs and activities.   1   2   3   4   5

INTERACTIVITY   NEVER   ALWAYS

5. Our media plan is a strategic balance between mass media and one-to-one media.   1   2   3   4   5

6. Special programs are in place to facilitate customer inquiries and complaints.   1   2   3   4   5

7. In our databases we capture customer inquiries, complaints, compliments, offers, and sales behavior (e.g., trial, repeat, frequency of purchase).   1   2   3   4   5

8. Our customer databases are easily accessible (internally) and user friendly.   1   2   3   4   5

MISSION MARKETING   NEVER   ALWAYS

9. Our organization's mission is a key consideration in our communication planning.   1   2   3   4   5

10. Our mission provides an additional reason for customers and other key stakeholders to believe our messages and support our company.   1   2   3   4   5

11. Our corporate philanthropic efforts are concentrated in one specific area or program.   1   2   3   4   5

Integrated Audit Mini-Audit Concluded

STRATEGIC CONSISTENCY   NEVER   ALWAYS

12. We periodically review all our planned messages (e.g., advertising, sales promotion, PR, packaging, direct marketing, events) to determine the level of strategic positioning consistency.

                                         1   2   3   4   5

13. Our current big idea is conceptually broad enough to allow for compatible subcampaigns aimed at all key stakeholder groups.

                                         1   2   3   4   5

14. We think carefully about the messages being sent by our pricing, distribution, product performance, service operations, and others beyond the control of the company.   1   2   3   4   5

PLANNING AND EVALUATING   NEVER   ALWAYS

15. A SWOT analysis is used to determine the strengths and opportunities we can leverage, and the weaknesses and threats we need to address, in our marketing communication planning.

                                         1   2   3   4   5

16. We use a zero-based approach in marketing communication planning.   1   2   3   4   5

17. When doing annual marketing communication planning, first priority is given to fully utilizing intrinsic brand contact points before investing in creating new brand contact points.   1   2   3   4   5

18. Our company uses some type of tracking study to evaluate the strength of our relationships with customers and other key stakeholder groups.   1   2   3   4   5

19. Our marketing strategies maximize the unique strengths of the various marketing communications tools.   1   2   3   4   5

20. The overall objective of our marketing communication program is to create and nourish profitable relationships with customers and other stakeholders by strategically controlling or influencing all messages sent to these groups and encouraging purposeful dialogue with them.   1   2   3   4   5

             Score _____

BARRIERS TO INTEGRATED MARKETING

Every CEO and marketing manager we know wants communication and relationship-building efforts integrated. Why then, are so many companies still dis-integrated? Following are the most frequently encountered reasons and situations that prevent integration.

- Ego and turf battles between individuals and departments.
- Compensation and reward systems that feed egos and fertilize turf battles.
- Lack of a corporate discipline to put the customer first (as in the ability to pass up a sale when it is in the best interest of the customer).
- Absence of databases and accompanying technology to track and profile customers and other key stakeholders.
- Lack of an internal communication system (e.g., groupware) to facilitate cross-functional planning that could maximize the use of databases when they do exist.
- Lack of a core competency in marketing communications among those responsible for managing marketing and sales.
- Lack of understanding among departments of the relative and changing importance of stakeholders.
- Lack of agreement on marketing and marketing communication objectives.
- Overdependence on mass media and a misunderstanding of how best to use one-to-one media.
- Suboptimization of functional areas without regard to the overall good of the organization in building and sustaining customer relationships.

Companies that Don't Get it

An example of the negative effects of turf battles was provided by a general manager of a leading U.S. advertising agency that got an assignment from the promotion department of one of its major clients. One of the stipulations the promotion manager placed on the agency was that it could not, under any circumstances, mention the assignment to the client brand group. It was made clear that if the brand group learned of the project, the assignment would be taken to another agency. The explanation for the secrecy was the ego and turf battles that plagued the client organization.

An example of the organizational problems that can create disintegrated marketing comes from an international greeting card company. In this company, as in many, brand management is separate from marketing services, and as a consequence the marketing service managers are seldom involved in the marketing planning or even in setting marketing communication objectives. Typical procedure is for the brand group to send down a memo requesting the execution of a particular ad, promotional piece, or sell-in kit, such as "a direct mail piece, two colors, with a 25 cent coupon, quantity: 50,000." Seldom is there an explanation of who the target is, when or where the mailing will be used, or anything else to guide the creative work. When the brand group is asked for more detail, marketing services people are told they don't have to worry about anything else—just do the piece or else the brand manager will take it to an outside agency.

AREAS OF DIS-INTEGRATING RELATIONSHIPS THAT IM CAN ADDRESS

The efficiency and effectiveness of brand communications cannot withstand the effects of confusion, contradiction, and inconsistency that are characteristic of marketing dis-integration. Ten years after writing *In Search of Excellence*, Tom Peters found that many of the companies he cited as being excellent no longer were and observed that sales and service have become two of the "most neglected elements" in organizations.[3]

As companies increase their production abilities to achieve mass customization, sales and marketing are not prepared to handle the increased quantity of information and communication needed to support this customization. Consequently companies often do not leverage what could be significant brand advantages because they are not capable of customizing (that is, personalizing) their communica-

> As companies increase their production abilities to achieve mass customization, sales and marketing are not prepared to handle the increased quantity of information and communication needed to support this customization.

tions.[4] By incorporating new communication technology, such as group-ware systems and database-driven contacts, IM offers a process for managing these communication challenges. Information overload can be turned into a manageable, competitive advantage.

Most companies continue to use the marketing practices that made them successful, failing to comprehend that both the marketplace and the marketing tools have changed. IM, however, leverages the new marketing tools to address the causes of dis-integrating relationships (which exist both externally and internally). The more these red flags of dis-integration are recognized and understood, the easier it is to develop an IM program that will create stronger brand equity and more enduring relationships. Following is a list of some of the specific causes of dis-integration that IM is designed to address and cure. (Further explanations and examples as to how IM addresses and cures these causes appear in the following chapters.)

> **Most companies continue to use the marketing practices that made them successful, failing to comprehend that both the marketplace and the marketing tools have changed.**

- ◆ **IM takes the emphasis off promotions that have conditioned many customers to buy on price.** A study more than 15 years ago found that top managers were frustrated with the increasing costs of marketing communications and were further frustrated by their marketing departments' lack of innovation and inability to find more efficient ways to communicate with customers.[5] The result of this frustration has been a shift in marketing spending away from brand building to sales promotion. Too often, sales and brand share increases have been the result of sales promotion steroids. The short-term increases have been good, but at what cost to the health of the brand?
- ◆ **IM helps counter the effects of brand and product proliferation.** There are too many products, too many brands, and too many commercial messages for most people to sort out. And these are increasing, not decreasing. Production

efficiencies, driven by technology, enable companies to offer
more choices which, in turn, diminish brand loyalty. Although
the heart of branding is developing relationships, research
indicates that these relationships, as manifested in brand
loyalty, have been declining. It's not just that brands are
getting weaker, but that the menu of acceptable choices has
expanded dramatically in most categories. Therefore, as brand
loyalty continues to decrease, the relationship between
customer and the brand becomes thinner and weaker.

◆ **IM helps create a competitive advantage in product
categories that have become commoditized.** One of the
reasons for product proliferation is that most companies are
able to match competitive product, pricing, and distribution
improvements in a matter of months. Toothpaste, for
example, has 671 stock keeping unit (SKUs) and 107 brands.
New products and new line formulations have shorter and
shorter periods of differentiation, and this truncated
competitive advantage means products move quickly to the
highly competitive maturity stage of their life cycle.

This does not mean product differences are no longer
important, but rather, they cannot be sustained; they function
more like the ante that allows a company to enter the game.
Sustained differentiation now must come from the soft side of
business—superior customer service, useful information, and
a commitment to shared values. IBM, for example, lost its
competitive advantage as other computer companies entered
the market with comparably engineered, lower priced, and
easier-to-use PC products. "We were simply selling iron in a
world that wanted help," says George Conrades, head of IBM
sales and marketing from 1988 to 1992.[6]

It's harder to maintain competitive advantage, but it is
even more difficult to grow new products. Many consumer
companies are struggling to replicate their historical successes
which isn't easy given global competition and all the other
changes in the marketplace. In the packaged-goods industry,
for instance, which is normally thought to house much of the
industry's marketing talent, developing competitive new
products has become largely ineffectual.

- **IM decreases brand switching.** In earlier days, when loyalty to a single brand was common, one of the things that motivated customers to stay loyal was the risk of "going to a new brand"—the risk of the unknown. Today, this risk no longer exists because products are so similar. This means that as the tangible side of business increasingly becomes ground zero for competitive advantage, the intangible side—effective communication that leads to brand relationships—becomes the critical brand-defining factor that provides sustainable differentiation.

- **IM provides a way to link the additional groups involved in "marketing."** Customers no longer depend just on ads or sales representatives to learn about brands and a company; they have many sources of information. As communication technology improves and expands, brand information is more easily and more quickly shared among customers—the Pentium chip problem spread worldwide in a matter of days over the Internet. Business customers demand to talk to others in the company, not just the salesperson. Consumers now relate more to their local retailers than they do to the faceless producers of their favorite brands. The sources of marketing information are diffused and, in many cases, beyond the direct control of the marketer.

- **IM provides a strategy for minimizing negative stories in the media.** Increasingly, what businesses do—open or close plants, give their CEOs a million-dollar raise or fire them, inappropriately use pension funds, or announce record earnings—appears on the evening news, or next morning's newspaper, or next week's news magazine. Stories about business and brands are no longer restricted to the business pages. In fact, business activities and products are increasingly fodder for stand-up comedians.

- **IM leverages the technology that produces new brand contact points.** The expanding installation of fiber optics and the telecommunication convergence of television/computers/telephone/cable will provide a virtually infinite number of "channels." It will operate much as phones do today, allowing us to dial up almost any person, company, or database in the world. Computer users will be able to connect with any other on-line user, any available database, any company that is on-line, and any commercial on-line information system.

♦ **IM helps customers deal with commercial message overload.** Unfortunately, the majority of people in developed countries have grown up in a commercial message cocoon, having been inundated with brand messages since the day they were born. Take television—the average person watches four hours a day and is exposed to 42,000 TV commercials every year, even with zipping and zapping. Add to this radio commercials, ads in newspapers and magazines, ads on packages, billboards, and all the direct mail we receive everyday. Then there are all the commercial messages a person sees when shopping—the in-store promotional signage and merchandising in discount, food, specialty, department, and drug stores, as well as the messages delivered at sporting and other events, including symphonies and operas, where it is not unusual to see a shiny luxury car on display in the auditorium's chandeliered lobby. In addition to consumer commercial messages, those in business and industry also receive an *additional* bundle of business-to-business messages. The result is that many consumers have developed psychological commercial message fire walls that block most brand messages.

♦ **IM makes customers less resistant to commercial information.** It's tougher each year to get customers of both business and consumer products to watch and listen to commercials and to read ads. As Coca-Cola's former director of marketing, Peter Sealey, said when he introduced Coke's new creative strategy in 1993, "Customers no longer have to watch commercials anymore, they must want to." Customers have learned how to psychologically screen out most commercial messages and they now have devices to help keep them from being exposed to these messages. Consumers can buy "agent" software that, when a commercial pod (a group of commercials in a commercial break) appears, will automatically change to the viewer's next favorite channel, only returning to the primary channel at the end of the "intrusive" commercial pod.[7]

◆ **IM recognizes that mass media advertising appeal continues to decline.** Advertising, which has been the standard bearer for building brand image, is liked less and less, at least in the United States.[8] One of the criticisms Europeans level at American advertising is that while its best creative work is wonderful, they feel that most of it insults the customer. Consequently, people brag about not watching commercials and use the remote control like a sword, cutting off ads in mid-air. And when they do watch but don't like the message, they are more likely not to like the product as well. One way advertising creates brand equity is through association; e.g., place a car sitting in front of an elegant mansion or swanky country club, and the car takes on the status of the mansion or club. When advertising is disliked, the same association principle is at work for liking of the brand.

◆ **IM provides a cure for companies that have become overly departmentalized.** As a result of years of "command and control" management, most organizations today consist of highly separated departments and divisions, each being assigned a certain function in the overall process. As companies grow, the problem of integration worsens because departments are further subdivided in order to maintain accountability and control.

Consider marketing, for example. The original concept of brand management was to integrate and coordinate all selling efforts, but the opposite—dis-integration—has happened. First sales and marketing failed to work together, then marketing subdivided into brand/product group and marketing services. To make things even worse, marketing services, especially in larger companies, further subdivided into specialty areas such as sales promotion, advertising, packaging, marketing, public relations, direct response, and event sponsorship. Each of these functional areas is served by separate, external agencies.

◆ **IM helps prevent the negative effects of suboptimization.** Each new division brings increased competition for budget, staff, and recognition. More importantly, each division creates suboptimization, with divisions and departments having less and less accountability for the big picture. As Peter M. Senge, author of *The Fifth Discipline*, explains: "functional divisions grow into fiefdoms, and what was once a convenient division of labor mutates into the 'stove-pipes' that all but cut off contact between functions. The result: analysis of the most important problems in a company, the com-plex issues that cross functional lines, becomes a perilous or non-existent exercise."[9] Traditional organizational structures sup-porting command and control management systems, and all that shapes these—compensation schemes, hiring policies, performance analyses—are major obstacles to integration.

◆ **IM helps keep expertise from becoming a two-edged sword.** Suboptimization of the various corporate functions means an increase in expertise, which is the good news. The bad news is that by becoming extremely proficient in their respective areas, departments optimize their processes at the expense of the overall corporate good. Although a principle of TQM is specialization, a higher TQM principle is optimization of the whole.

We are not arguing against expertise, merely pointing out that specialization can become counterproductive unless it is integrated into accomplishing the larger, cross-functional objective of creating and nourishing relationships. As functional specialists develop expertise, they each have their own strategies on how to build the brand. Although many can contribute in the search for positioning and the big idea, in the end there must be only one strategy if the brand is to remain cohesive. Expertise is a desired corporate asset at the execution level; at the strategic level of relationship building, however, compromise and flexibility are required. For example, as Montblanc learned in the 1980s, merely because distribution of a luxury item can be increased via mass merchandisers or convenience stores, these new distribution points can send messages that contradict the brand's position.

◆ **IM compensation systems discourage rather than encourage disingegration.** Since most organizations tie compensation to responsibility, and since more responsibility is generally determined by the size of a person's budget and staff, managers wind up building empires in order to increase their salaries and bonuses. In other words, the motivation for building departments is not to more effectively grow and nourish stakeholder relationships, but to increase the size of budget and staff—the edifice complex.

Turf battles are a natural outgrowth of a combination of specialization and the traditional competition for budget and staff. Since departments must justify annual budget and staff requests, if a department doesn't use its full budget or keep all its people busy, it will suffer in the next budget allocation. In other words, the reward structure is designed to build fiefdoms and empires rather than to foster integration, which requires that departments be willing to transfer dollars and staff to other departments when it is determined to be best for building relationships and brand equity. Several studies have confirmed that turf battles and egos are the main barriers to integration.

- **IM processes apply to local as well as to global brands.** More and more companies, even small ones, are moving into international marketing. If they aren't actually marketing outside their own country, then they face competition from foreign companies trying to enter their markets. The challenge of maintaining a consistent brand image is further complicated by the difficulties of multinational marketing management.
- **Finally, IM provides a way for companies who have integrity to get greater benefit from it.** There is growing public distrust of the business community. High CEO salaries, along side massive layoffs, product failures, and poor service, have led customers and other stakeholders to be wary of business practices. Many feel the *only* objective of business is to make a profit, regardless of how this affects customers, employees, and the environment. When a company has a mission that goes beyond just making a profit, however— such as Merck's, which is "preserving and improving human life"—employees and other stakeholders have an additional reason to support the company. (Integrity and integration are both derived from the same Latin root.)

In this day of multiple stakeholder influences and interactions, managing relationships using traditional marketing strategies and processes is like trying to herd cats—an impossibility.

Overspecialization, departmentalization, and turf battles are all signs that an organization has dis-integrated; each function doing its own thing. In most organizations, internal conflicts, uncoordinated thinking, and isolated program execution are greater barriers to success than the company's leading competitor. These are the hidden competitors, and when unchecked, they can cause marketing programs to underperform or completely fail.

E N D N O T E S

1. Anders Gronstedt, "Integrated Communications at America's Leading TQM Corporations," doctoral dissertation, University of Wisconsin-Madison, 1994, p. 24; Robert Haavind and the Editors of *Electronic Business, The Road to the Baldridge Award* (Boston: Butterworth-Heinemann, 1992), p. x.

2. This audit has become a major part of the University of Colorado's graduate program in IMC as students spend their spring semester auditing major companies.

3. Tom Peters, *Thriving on Chaos: Handbook for a Management Revolution* (New York: Harper & Row, 1988), p. 426.

4. Frank Cespedes, *Concurrent Marketing* (Boston: HBS Press, 1995), p. xv.

5. Fred Webster Jr. "Top Management's Concerns About Marketing Issues for the 1980s," *Journal of Marketing* 45 (Summer, 1981), p. 9–16.

6. Ira Singer, "The Few, The True, The Blue," *Business Week* (May 30, 1994), p. 125.

7. Watts Wacker, "Cultural Schizophrenia," presentation to National Demographics & Lifestyle Summit '94, Denver, Colorado, July, 1994.

8. Esther Thorson, "Likability: 10 Years of Academic Research," ARF Copy Research Workshop, New York, 1991; Rance Crain, "Agencies: Get With the Program," *Advertising Age* (May 3, 1993), p. 29.

9. Peter M. Senge, *The Fifth Discipline*, (New York: Doubleday Currency, 1990), p. 24.

PART TWO

IMPLEMENTING INTEGRATED MARKETING

3

CHAPTER

Focus on Brand Relationships

The unit of value in business today and the coming years is no longer products but relationships. A company with a warehouse full of products is not nearly as rich as a company with a database full of profitable customers, prospects, and other supporting stakeholders.

Most companies, however, focus on transactions, not relationships, chasing the business equivalent of one-night stands. In a survey of business marketers it was found that only a third of the responding companies were using relationship-building strategies. A high churn rate, for example, generally indicates a company is selling on price rather than brand value. By definition, a high churn rate means low customer retention. This does not mean a company should do everything it can to keep every customer, however, because some are significantly more profitable than others.

Baxter International, a $9 billion health care products and services company, found that one reason for its profitability was that 80 percent of its incremental sales was coming from current customers with whom it has a relationship. Baxter negotiates risk-sharing partnerships with hospitals and health maintenance organizations to set cost targets for supplies and share the savings—or the additional costs, if expenses overshoot targets.

Baxter brings in consultants to streamline distribution and works with hospitals to standardize instruments and bandages used for given procedures. It even delivers products to the site of the operation. Baxter's executive vice president Kim Cleland states in *Advertising Age* (February 27, 1995, p. 10), "This goes beyond loyalty; you are sharing a common P&L. You both can make money by bringing costs down." Participants in Baxter's ValueLink inventory management program cede ownership and management of inventory to Baxter, which will deliver supplies direct to hospital floors and departments. Baxter has even taken over the task of cleaning and sterilizing equipment, freeing hospital staff to care for patients. At some hospitals, Baxter employees are on site 24 hours a day.[1]

The primary benefit of focusing on relationships is increasing retention and optimizing *lifetime customer value* (LTCV). And just as you will find that it is more economical to retain a customer than to acquire a new one, the same is true for most other stakeholders, especially shareholders and employees. The objective of focusing on retention, of course, is to build loyalty. But companies must be realistic in what constitutes loyalty: Because of brand proliferation and brand parity, a company is doing well if it receives over 30 percent of the purchases made by heavy users in its product category.

Garth Hallberg studied Market Research Corporation of America (MRCA) panel data, which track food and drug purchases (e.g., packaged goods), and found that a brand's average share of its heavy users' buying is only about 20 percent. This means heavy brand users have a relatively large menu of brands from which they routinely choose. The brand with the highest share-of-customer in this particular study was Butterball turkeys, which still only had a 48 percent share-of-customer. It was found that heavy fast-food users buy from 2.9 chains and heavy credit-card users spread their buying over 6.2 cards. Most disturbing, customers who were totally loyal were, on the average, low-frequency buyers and therefore low-profit customers.[2]

As this study shows, most companies are still losing a large percentage of their customers' buying to competitors. In the automotive field, for example, Bain and Company has found that over 55 percent of new car buyers don't buy the same nameplate they are replacing. Saturn, however, only loses 45 percent and Infiniti 30 percent because both of these car companies put much more emphasis on relationship building. One reason most companies lose customers is that they perceive their level of customer satisfaction to be far higher than what it really is (similar to how parents perceive their child's IQ and athletic abilities).

These and other similar findings dramatize the need to redefine brand loyalty. It no longer means, especially for profitable customers, that you get 100 percent of their business. In most business categories, a margin optimization analysis will show that spending to get 100 percent of a customer's business is not profitable because it is nearly impossible to do. Acquiring a customer merely means getting on their menu of "okay to buy." Retaining a customer means staying on that menu. Growing a customer means increasing your share of his or her spending.

There have been many estimates of the cost differential of acquiring versus retaining a customer. Most of these have been based on the cost of selling to a customer for the first time versus the cost of making a repeat sale. The cost of making the first sale is generally considered to be 5 to 10 times more than the cost of making additional sales. Sears, however, estimates the difference is 20 times more—$100 to acquire and $5 to sell to again.[3] The businesses with the best handle on this are direct-marketing companies where it is easiest to measure cost-per-sale (CPS). In most direct-marketing programs, a customer isn't profitable until the third time he or she buys. Focusing on current customers, then, is a critical way to reduce average cost per sale.

These calculations don't take into consideration the fact that an acquisition investment is lost when a customer is lost. Another cost of losing a customer who has a bad experience with a brand is the subsequent negative word of mouth. It is not unusual for unhappy customers to tell at least 10 others of their dissatisfaction.[4] If and when the Internet becomes a standard household communication tool, this number will skyrocket into the thousands.

> When a strong brand relationship is formed there are other benefits for your company than repeat sales.

LEVERAGING BRAND RELATIONSHIPS

But thinking of relationships only in terms of repeat sales is still transactional thinking. When a strong brand relationship is formed there are more benefits for your company than repeat sales. It has been found, for example, that profits per customer increase with customer longevity (read: relationship) because the longer customers are with a company the more willing they are to pay premium prices.

An analysis of MRCA panel data found that "loyal" packaged-goods customers generally pay 7 to 10 percent more than nonloyal customers.[5] In addition, loyal customers make more referrals and demand less service because they know how the company's system works, and their annual buying tends to increase over time.[6] And finally, and often most important, because current customers are known in many product categories, they can be reached with individualized media, thus reducing the selling cost.

Barry Blau & Partners, a direct-response company, reports that over a 5-year period the cumulative profit for a 5-year loyal customer is about 7.5 times the first year's profit.[7] Robert Reichheld of Bain & Company found that a 20-year bank customer is worth 85 percent more in profits than is a 10-year customer. He also found that a 4 percent decrease in the customer defection rate can boost profits by 25 to 95 percent.[8]

A study of 83 grocery chains found that the top 10 percent of customers using electronic membership cards spend double what those customers in the next-best decile spend, and that the "top 30 percent of shopping-card holders account for approximately 75 percent of the store's total sales, versus only 2 percent for the bottom 30 percent."[9]

Benefits of a good brand relationship accrue both to the company and the customer. Table 3–1 depicts these benefits.

T A B L E 3-1

Value of Loyalty

To Company	To Customer
Buys more per year	Reduces risk
Less costly to sell to	Simplifies choices
Less costly to service	Saves search time
Willing to pay higher prices	More efficient transactions
Provides valuable feedback	Eliminates switching costs (finding, screening, setting up new systems)
Makes referrals	Minimizes cost of educating suppliers
Convenient test pool	Recognized by company

The value of referrals was discovered by an English company, Direct Line Insurance, which depended heavily on insurance brokers who sold on commission. Cost savings were achieved after the company did customer research and found that 50 percent of its new business was coming from referrals. With this information, marketing began to put more effort on motivating current customers to recommend others and therefore was able to bypass the brokers. The company now has a 30 percent share of the U.K. insurance market.[10]

THE ADDED VALUE OF RELATIONSHIPS

Avon is an example of a company whose brand differentiation was built on relationships, but which failed to consistently manage the relationships with its dealer network, the basis for its differentiation. Avon's success was founded on a network of housewives going door-to-door selling cosmetics to friends and neighbors, a strategy of relationship building that it has used since 1886. But in the 1980s, when more women were working outside the home, Avon was reaching fewer customers and profits began to slip. In a cost-cutting move it eliminated many of the sales incentives, such as awards and trips, that it had used for years to motivate its sales representatives to build these one-on-one relationships.

It also laid off 600 employees. Nevertheless, United States profits were off 10 percent in the first quarter of fiscal 1993, 7 percent in the second quarter, 36 percent in the third quarter, and 29 percent in the fourth quarter.[11] The cost-cutting moves turned out to be short-sighted. In November 1993 a new CEO, Christina Gold, was appointed. One of her first moves was to rebuild the relationships with Avon's channel members—the Avon ladies. She reinstated giving birthday presents, anniversary plates, and annual pins to the sales representatives, and morale improved immediately. Her number one priority, she said, was to re-integrate the company and the sales representatives—to rebuild Avon's relationships with its sales representatives as well as with its former customer base. The results speak for themselves. In just three years, the company's stock price increased 148 percent and its earnings were up 41 percent over 1993.

Another example of the positive results of focusing on relationships rather than transactions is the success of the Edward D. Jones brokerage company. Jones is the Wal-Mart of brokerage houses, concentrating on smaller, out-of-the way towns. Jones closely monitors its salespeople to make sure they are sending messages that create trust among customers and potential customers. To this end salespeople are continually reminded that they are selling mostly to people who are not familiar with the stock market and therefore should steer customers away from risky investments. It also has a system to identify and check when accounts show excessive trading, to make sure customers aren't being motivated by buy and sell unwisely to generate commissions. And, most importantly, it has designed its compensation system to encourage its brokers to put the interests of their customers first, sales second.[12] The company's success did not come from focusing exclusively on existing customers, but instead it built its business on a strategy of acquiring customers for the long term and providing them with the services they need to stay loyal.

The result is that Jones' customers hold their funds for nearly three times the industry average. Today the company has over 3,350 offices and has watched its revenue nearly triple in the last five years, despite having a "meager advertising budget." Although Jones' rate of growth has leveled off as the big brokerage houses have begun moving into the smaller markets, the company is beginning to expand into larger markets with its successful customer relationship strategy.

Compare this to the types of messages Prudential Securities (formerly Prudential-Bache Securities) used in building (or destroying) many of its relationships. In 1994 it was forced to pay $1.4 billion to settle state and federal securities fraud charges that it supplied its brokers with misleading promotional literature. According to a *New York Times* investigation, one of the primary reasons for the misleading promotional material was the company's culture, which emphasized transactions—short-term sales—over long-term relationships with customers. Unlike Edward D. Jones, Prudential Securities had "utter disregard for the ultimate harm it might do to the customer."[13]

RELATIONSHIP LINKS, TIES, AND BONDS

Before brand relationships can be managed, the nature of a commercial relationship must be understood. Commercial relationships are not the same as personal relationships. By recognizing how and why commercial relationships are formed and maintained, you can better focus your relationship-building efforts, zeroing in on those areas that need strengthening and leveraging those that are already strong.

One aspect of brand relationships is how customers are linked to your brand. *Social* links are one of the oldest and most commonly used ways of building a business relationship, predominantly in business-to-business dealings and retail services where there is a lot of personal interaction and the transactions are relatively large, such as brokerage and legal services. *Psychological* links are often the main connectors between consumers and packaged goods. These are most common where the brand image or personality provides a lifestyle association, satisfies a status need, or helps customers express themselves in some desirable way.

Financial relationships are those that provide economic services and rewards, such as frequent buyer/user programs. In banking, the more accounts and services a customer uses with one bank, the longer that customer will stay with that bank. Such things as direct paycheck deposits and automatic payment of utility bills are financial links, as are normal checking and savings accounts. The more links, the higher the switching costs.

Structural relationships are those where there is a physical connection, such as EDI (electronic data interchange). Some communication agencies, for example, have set up computer on-line links between their offices and their clients.

Although some links are obviously more suited to some businesses than others, all possibilities should be considered in developing your relationship strategies. The more links a company has with a customer, the stronger the relationship, and the more opportunity for dialogue.

Another way to analyze relationships is by looking at how customers, potential customers, and other stakeholders perceive your company. Recent years have seen much discussion and analysis, especially in business schools, on relationship marketing. Although most of these analyses have focused more on business customers and distribution channel members, the relationship "constructs" that have been identified can be used to help measure almost all brand relationships, regardless of type of product or customer. The constructs that have most often been found to define a strong brand relationship are:

- **Trust.** Does it do what it says it will do? Do products and employees have integrity?
- **Consistency.** Is product performance and service predictable? Are company policies and procedures consistent?
- **Accessibility.** Is it easy to reach the company?
- **Responsiveness.** Are questions, inquiries and complaints quickly and thoroughly handled?

- ◆ **Commitment.** To what extent is the company really interested in customers?
- ◆ **Affinity.** Do customers identify with this brand or company? Do they relate to other people who use it?
- ◆ **Liking.** Do stakeholders like to be associated with this company/ brand? Do they like the things it does and stands for?

Cross and Smith's hierarchy of bonding levels also provide a set of constructs that are important in relationship-building programs[14]. He proposes a hierarchy that starts with awareness, where most advertising objectives focus, and ends with advocacy, where your customers (and other stakeholders) speak on your behalf with testimonies about the effectiveness or quality of your product or brand.

Cross and Smith's Five Levels of Bonding

- ◆ **Awareness.** Brand is included on customer's menu.
- ◆ **Identity.** Customers proudly display the brand.
- ◆ **Relationship.** Customers communicate with company between purchases.
- ◆ **Community.** Customers talk to each other.
- ◆ **Advocacy.** Customers recommend to others.

These levels, when analyzed in terms of the relationship characteristics on which they are built (trust, consistency, etc.), provide insight into the relationship-building process. From a strategic standpoint, over time, if relationships are being built and properly strengthened, the percentage of customers that fall into the *relationship, community,* and *advocacy* levels should increase.

TRACKING BRAND RELATIONSHIPS

Brand relationships vary by product category as the number of brand contacts and transactions in each product category vary by frequency, dollar size, complexity, and degree of personal interaction. The extent to which relationship building is profitable depends on the cost of collecting customer information, the cost of analyzing and using the information, the return on using database-driven programs that track customers and other stakeholders, and the cost of personalizing brand messages. Relationship modeling is based on tracking transactions and all other forms of customer interaction and responses to company/brand experiences.

Most relationship models are based on business-to-business operations because individual customer data from orders, shipping, and billing already exist; there is more personal contact between company and customers where additional customer data can be collected; the average annual sales volume can justify customer tracking; and the average business account is relatively more important. However, there are many consumer product categories, especially services, where customer data already exist and can be used to customize communications. The following outline breaks down product categories in terms of their ease in tracking relationship information.

Easy-to-Track Relationships

Companies that have or can get consumer profiles and can easily track business:

> Financial institutions: banks, brokers, insurance.
> Monopolies: public utilities.
> Contractual services: club memberships, trash removal, lawn care.
> Personalized services: doctor, dentist, lawyer, hair care, car repair.
> Large ticket goods: real estate, cars.
> Retail stores with their own charge cards: department and specialty stores.
> Rental agencies: video, car, hotel, sporting equipment.
> Direct response companies: mail order, telemarketing, on-line services.
> Business-to-business companies.

Difficult-to-Track Relationships

Companies that must make a special effort to profile consumers and track business:

> Manufacturers of packaged goods and consumer durables.
> Retail stores: food, drug, discount.
> Retail services: restaurants, movie theaters, dry cleaners.

For consumer products and retail businesses, where capturing customer data is not intrinsic to the transactions, such data can be collected in other ways. For consumer products, manufacturers can buy customer information from retailers who have set up customer tracking systems or take it off warranty cards. Manufacturers of consumer products can also create affinity clubs and develop promotional offers that require customer names, addresses, and whatever other information is helpful in profiling and qualifying these customers.

With consumer products, the number one priority for building relationships should be with a company's primary customers—channel members. As for end users of packaged goods, information gathering can only be cost justified when a company like Kraft has a variety of complementary products which can be integrated and promoted to identifiable customer segments, affinity groups, or high usage purchasers. For many consumer goods manufacturers it makes more economic sense to support retailer efforts to track their customers and then use this input to support that retailer's merchandising strategies.

FACTORS AFFECTING LIFETIME CUSTOMER VALUE

The most important reason to track customers, besides being able to have a purposeful dialogue with them, is to determine their life-time value to the company. Various software programs have been developed to do this based on the type of product category and the cost associated with servicing customers. Basically, LTCV is determined by multiplying the average length of time a customer stays with a brand times that customer's average annual contribution to profit, minus the cost of maintaining the relationship. Finally, the LTCV estimate should be discounted based on the current cost of money to represent net present value. A worldwide luxury hotel chain has estimated that its average LTCV is $175,000. A men's retail store that has done this analysis came up with a LTCV of $100,000.

> The most important reason to track customers, besides being able to have a purposeful dialogue with them, is to determine their lifetime value to the company.

Many companies do not measure lifetime customer value because it is complicated. Part of the problem is accounting systems that don't accurately reflect the true costs of poor service, lost business, and the value of cash flow over the lifetime of a client relationship. Marketers naively tend to think that if a transaction is handled badly, the cost is simply the loss of a single sale rather than a potential lifetime series of transactions. Other costs that are difficult to determine include the cascading impact that one dissatisfied customer can have through negative word-of-mouth testimonials. Opportunity costs—the lost revenue that comes from a missed opportunity—is a huge problem in planning and evaluating relationship strategies.

To determine which relationships are profitable, you must also consider that different customers provide different types of support. For example, one customer could be a strong brand advocate and be responsible for bringing the company new customers, even though that customer's sales level might not be very high. Also, the largest customers are not necessarily the most profitable because they often use their size to bargain for the lowest prices. Also, as communication agencies well know, the larger the volume the more a customer will demand extras in service. In analyzing customer profitability, however, it should be kept in mind that both high-volume/low-margin customers and low-volume, infrequent customers make a contribution to overhead. On a pro forma the profit margin might be 7 percent, but the overhead contribution 10 percent. The problem is that these behaviors cannot be determined and quantified unless such customer actions are tracked and recorded.

Another consideration in segmenting customers is that today's break-even customers might become tomorrow's high-volume customers as their businesses grows. During IBM's glory days, the company was reputed to not want to talk to potential customers who could not afford to spend over $40,000 on computer ware. When competition forced IBM to look for new revenue steams, it found that many of those it once rejected were now high-volume customers of its competitors who had been willing to help the small companies grow.

Not only do most companies not estimate lifetime customer value, they don't have a proper balance of acquisition and retention programs. A survey conducted by *DIRECT* magazine found that marketers are more likely to use their direct marketing budgets, which are based on individualized media and messages, to gain new customers rather than retain current ones.[15]

REMINDING CUSTOMERS OF RELATIONSHIP BENEFITS

There are a number of benefits to a customer for being brand loyal, even when they are being loyal to several different companies at once. Loyalty reduces the risks encountered when switching to a new brand (or even returning to a brand formerly used, as it may have changed in the interim). It also simplifies choice since the customer is familiar with the company's offerings and doesn't have to learn new model numbers and such. Staying with a brand eliminates switching costs—that is, learning about a new company or product: how to make returns, who to call to solve various problems. The more relationship links and bonds in place, the higher the cost of switching. These three benefits result in the loyal customer being more efficient in his or her buying, which can save both time and aggravation.

In addition to efficiency, there is a psychological comfort in association and familiarity. The added value of a relationship to a customer is recognition. Recognition of a brand, or being recognized by a brand representative, improves self-esteem. Most customers want to be recognized on the basis of their relationship history—a long-time, brand loyal customer is insulted when a clerk treats him or her as a newcomer. Investment in a well-known and well-liked brand also means some of the brand's aura may rub off on customers as well. If you like the brand you are using, why gamble on trying a new one and risk disappointment? Likewise, the need for affiliation is deeply rooted and it applies to commercial situations as well as personal relationships. Saturn cultivates this feeling as it builds a special relationship involving the car, the owner, the company, and its employees.

The benefits we have been discussing are customer focused; however, they also apply to other stakeholders. The higher the level of employee loyalty, for example, the less likely they are to leave. The higher the commitment of the financial community, the less likely people are to churn their investments. According to studies by Bain and Co., investors are the most fickled stakeholder group, turning investments over 50 percent a year.[16] A relationship program with investors, then, will try to extend the relationship by creating a sense of commitment. And with the commitment will come a willingness to invest on the basis of the long-term health of the company rather than short-term profits. Loyalty benefits, in other words, apply to all relationships; well-managed communication programs uncover these feelings and address them.

Because these benefits can be taken for granted, a company should periodically remind customers of the benefits produced by their loyalty. Most companies, however, do a poor job of reminding customers of these benefits. As mentioned earlier, most planned messages are designed to acquire new customers rather than retain old ones. As part of customer retention, a certain portion of planned messages should be designed to recognize loyal customers, reward them, and show them how they are saving by staying loyal even if they are paying slightly higher prices. The Marlboro Country Store, for example, is a frequent purchase program that is a constant reminder of the advantage of staying loyal as well as a way of reinforcing the brand's positioning and image.

A successful brand is nothing more than a successful relationship, according to Regis McKenna, author of *Relationship Marketing.* He makes a direct link between integrated marketing and managing relationships: "The marketer must be an integrator, both internally—synthesizing technological capability with market needs—and externally, bringing the customer into the company as a participant in the development and adaptation of goods and services."[17]

A relationship strategy, by definition, involves more than transactions. It calls for coordinated planning in order to make the long-term engagement mutually beneficial. But before you can plot a relationship strategy, it is important that you understand the diversity of stakeholders whose interests must be addressed strategically.

ENDNOTES

1. Rahul Jacob, "Why Some Customers Are More Equal Than Others," *Fortune,* September 19, 1994, pp. 215-224.

2. Garth Hallberg, *All Consumers Are Not Created Equal* (New York: John Wiley & Sons, 1995), pp. 56-57.

3. Jock Bickert, President of Looking Glass, "A Look as We Leap Into the Mid-1990s: Databases, Brand, and Common Realities," National Direct Marketing Institute for Professors, Sponsored by the DMED, San Francisco, March 20, 1996.

4. Bickert, op. cit.

5. Hallberg, p. 50.

6. Frederick F. Reichheld, "Loyalty-Based Management," presentation to NDL Summer '94, Denver, Colorado, July 1994.

7. Kenneth Wylie, "Database Development Shows Strong Growth as Shops Gain 16.9% in U.S.," *Advertising Age*, July 12, 1993, p. S-8.

8. William H. Davidow and Michael S. Malone, *The Virtual Corporation* (New York: Edward Burlingame Books/Harper Business, 1992), p. 153; Kim Cleland, "Few Wed Marketing Communications," *Advertising Age*, February 27, 1995, p.10.

9. Arthur Middleton Hughes, "The Real Truth About Supermarkets—and Customers," *DM News,* October 3, 1994, p. 40.

10. Michael Green, President of Direct Marketing Research Association, presentation to National Direct Marketing Institute for Professors, sponsored by the DMEF, San Francisco, March 20, 1996.

11. Suein L. Hwang, "Updating Avon Means Respecting History Without Repeating It," *The Wall Street Journal,* April 4, 1993, p. A4.

12. Greg Burns, "Can It Play Out of Peoria?," *Business Week*, August 7, 1995, p. 58.

13. Kurt Eichenwalk, *Serpent on the Rock*, book excerpt published in *Sales and Marketing Management,* September 1995, p. 83.

14. Richard H. Cross and Janet Smith, *Customer Bonding: Pathway to Lasting Customer Loyalty* (Lincolnwood, IL: NTC, 1995), pp. 54-55.

15. "What's in store? *DIRECT's* second annual reader survey tracks where marketers are putting their money. Database development is a top priority," *DIRECT* 4.:12 (December 1992), p. 26.

16. Frederick F. Reichheld, "Loyalty Based Management," presentation to National Demographics and Lifestyle Summit '94, Denver, Colorado, July 21, 1994.

17. Regis McKenna, *Relationship Marketing* (Reading, Mass.: Addison-Wesley, 1991), pp. 4-5.

4

CHAPTER

Manage Stakeholder Impact and Overlap

IM should not be limited to managing relationships with customers but used for planning and monitoring relationships with all stakeholder groups. By definition, all of your stakeholders have a vested interest in the success of your company. What your company does affects them, and what they do affects your company. The broader and deeper the support of your stakeholders, the greater your stakeholder capital and thus the greater your brand equity.

What marketing managers often forget is that profitability is a result of the actions of all stakeholders, not just customers. This is because each of the key stakeholder groups—employees, investors, suppliers, resellers, distributors, financial analysts, the media, the community (which for some companies is transnational or even global), special interest groups, and regulators (e.g., government)—can *affect* profitability just as much, if not more, than customers. Just as brand share is the result of your brand's customer franchise, brand equity is the result of your company's *stakeholder franchise*. The marketing department, therefore, must be willing to work with other areas of the company and even be willing to give up budget when resources can be better spent to address a problem or leverage an opportunity with a stakeholder group besides customers (and, of course, the reverse is also true).

There are two basic ways to affect profitability: increase revenues and decrease costs. Sales revenue and stock prices (in the case of public companies) can either increase or decrease depending on the efforts, attitudes, and ideas of various stakeholders. Likewise, costs can either increase or decrease depending on the *same factors*. In other words, a broad range of stakeholders impact costs, as well as revenue—and thus profitability.

Often overlooked is the fact that all stakeholders, not just customers, choose to what extent they provide or withhold support for your brand or company. People, especially those that are skilled, have a choice where they work; investors have a wide choice of investment opportunities; and customers have a choice as to what to buy and where to buy it. In other words, most people *choose* to be stakeholders. And when they do so, that automatically gives them the right and opportunity to *understand* and *influence* what your company does and doesn't do.

The benefits of having a multiple stakeholder focus has been proven by Kotter and Hesket. They found that companies that emphasized three groups—customers, employees, and shareholders—significantly outperformed those that only focused on one or two of these groups. Looking at an 11-year period, they found that companies that focused on all three groups had revenue increases of 682% versus 166% for the groups with a more limited stakeholder focus. In addition, the multi-stakeholder focused companies saw their stock appreciate 901% versus only 91% for the other companies. An internal analysis of the multi-focused companies found a value system that communicated the importance of all three stakeholder groups integrated into their total operations. Employees in these companies described it as corporate integrity and "doing the right thing."[1]

The importance of a stakeholder group other than customers is illustrated by Coke chairman Roberto Goizueta's involvement with financial analysts. To most corporate executives, financial analysts are a group to be feared. Goizueta pours over every word analysts write about the company.[2] He frequently writes letters back, blasting analysts who denigrate Coke's stock. His letters pick apart their calculations and gloat when their forecasts don't bear out. It's an intimidating approach, but it has earned him the respect of the industry and the assurance that analysts treat stories about Coca-Cola very carefully.

HOW STAKEHOLDERS IMPACT THE BOTTOM LINE

How and to what extent stakeholders support your brand depends on your company's relationships and interactions with them. Stakeholder support and cooperation also depends upon communication. In some cases, stakeholder support is proactive—such as buying your company's products—and in others it is reactive—such as choosing whether or not to complain or interfere with what your company wants to do. Following are examples of the different ways in which different stakeholders can provide or withhold brand support.

- ◆ **Investors** can choose to sell their stock, hold on to it, or buy more—each decision affecting the price of the company's stock.
- ◆ **Financial analysts** can choose to be either bearish or bullish, advising clients to either buy, sell, or hold a company's stock.
- ◆ **Standard and Poors** can raise or lower its financial rating of a company which will increase or decrease its cost of financing expansions, acquisitions, or any other venture. The **financial press** can extol a company's performance or criticize it.
- ◆ **Suppliers** can support a brand by bringing new ideas to it before taking them to competitors, by making extra efforts to meet product specifications and delivery schedules, and, in times of product allocation, by making sure the brand receives at least its share of support if not more. Ironically, the number one thing most companies squeeze their suppliers on is price. Although cost control is important, with everyone squeezing suppliers on price, the resulting benefit seldom provides a competitive advantage. Where companies can get a competitive advantage is getting their suppliers' best thinking on improving products and processes. One significant idea from a supplier can be worth many times more than the few pennies squeezed from each order. The Japanese discovered the power of supplier relationships long ago. *Keiretsu* is the term applied to the relationships among business-to-business companies. During the last several decades, much of Japanese businesses' marketing success has been due to their stakeholder synergies and integration culture.

- **Customer** support goes beyond just buying a brand. Customers can refer the brand to others, not be overly demanding of service and unwarranted repairs, and remain loyal even when a product or service experience has been problematic. Club Med, for example, has done surveys showing that as many as two-thirds of its first timers signed up because friends or relatives recommended that they do so. When a good dialogue has been established with customers, they will also provide insights that will produce new, creative ideas for products and services.

- **Employee** support can vary greatly depending on morale and commitment to the brand/company. When fuel prices skyrocketed in the 1970s, employees at Southwest Airlines voluntarily took a pay cut so the airline could remain operating in the black—it is the only American airline to never have had a red-ink year. Employees can choose to strike or continue working while a settlement is being negotiated.

- **Government regulators** can support a company's plans by permitting or denying it the right to introduce new products, expand distribution, increase prices (in a controlled product/service category), and change ingredients. Regulators also affect the bottom line by providing input and time to correct problems and meet requirements (e.g., regulations can be interpreted very tightly or very loosely depending on a government agency's or inspector's predisposition toward a company).

- **Competitors** can also impact on a company's bottom line through partnerships and joint ventures, as Apple and IBM have discovered in teaming up to produce a personal computer that can read both platforms. Even Japanese competitors come together in industry conglomerates to compete against outsiders and in international markets.

- **Media** can not only choose which positive and negative stories to run about a company, but also the extent each type of story is featured. They can contact a company's spokesperson as an expert resource or someone to be challenged and discredited. Other stakeholders who read these stories are likely to be influenced accordingly.

We often find little or no consensus among managers on the relative importance of the company's various groups of stakeholders. In an IM audit of a health care facility, all executives were asked to rank stakeholders in order of importance to the organization (not to their individual department). The public affairs/public relations managers ranked political leaders third although this stakeholder group was ranked ninth by all other executives. Patients and families were ranked third overall, but eighth by senior management. When a "communication network" analysis was made it was discovered, not surprisingly, that there were few discussions of target audiences and communication objectives for each of these stakeholder groups. Although total agreement may be too much to expect, it would be an improvement if the managers at least understood each other's strategic needs.

Although each department's focus must be on the stakeholders for whom it is responsible, all departments must keep in perspective the overall corporate stakeholder priorities. Otherwise, counterproductive messages can be sent. In one company, for example, it was found that 24 percent of all print messages were not targeted to any of the high-priority stakeholder groups, and only 1 percent was directed to the target audience rated most important overall.

The relative importance of each stakeholder group depends on a variety of factors. In highly regulated product categories such as drugs and alcohol, the support of government agencies will be more important. If a company is publicly owned, the investment community and financial media will be more important. If mass rather than niche distribution is being used, channel members may be more important. Finally, the larger a company is, the more likely it is to attract both media and special interest group attention.

Stakeholder support will also change over time, depending on the situation. For example, in a crisis, the most important stakeholder group

> **Although each department's focus must be on the stakeholders for whom it is responsible, all departments must keep in perspective the overall corporate stakeholder priorities.**

may be the media. During a stock offering or merger of a public company, the most important stakeholder group may be the financial community. During a restructuring, the most important group may be employees who need to be kept informed to minimize negative rumors that can lower morale and productivity. Because integrated marketing is a cross-functional process, it provides a mechanism that allows your company's communication efforts to automatically change, regardless of prior budget allocations, to deal with these new situations.

DON'T OVERLOOK STAKEHOLDER OVERLAP

A major reason for using integrated marketing is stakeholder overlap, as shown in Figure 4–1. An employee can be a shareholder, a local government official, and a neighbor to your plant or office, as well as a customer. For example, we found in an IM audit of a bank that over three-fourths of its employees were shareholders and over 90 percent were customers of the bank. This type of overlap is a serious problem for companies going through reengineering. If shareholders are told that the value of their stock is rising and they should rejoice, how does that square with the message received by the employee who is also a shareholder but who fears downsizing and job cutbacks? Interestingly, over

FIGURE 4–1

Stakeholder Overlap

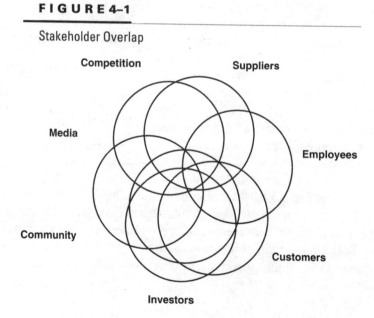

40% of U.S. pension funds are invested in the employees' own company. Depending on what proportion of the outstanding shares this represents, employees can increasingly influence board room decisions.

An example of what can happen when messages to overlapping stakeholders aren't integrated is illustrated by a women's retailer that did significant business in the professional women's market. The chain decided to reposition its merchandise line and feature more youthful styles. Some of the store's customers were fashion writers and financial analysts (representatives of two of this chain's critical stakeholder groups) who quickly found the new offerings inconsistent with the chain's normal offerings and their needs. The journalists wrote negative stories and the analysts began talking in the financial community about what appeared to them to be a wrongheaded strategy. The result was a significant drop in share price at a time when the stock market was rising.

Although the day-to-day job of managing stakeholders is generally assigned to different departments or individuals within a company, the planning and monitoring of interactions and transactions with all of them must be integrated. Without integration it is unlikely the various departments will take into consideration what other departments are doing and saying even though they may be talking to the same people. Also, if the various departments' objectives and strategies aren't integrated, the brand positioning can become inconsistent. Finally, the expectations created by one department may not be delivered by another which is either unaware of the promise or doesn't agree with it.

A situation at Ford in Europe demonstrates what can happen when marketing, the advertising agency and the PR department don't work together. A photo of Ford-Europe employees had been taken originally to celebrate ethnic and cultural diversity. This photo was later manipulated by changing all the black and Asian faces to white for an ad scheduled to run in Poland, where there are few dark skinned people. In defending the manipulation, one marketing professional (not with Ford) said, "It was the wrong decision in political-correctness terms, but a right one in marketing terms."[3]

Although the consumer group in Poland may have had no problems with the ad, the employee stakeholders, particularly those pictured in the photo, found the ad to be a negative message of exploitation and insensitivity. Not only did the company risk insulting all employees of color, but the story, including both the original and retouched pictures, received wide exposure in the mass media. It would have been far less costly to simply shoot a new picture for the Polish ad.

The decision to retouch the photo illustrates the rock and the hard place faced by management every day. The dilemma is resolved through a relationship sensitivity and a core values perspective. What Ford and the marketing pro defending the action didn't realize is that there can no longer be a gap between marketing strategy and other stakeholder relations. In an integrated marketing program, the focus shifts to targeting all key stakeholders sensitively, be they employees, neighbors, investors, or customers.

RELATIONSHIP BUILDING PLAN NEEDED FOR EACH STAKEHOLDER GROUP

As companies more closely integrate their business operations with the operations of their suppliers (including marketing communication agencies), their distributors, and their customers, the question becomes not whether to form relationships but how those relationships should be managed. Unless a company has a recorded history of its interactions with its partners, however, it will be less efficient in its dealings with them. As employee turnover and transfers occur, promises, guarantees, programs, and schedules get lost unless there's a process for the long-term management of these points of interaction. Developing a strategy of retaining relationship history information is the first step in having a stakeholder focus.

As organizations become increasingly and systemically locked into an efficient working relationship with suppliers, distributors, and customers, the nature of the marketing function will inevitably have to change to take into consideration these other relationships. Although there are certain types of support that a company needs from each stakeholder group, few of the departments responsible for these relationships now develop formal relationship strategies. Most departments do not have a stated set of objectives and strategies detailing how to most efficiently strengthen these relationships and maximize the support the company will receive from each stakeholder group.

In an integrated program, each stakeholder group is tracked and profiled in the same way the company profiles customers, target audiences, or customer segments. Then the overlaps are plotted and analyzed. This profiling can be extended by considering the "sphere of influence" of each group. Suppliers, for example, work with industry associations and other buying groups. The media, in particular, are important because they potentially reach customers, employees, shareholders, and all other stakeholders.

Then the stakeholder groups (and key individuals within them) are prioritized based on their impact on profit (both short- and long-term) and the cost to reach them and influence or control their behavior. Objectives and strategies are set with a plan for each that incorporates the company's overall objectives and positioning strategy, as well as objectives and strategies specific to each function and stakeholder group. Both one-way messages and two-way communication systems are designed and executed, their impact measured, and corrections agreed upon to better improve communication in order to achieve the support objectives.

Weighing the importance of each stakeholder group and estimating its impact on the company is an important strategic decision. During the last two decades many public companies have focused their efforts solely on investors and creating shareholder value. When this is the only objective, it often leads to short-term planning. Companies are beginning to realize that investors have been given too much emphasis in corporate planning.[4] Just as the overuse of sales promotion has conditioned consumers to shop on price, the corporate emphasis on quarterly profits has conditioned many investors to buy and sell based on quarterly returns.

Although analysts have found that 50 percent of stock is turned by fund managers every year, Warren Buffet's successful Berkshire Hathaway investment firm's philosophy has been to invest for the long term. Its performance has received much attention, outperforming most of the investment houses that are driven by quarterly profits. More and more investment fund managers have evidence that shows that moving money around quarter by quarter and chasing short-term profit produces lower returns in the long term.[5]

INTEGRATING THE STAKEHOLDER VALUE FIELD

Integrated marketing is important in managing stakeholder relationships because of the overlap and interaction between and among stakeholders in the value field. Unlike in decades past, when each stakeholder group was only involved in one or two parts of the value stream, today they are increasingly involved in the way the product or service is designed, assembled, promoted, and delivered.

Stakeholder groups are offering, asking, and in some cases demanding to be involved in planning, production, and the distribution processes. This integration is taking place. The question is, how well is it being managed? Integrated marketing recognizes this increased level of involvement, encourages it, and provides a structure for managing it as well as a philosophy that provides this relationship-building process with a sense of direction.

An example of integrating a relationship within the value field is IBM's licensing of its operating system to competitors and software manufacturers. By making it easier for these other companies to work with DOS, the IBM platform soon came to dominate the marketplace. Customers valued DOS-based systems because there was more hardware and software support for their computers. In contrast, Apple waited until 1996 to license its operating system to Motorola in an attempt to gain greater worldwide acceptance of its operating platform. Motorola is not only one of the first companies to win the right to "clone" the Macintosh; the agreement also means that other manufacturers that buy Motorola boards and systems can make machines running Mac software without having to negotiate individual agreements with Apple. One of Apple's objectives with such a deal is to encourage software developers to write programs for the Macintosh. If Apple had been more open to such relationships perhaps it wouldn't have found itself on the ropes in the mid-1990s.

UNDERSTANDING STAKEHOLDER PERCEPTIONS

Because relationships are communication driven, analysis of brand communication, especially the two-way communication, can provide insight into the nature of these relationships. From a company's point of view this means learning what type of support is needed from each group. From the stakeholders' perspective this means learning what they expect and what they are willing to pay (in both time, money, and effort) for having these expectations met.

Before communication objectives and strategies can be determined for strengthening each stakeholder relationship, you first must know how each group perceives your company and what it expects in return for its support. Few people or departments responsible for managing stakeholder relationships systematically do this type of ongoing analysis. There is rarely a disciplined process for profiling and tracking the behavior, let alone the perceptions of stakeholders, and most of the information is filed in the heads of individual staff members, where it is inaccessible to others dealing with these same stakeholders.

Market research has always been an important tool for understanding customer needs. The more recent emphasis on consumer insights, however, has shifted the focus from aggregating numbers and consumer descriptors to qualitative tools that better explain consumer feelings and motivations and better methods of capturing relational information in databases.[6] Integrated marketing uses these same methods to monitor and evaluate all stakeholder relationships, not just customer relationships. Like customers, all stakeholders have needs, wants, and concerns regarding the company, as well as a history of being involved with the company. Unless these factors are taken into consideration, the relationships with each cannot be adequately managed.

The premise of this chapter is that all stakeholders impact a company's relationship with customers and the company's bottom-line. Stakeholders' collective support determines profitability because their support determines revenues as well as costs. Their level of support is based on their relationship with the brand and their perceptions of it and the company.

Because brand equity is determined by the net-sum support of all stakeholders, it is important to develop and manage relationships by treating each stakeholder group as a target market with its own objectives and message strategy. The problem with failing to manage stakeholder groups and their diverse communication needs is it opens the door to inconsistency, and inconsistency is a barrier to supportive relationships.

> Because brand equity is determined by the net-sum support of all stakeholders, it is important to develop and manage relationships by treating each stakeholder group as a target market with its own objectives and message strategy.

Integrated marketing stakes out the various types of support needed for maximum profitability. It helps companies create stakeholder capital by managing its relationship investments. In the long term, such a focus will generate greater brand equity and thus even greater customer value. The problem is that relationship R&D doesn't exist in most industries. There is little tradition in most companies of researching relationships other than with customers; nor is there a department or functional area charged with the management of critical relationships, other than public relations.

Integrated marketing provides a model to each department responsible for a group of stakeholders by which it can better manage these relationships. Strong relationships with stakeholders can minimize the potential damage to a company or brand when a crisis occurs. Just as plane or car seatbelts are rarely needed, when they are, having them fastened can mean the difference between life and death. The same is true for a company. It too must continually keep its stakeholder seatbelt (read: relationship) strong and fastened.

ENDNOTES

1. John Kotter and James Haskett, *Corporate Culture and Performance*, (New York: Free Press) 1992.
2. Robert Frank, "Seeking a Pen Pal? Try Writing Reports on Matters at Coke," *The Wall Street Journal*, February 16, 1996, p. A1.
3. Tara Parker-Pope, "Ford Puts Blacks in Whiteface, Turns Red," *The Wall Street Journal*, February 22, 1996, p. B5.
4. John Byrne, "Time to Stop Toeing the Same Old Bottom Line," *Business Week*, April 14, 1994, p. 20.
5. Michel Robert, *Strategy Pure and Simple* (New York: McGraw-Hill, 1993), p. xi.
6. Lisa Fortini-Campbell, *The Consumer Insight Workbook* (Chicago: The Copy Workshop, 1992); Don Schultz, "We Simply Can't Afford to Go Back to Mass Marketing," *Marketing News*, February 15, 1993, p. 20; and Michelle Foster, "Understanding Customers: Integrated Marketing Communications," Association for Education in Journalism and Mass Communication (AEJMC), August 1993, Kansas City.

PART THREE

IM PROCESSES

5
CHAPTER

Develop Strategic Consistency

Examples of marketing confusion are not difficult to find, and they plague big, sophisticated marketers as well as small ones. Pepsi, for example, announced in 1996 that it was scrapping its familiar red, white, and blue design and switching to a radical new electric blue design. The reason is that Pepsi's message, particularly in international markets, had been losing something in translation. As *The Wall Street Journal* observed in reporting on "Project Blue's" launch, "its image is all over the map." The story explains that a grocery store in Hamburg uses red stripes, a bodega in Guatemala uses '70s-era lettering, a Shanghai restaurant displays a mainly white Pepsi sign, and a hodgepodge of commercials feature a variety of spokespeople, ranging from cartoons and babies to doddering butlers.[1]

And it's not just the marketing communication that sends different messages to different people about Pepsi. Consumers say the cola tastes different in different countries, so PepsiCo's plans also call for revamping manufacturing and distribution to get a consistent-tasting drink marketed throughout the globe. This story dramatizes the point that consistency is a systemic problem. It has to be approached from the viewpoint of the whole company and its total business operations, not just the company's marketing communication messages.

MAINTAINING STRATEGIC CONSISTENCY

Maintaining product and service consistency has always been a basic marketing principle, and in recent years TQM has reinforced this goal. But as the Pepsi situation shows, product consistency cannot be guaranteed when there are so many other inconsistent messages being sent about the brand.

Brand equity is a multi-functional product: the result of all brand communications relating to your company and its brands. To build brand relationships requires managing a brand's total "communication package"—everything it says and does. All the messages being delivered at all the various contact points must be monitored to see if they are working in concert with your overall business and marketing strategy.

Strategic consistency is the coordination of all messages that create or cue brand images, positions, and reputations in the minds of customers and other stakeholders. The less consistency in what your brand says and does, the more your brand will be unfocused, diffused, and fuzzy. Strategic consistency, from the customer point of view, means "no negative surprises" as well as "easy recognition" of the brand.

This does not mean, however, that every brand message should be the same. Obviously messages need to vary by stakeholder and customer segment. Also, messages will differ by situation. Therefore it is important to understand how consistency is applied and when and where individualized messages are needed.

THE CONSISTENCY FACTORS

A total integrated communication program ensures that there is strategic consistency on several different levels. That is why IM is far more complex that merely having one voice, one look. The multiple levels of strategic consistency make up a Consistency Hierarchy as shown in Figure 5–1.

As shown, having consistency of the marketing communication messages is merely the tip of the consistency iceberg. It should also be kept in mind that consistency at this executional level will vary by customer segment and of course by each stakeholder group. And the more a company is able to have one-to-one communication with stakeholders, the more the executional consistency will be individualized (which is made possible by having in-depth customer information files which will be explained in the next chapter).

FIGURE 5-1

Consistency Hierarchy

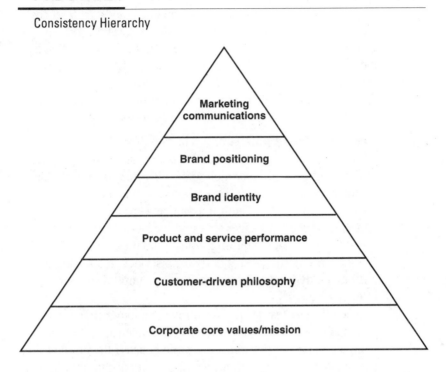

The fact that most companies, especially larger ones, have difficulty maintaining executional consistency of planned messages is because they don't have consistency in the other more critical, supporting areas. There is little to be gained by trying to have executional consistency until consistency is assured in the more strategic foundation areas such as core values and mission, business philosophy, and brand identity. The more consistency there is in each of these, the more distinct, clear, and predictable a brand will be in customers' minds. And the more distinctive and predictable a brand is, the easier it is to identify, recall, and most importantly, trust.

- ◆ **Corporate core values and mission.** One of the reasons companies like Hewlett-Packard, McDonald's, Nike, and Disney have been so successful is that they have distinguished between core values and practices. They have kept the former constant, but changed the latter as business has demanded. Core values are the soul of an organization and should be reflected in how brands are presented. They help define the mission and integrity of a company and its brands. As a recent *Harvard Business Review* article pointed out, successful companies "have aligned their entire operating model—that is, the company's culture, business processes, management systems, and computer platforms—to serve one value discipline. Knowing what they want to provide to customers, they have figured out what they must do to follow through."[2]

◆ **Customer-driven philosophy.** The company's business philosophy is also a foundation for a consistent strategy. One of the toughest areas in which to be consistent is putting the customer first. This is an easy promise to make in planned messages but often difficult to practice, especially when it comes to service messages that involve sales, customer service, repairs, and handling returns and make-goods. Land's End is particularly good at delivering service in advising its customers, delivering its merchandise promptly, and handling returns efficiently.

The ultimate test in really putting a customer first is when a company advises a customer or potential customer to buy from a competitor this particular time because the product is not in stock, the competitor just made a break-through, or the competitor's price is better even when taking into consideration all supporting services. When a company is willing to risk losing a transaction in order to better serve a customer, it has obtained the pinnacle in consistently putting the customer first. Obviously, practicing this policy requires a corporate confidence and a strategic plan for ensuring the customer is not lost permanently because of the one-time transaction. If customer relationships are so vulnerable that this might happen, a company has bigger problems than losing one customer.

◆ **Brand identity.** In order for customers and other stakeholders to quickly and accurately recognize and identify a company and brand, it is important to maintain a consistency of brand identification marks and logos. If these are not consistently displayed and reproduced, it will make picking out brands, especially in the case of consumer packaged goods, that more difficult. Companies successful at maintaining a consistent look and identity, such as Marlboro, adhere to a set of graphic standards. These are rules for how to use logos and brand marks whether for signage, truck side panels, letterheads, ads, or packaging. Having and enforcing graphic standards also helps to legally protect trademarks and logos.

◆ **Product and Service messages.** Maintaining consistency in product performance and the accompanying supporting services has been a primary thrust of TQM and is critical in IM. As we have mentioned before and will be explaining in more detail in the next section, product and service performance have communication dimensions that send some of the most critical brand messages.

◆ **Brand positioning.** Positioning defines how a brand compares to competing brands. If the positioning is upscale status, then that positioning should be reflected in product design, packaging, pricing, distribution, and marketing communication messages. As Montblanc found in the mid 1980s, it had to be consistent in pricing, packaging, distribution, and its marketing communications before it was able to reverse its sales trend and create a coherent, upscale image.

Positioning provides contextual meaning for a brand. Ford Escort is *the most economical* car, Mercedes *the most prestigious*, Corvette *the most sporty*, and so on. The CEO of SMH, the company that makes Swatch watches, explains how the long and short-term elements interact to create a position. His comments dramatize the complexity of the cues being managed in the various Swatch messages: "There are many elements that make up the Swatch message. High quality. Low Cost. Provocative. Joy of life. But the most important element of the Swatch message is the hardest for others to copy. Ultimately, we are not just offering watches. We are offering our personal culture."[3]

A company cannot be something one instant and something different the next. Swatch has positioned itself as a fun, pop fashion watch; that position is consistently integrated into all its messages, whether ads, product designs, special promotions, or packaging.

Examples of how inconsistency can weaken a position abound in bank marketing. Because "friendly service" is always a top customer priority in banking, nearly every bank, at some point, directs its advertising agency to create "the friendliest bank in town" campaign. Unfortunately, operations is rarely told about the campaign, and tellers and loan officers continue to perform as they always have. This creates two problems. First, the campaign sensitizes customers to look for, and expect, friendlier service. While customers may have been satisfied with the service before, now they are not because expectations have been raised. Second, if it doesn't do what it promised, it sends a subtle message that you can't trust this bank—not a message that banks, especially, want to send out. In these situations, marketing communications are actually counterproductive because the bank's position becomes nebulous.

When a brand is repositioned, integrated marketing requires that all messages—not just the planned messages—be strategically changed. A good example is how McDonald's has strategically managed its repositioning over the years as it has expanded its offerings. Its current positioning as a full-menu restaurant (serving breakfast, lunch, and dinner) with sit-down and drive-through as well as carry-out, is a significant change from its original positioning as a fast-food hamburger and fries carry-out only chain. And yet the McDonald's *brand* has remained constant—inexpensive but dependable quality fast food served in a clean, family environment. Like Hewlett-Packard, McDonald's has changed its positioning but has kept its values consistent.

- ◆ **Executional consistency.** This is maintaining one voice and one look for each customer segment, specific stakeholder group, and as mentioned above, with each customer when individualized messages are being sent. Within the various IMC executions that present different promotional offers and stress different brand claims to different customer segments, however, certain design, tone, and other image elements should remain constant.

MANAGING MESSAGE CHAOS

Messages to the various stakeholders are sent by many different areas within a company. Take business customers, for example: They frequently interact with production, accounting, sales, research, customer service—as well as receive planned messages through marketing communication. Furthermore, a customer may also be an employee and/or a shareholder. So customer communication is not just the sole responsibility of marketing.

Within the more traditional area of marketing communication in large companies, different messages are often developed by different marketing services areas and their agencies, such as advertising, direct marketing, sales promotion, and packaging.

When confusion arises, the brand positioning, as well as notions about who the company is and what it stands for, are left to the receivers of these messages to decipher. This does not mean that individual departments should not be allowed to produce planned messages, but rather that they should conform to a central positioning strategy and core values and coordinate their activities with other departments who are interacting with the same stakeholders.

When the full array of brand messages is considered, one can quickly see the complexity involved and the challenge of maintaining strategic message consistency (see Figure 5–2). The larger the organization, the more people and departments are creating and sending messages and responding to customers and other stakeholders, and the more the company is discussed by the media, suppliers, competition, analysts, and customers.

In IM, integrating and coordinating communication and marketing planning extends across stakeholder groups. For example, a number of companies are offering special benefits, discounts, and other incentives to investors and suppliers to encourage them to use the company's products and services so they can learn more about the company and its products and gain a greater sense of involvement. A number of service companies, like The Incredible Universe and the Lettuce Entertain You restaurant chain in Chicago, have found that the place to begin with customer retention is to emphasize employee retention. In both of these cases, the lower the turnover, the more committed the employee is to the company and its philosophy. And that is evident in the

FIGURE 5-2

The Challenges of Maintaining Strategic Consistency

1. **Organizations have multiple audiences/stakeholders.**
2. **Each audience/stakeholder group has different message needs.**
3. **Stakeholder audiences overlap and therefore receive multiple brand messages.**
4. **Companies are increasingly using co-branding, ingredient branding, and multi-tier branding.**
5. **Brand messages originate from a wide variety of sources (many from within an organization, and some from outside sources).**
6. **Brand messages are received at many different brand contact points.**
7. **Message impact greatly varies.**
8. **Messages that can be least controlled often have the greatest impact.**
9. **Increased expertise in marketing communication functions creates greater completion for control of the marketing communication budget and planned messages.**
10. **The number of employees from different departments who communicate with stakeholders has significantly increased.**

better quality of customer service delivered by the employees. In other words, it is difficult to manage stakeholder groups in isolation.

When message planning is not integrated, some or most is likely to be off strategy. In an IM audit of a hospital, for example, we found that several of the medical units (e.g., pediatrics, cardiology) were producing their own brochures to promote their respective areas. They claimed that not only were they more qualified to write about their areas, but also that the hospital's marketing department refused to do the brochures. (That was because, according to marketing, individual departmental brochures were not a part of the hospital's marketing communication plan that year.) Because of the political power of the medical units, however, they were able to get away with producing these "renegade" messages, most of which did not even address the hospital's number one communication objective for the year—cost containment. The result was uncoordinated collateral materials as well as a reduced level of strategic synergy.

Because the hospital marketing department, in its annual marketing plan, had targeted "cost reduction" as its number one concern, it wanted to position the hospital as a cost-sensitive health care provider to all of its important stakeholders in order to focus everyone on this critical issue. However, the audit found that the cost-sensitive message was seldom present in any of the hospital's messages except those going to insurance companies. The recommendation, therefore, was that cost sensitivity be a consistent element in *all* messages, making it relevant to each. Following are examples of how this could be done.

◆ **Employees.** Each employee newsletter would contain at least one story on steps being taken to reduce cost; all stories in the newsletter would be examined to find further tie-ins to cost containment.

◆ **Primary care physicians** (who refer patients to the hospital). In newsletters and brochures written for this group, cost containment would be the primary focus. When announcing a new procedure or new piece of equipment, for example, care would be taken to discuss how this either helped save cost long term or provided better service to the primary care doctors so they could operate more efficiently.

◆ **Government officials.** Discussion of current and proposed regulations would be related to cost whenever relevant.

◆ **Donors** (with whom the hospital's foundation communicated on a regular basis). Communication with donors would emphasize that their money was being used most efficiently because of cost containment steps being taken throughout the hospital.

◆ **Volunteers** (who were donating thousands of hours a year in time). These people were consistently thanked and in other ways psychologically rewarded for their time and efforts, which allowed the hospital to provide more services to patients without raising prices. They would be reminded that it was through their efforts that the hospital was able to provide care to those unable to pay the regular fees.

THE FOUR SOURCES OF BRAND MESSAGES

Because controlling or influencing brand messages is the basis for managing brand relationships, it is critical to identify where these messages originate. In other words, who or what departments, products, services, programs, or people are the sources of the messages? As explained at the beginning of this book, all elements of a company and its processes have a communication dimension. Once these critical message sources are identified, strategies and tactics can be developed to control or influence them, ensuring that the messages are consistent, reinforce each other, and, most importantly, do not contradict each other. An analysis of brand contact points shows four major sources of brand messages: *product, service, planned,* and *unplanned.*

Planned Messages

These are traditional marketing communication messages, which include advertising, sales promotion, personal sales, merchandising materials, PR releases, events, sponsorships, packaging, and events, to name a few. While much of the emphasis is on customer targeted materials, planned messages also are directed at employees, investors, and other key stakeholders and can include annual reports, annual sales meetings, notices in pay slips, bulletin boards (on-line as well as on a wall), and newsletters.

Also overlooked are messages initiated by the finance department, such as announcements of new stock issues or profit reports; human resources' advertising for new employees; and the engineers who write articles for, or are interviewed by, trade journals. Without a cross-functional planning and monitoring process, these people can produce "renegade" messages saying a variety of things that may even contradict those produced by marketing, which are designed to create a specific corporate or brand image and reputation.

Planned messages, in most cases, make a promise about what the brand and company can or will do. Planned messages are generally responsible for creating brand awareness, brand positioning, and brand knowledge and motivating some type of behavioral response, such as buying, sampling, requesting additional information, or increasing purchase frequency or quantity. Because most planned messages have relatively low credibility, they are best used for carrying noncontroversial information.

Planned messages are often seen as failing when they are inconsistent with the product performance (or other marketing mix factors) and perceptions of the product. A good example is Oldsmobile's campaign a few years ago, "This isn't your father's Oldsmobile." Although the product had been significantly improved, the planned messages were so different from potential customers' perceptions of the car that market share actually decreased and the agency that had the account for decades nearly lost it. Another example is the Joe Isuzu campaign, which made fun of common images of car salesmen. Unfortunately, the campaign primarily worked to create this negative association with the car, and potential car buyers avoided Isuzu for years because what it said in jest overpowered the message delivered by its car.

Keeping planned messages consistent is "beginner's level" integration. This doesn't mean it is not difficult or not important. It merely means that relative to the other message types—product, service, and unplanned—it is easier to maintain consistency within the arena of marketing communication because these messages can be controlled, not just influenced.

The marketing and marketing communication objectives are the first place to start in managing planned messages for consistency. An IM audit of a major beverage brand (marketing communication budget of $150 million) found that the marketing services managers and brand managers were working against 10 different marketing communication objectives, not the one basic marketing communication objective stated in the brand's annual plan. When a content analysis was done of a year's worth of this brand's planned messages, not surprisingly, the advertising and sales promotion messages were all over the place. In all the audits we have done, we have yet to find a company which is effectively integrating its planned messages with a consistent position.

Good campaigns are based on a strong central idea integrated into all planned messages. This idea is the focal point around which the various efforts and executions are balanced. The big, central idea is also important for locking the brand into the consumer's mind because it tends to intensify recognition and recall. The richer the idea, the more easily it can be integrated into any type of planned message.

An example of a successfully integrated big, central idea was the "Color of Money" campaign used by A.B. Dick, known as a manufacturer of duplicating machines that produced relatively low-quality reproductions. The company used an integrated campaign to expand its position into the full-size printing press market. Using a theme borrowed from the Paul Newman/Tom Cruise movie, *The Color of Money,* the idea of color reproduction in printing was linked with the idea of making (printing) money. The theme was incorporated into a six-minute product video, ads, direct marketing, public relations, trade show exhibits, sales promotions, and sales efforts—all designed to lead to the development of a sophisticated database of prospect information.[4]

As many companies have learned the hard way, the chances of coming up with a really big, creative idea—one that cuts through the commercial message clutter and manifests the brand positioning—are low. We call it the *creative lottery*. Only one out of a thousand creative ideas really wins big, yet it is interesting to note that some companies consistently develop great advertising. One reason is because the client has a relationship with an agency that fosters creative ideas and knows, respects, and champions great work. It is also important to note that great creative ideas can come from other areas of marketing communication, such as sales promotion, public relations and event marketing, just as they do from advertising.

Rather than playing the creative lottery every year, IM takes a good, solid strategic idea, integrates it into all planned messages (and other message types where appropriate), and stays with that big idea over an extended period of years, as Green Giant, Pepsi, Marlboro, and United Airlines have done. Campaigns and executions need to change to keep a fresh feel; however, the positioning and the central idea remain constant.

A classic example of how consistency can take an "okay" creative idea and make it powerful was the use of Joe DiMaggio as spokesperson for Mr. Coffee. The creative idea of having a retired, all-star baseball player associated with an automatic coffee maker was not the brilliant part of this campaign, but rather the brand's decision to maintain the consistency of using DiMaggio for years. On a relatively limited budget, Mr. Coffee was able to become a leading brand of coffee makers by being consistent. The synergy that this approach produced definitely had more impact over the long run than if the brand had kept trying for the latest and greatest creative idea each year. This is not meant as a disparagement of advertising, but simply an acknowledgment that creative breakthroughs are rare although most agencies will tell a client that every idea they present is "breakthrough stuff."

Most early integration efforts attempted to create a one-voice campaign by standardizing strategy and the executions that brought the strategy to life. One of the best examples is Marlboro. It has religiously maintained the red and white elements in its logo and packaging along with the macho, independent cowboy image. The red and white elements are extended to every brand message, including the design on the grand prix race cars which Marlboro sponsors. Not only does the red and white logo appear on the car, the car itself is red and white—which makes it recognizable even at 200 miles per hour.

When a brand has multiple key stakeholders or a user base made up of multiple segments, it should keep its position consistent but modify its "one-voice, one-look" approach to better communicate to its various audiences. For example, in selling Kellogg breakfast cereals, the message to mom is different than the one aimed at kids and, of course, both are different from the one aimed at retailers and suppliers. Each stakeholder group generally has a completely different set of information needs because of the nature of its relationship with the company.

This does not mean, however, that there shouldn't be certain consistencies in all sets of messages. The brand's positioning cues must be consistent. In many cases, however, the positioning message will be secondary to the individualized selling propositions (for kids: the breakfast that's sweet to eat; for moms: contains less sugar than an apple; for retailers: nice profits). And underlying these audience specific messages is the message of Kellogg's quality.

A one-voice strategy is analogous to a choir singing in unison; however, multiple voices singing in harmony are much more engaging and enjoyable. That's what we call consistency with diversity. An example of an effort to deliver harmony with multiple voices is the "Always Coca Cola" campaign introduced in the spring of 1993. According to Peter Sealey, at that time Coke's director of marketing, Coke had many different audiences, and it decided it could be more effective talking directly to each one, which required different messages, tones, and images, as well as different media. As Sealey explained, "It's not one sight, one sound, one sell any longer."[5]

Consequently, the TV spots produced by Creative Artists Associates for Coke have had a wide range of creative executions directed at specific audiences and the television programs they watch. For example, in "Real Things Last," the old tune "When I'm Sixty Four" showed a couple still enjoying Coke together after their fiftieth anniversary. At the other extreme was "Digging Dog," aimed at teenagers. It was fast paced with stark, almost comic-book images about a dog that was always digging holes but would occasionally dig up a bottle of Coke for its owner. What held them together was a consistent set of execution elements—the red sphere with the Coke logo, the Spencerian font used for the brand name, the contoured bottle, the slogan "Always Coca-Cola," and a distinctive jingle and audio tagline.

Although Coke's multivoice approach has been criticized for a variety of reasons—no central strategy, no selling idea, message overlap—it appears to be working. (Between 1993 and early 1997, Coke's stock price increased more than 150 percent.) According to an editorial in *Advertising Age*, Coke's performance suggests that "in today's marketplace, a sound, clear, long-range strategy can still pay off big-time for smart, and patient, brand builders."[6]

Coke's approach demonstrates the more complex use of a multivoice strategy by a big company with a big budget that can afford to create and target multiple messages to multiple consumer segments.

Product Messages

These are the messages that customers and other stakeholders infer from the product itself (e.g., performance, appearance, durability), its pricing, its design, and where and how it's distributed. Although product messages generally do not involve human contact between customers and the company, they have a significant impact and can be anticipated and controlled, although the cost to control can be significant. For example, if it's found that the design of a motorcycle is sending negative messages (e.g., old-fashioned, slow, or undependable), the cost to redesign could be hundreds of thousands of dollars and require months or years of work.

Although product design of both goods and services is important, performance is even more important when it comes to sending brand messages. This is the rationale for spending large amounts on sales promotion to generate trial for a new product. As long as there are perceivable differences in product performance vs competition, such investments are wise.

Points of distribution, especially for retail products, can also send a strong message, although these no longer have the differentiating impact they once had. When a brand is seen in an upscale department store like Bloomingdales, Saks, and Nieman Marcus, it sends a message about the brand that is different than messages about brands displayed by mass merchandisers such as Kmart, Wal-Mart, and Target. But that's true only for certain product categories. The Yuppie generation taught us that not only was it okay to go into a Target or Wal-Mart, it was actually a smart thing to do as long as you were buying such things as garden supplies, health and beauty aides, toys, and paper goods. In other words, when a brand like Crest is seen in a Wal-Mart, the message sent is neutral. However, status products, such as Montblanc pens or Rolex watches, would find that being displayed in discount stores sends a message that contradicts those being sent by their planned messages and price.

Customers still use pricing as a cue about the quality of a product. Since there are a variety of brand choices for most product categories, the price of a particular brand is a statement of how it compares with competing brands (e.g., positioning on price). In addition, the frequency of brand promotions also says something about a brand. The more a brand is on sale and discounted, generally the more ordinary it is considered to be. Brands that compete consistently on price often have little else to say.

Seldom, however, can pricing messages stand alone. Take, for example a watch. If it is priced at $300, is the message "quality" or "overpriced?" Or, if it's priced at $15, is the message "bargain" or "cheap?" Pricing messages, like all others, must be strategically integrated with all other brand messages in order to send customers and potential customers a coherent, meaningful message.

One of the most important integration elements that needs to be managed throughout the marketing mix is the positioning strategy. An example of integrating a product message with a brand position is how Odwalla, a producer of natural juices, uses distribution to reinforce its "all natural" brand position. The company converted its 143 delivery trucks to natural gas. By polluting less, the company also helped itself to be perceived as more socially responsible.

An example of a product message that was not well integrated is the pricing strategy uncovered in an IM audit of a retail chain. The company had moved to an everyday low price (EDLP) strategy but was inconsistent in executing it. Some items went on sale, some didn't; some carried the EDLP tag, some didn't. The company's marketing managers couldn't even explain the strategy, so there was no way customers could know what EDLP really meant at these stores.

Service Messages

Service messages originate from interactions with an organization's customer service representatives, receptionists, secretaries, delivery people, and drivers—the live, real-time interface between brand and customer. As the Ukrop's story in Chapter 1 illustrated, these contacts have significant impact on customer relationships because they involve personal interaction, which is the most persuasive form of communication. They can be controlled with the proper training (or retraining), proper incentives, monitoring, and a strong corporate culture.

Companies should recognize that line employees are often aware of the value field in which they work. As one employee commented when asked about his thoughts of going on strike: "What's the point of going on strike when I can screw up the company a whole lot better by giving surly service to our customers?"

Because of the generalized negative attitude toward business and the low expectations that many customers have about encounters with companies, service messages have the potential to send strong, positive messages when situations are properly handled, such as a follow-up call to confirm that a service repair was satisfactory or that the family pet was improving after a visit to the vet.

An example of a negative service message occurs when bank customers are forced to wait in line for a teller while several bank employees are huddled together behind the counter talking. Even if these employees are not tellers, customers don't know this and assume they are being ignored. In most service organizations, what service people do is the responsibility of operations, not marketing. Nevertheless, as this example shows, their behavior can send negative messages, and just one of these can more than counter the effects of dozens of positive, planned messages produced by marketing. In IM, marketing works with operations to minimize negative service messages which undercut the planned messages.

> In IM, marketing works with operations to minimize negative service messages which undercut the planned messages.

A positive service message when handling customer requests and complaints is speed of response. A quick response shows the company is concerned because it has made the customer's problem a top priority. Customers who send in complaints are often more impressed with a quick response than with eventually receiving a free coupon. A quick response can add a positive element even when the message content is not what a customer wants to hear. For example, a customer that needs parts for a discontinued product doesn't want to hear these parts aren't available. However, if that is the case, letting the customer know sooner rather than later minimizes the overall disappointment.

One retail company that understands the importance of the service message is Radio Shack. Because it sells many different kinds of electronic products, it has anticipated that people will occasionally have trouble operating them. It has therefore (1) trained its store employees to expect and welcome these calls for help and (2) developed a system that provides easy access to instructions for products eliciting the majority of calls. This has become the theme of its advertising: "You've got questions, we've got answers . . . 24,000 of us at Radio Shack." Besides answering questions, this campaign also generates a communication contact point providing an opportunity to create relationships with new customers and keep current customers satisfied by selling them equipment upgrades or other useful, related products. This could not have happened if marketing had not worked with operations to prepare for and control these newly created customer communication contacts. This campaign was produced by Young & Rubicam, which won the account in 1994 with a presentation that emphasized integrated marketing.

An example of inconsistent service messages was found in an IM audit of a regional retail chain. Most of the clerks were knowledgeable, patient, and generally quite personable when helping customers make purchase decisions—positive service messages. However, although the chain had a liberal return policy, some of these same clerks became sullen, mechanical, and made limited eye contact when handling returns—sending negative service messages that overpowered those earlier positive messages.

Consistently supplying customers with the information they want, when and how they want it, is another type of strategic consistency. Like product messages, these must deliver on the positioning promise and selling premise. A service that is correctly delivered is a fulfilled promise.

Another aspect of delivering on a service promise is to make sure that operations and training programs are working to support the marketing strategy. A major resort and conference center stresses in its brochures and signage that "Our people make the difference." However, the resort has no formal or informal training program for new hires and no in-service training. The result is that guests experience not only inconsistent service, but often poor service even though the resort is very costly. What it says and what it does are two different things. Consistency doesn't exist. (It has stayed in business primarily because of its superb location.)

An example of how a company can unintentionally send a negative service message is the decision to use long, recorded telephone menus. Many callers hate these menus, particularly when they get complex. On the surface, the decision makes financial sense. If there are three full-time operators costing the company approximately $100,000 a year, replacing two with a recorded menu-of-options can save $65,000 a year. Because the savings are obvious, little or no consideration is given to the brand message this new system sends to customers, potential customers, and other stakeholders. It may be efficient for the company but it is not efficient for the caller. The real message may be: company first, customer second.

In nearly all service situations, it is necessary to standardize policies and procedures in order to maintain consistency and control. What happens, however, is that control sometimes becomes more important than consistency, depriving front-line people of the ability to act when it is in the customer's best interest to do so without violating the company's integrity. From the customer's perspective consistency means actions that deliver on their expectations, not adherence to rigid policies. For example, a policy that all checks over $500 must be approved by an officer of the bank is not strategically sound. Once a long-time customer becomes known to a teller and has been cleared, why should that person have to be approved every time for a check over $500? The policy should be to get approval for all checks over $500 from customers *unknown* to the staff. These "inconsistencies" of service in reality can provide individual customers with greater consistency through customized messages.

Unplanned Messages

Unplanned messages are brand or company-related news stories, employee gossip, actions of special interest groups, comments by the trade and by competitors, findings by government agencies or research institutions, and the proverbial word-of-mouth that one hopes will confirm the other brand messages. Like all other brand messages, unplanned messages can be positive or negative and affect customers and other stakeholders accordingly. Unplanned messages can have significant impact because the sources are seen either as experts on the company (such as employees) or objective protectors of the public interest (special interest groups, media, government agencies). Messages from employees can decrease support for a company as well as build it because employees are considered highly credible; they have "inside information." Therefore friends, acquaintances, and the reporters who talk to employees generally believe what they say.

The more the unplanned messages confirm that a company does what it says it will do, the greater the trust that is built with customers and other stakeholders. One type of positive unplanned message that is often overlooked is what we call the "steady as she goes" message, in which one gust of wind doesn't blow a customer off course. If, for example, a customer has a negative experience at a restaurant, but several friends say it's a great place, then the disappointed customer may be motivated to give the restaurant a second try. This confirming message leverages the social dimension of persuasion.

For most companies, the most critical unplanned messages are from the news media, as they generally reach the widest audiences. However, these messages often come from other unplanned sources, such as whistle-blowing employees and special interest groups who can get the media to carry their stories and points of view.

Influencing media behavior is difficult because most reporters distrust business executives and their comments and explanations even more than the general public does. A study of both journalists and business executives by the Media Research Center of the Freedom Forum found that over two-thirds of the business executives admitted they had lied to the media at some time.[7] (The study was overseen by Wallace Rasmussen, former CEO of Beatrice Foods, and *Miami Herald* editor Mike Haggerty.)

A significant gap was also found between the perceptions of business executives and journalists. More than three-fourths of the journalists said business coverage has improved over the years, but only 30 percent of the executives believed this to be true. Nearly three-fourths of the business executives said the news media provide a negative view of business, but only 31 percent of the journalists believed this to be true.

Unplanned messages create the most difficult consistency problems because they are not under the control of the organization and can only be influenced. To manage unplanned messages, the first step is to do a word-of-mouth analysis of the company's relationships. What are the employees and other key stakeholders saying about the company? The amount of inconsistency can be minimized through open employee relations with rumor control programs, openness with the media, proactive dealing with government and special interest groups, and accessibility to the financial community.

To build trust with the media a company must have a policy of openness in dealing with the media. Although a company can't control the media, with a strategic, proactive media relations program it can influence what and how reporters talk about a company, its products, and its people. Not all negative stories can be eliminated, just as all product defects cannot be eliminated, but their percentage and depth can be minimized when a process is in place that is designed to create positive media relations.

For years public relations professionals have counseled clients to be honest with the media and admit mistakes. In this age of hyper-litigation, however, corporate lawyers cringe at the thought of their CEOs publicly assuming liability when a disaster hits. An IM solution is to have a customer relationship focus. That means expressing concern, showing empathy, explaining the all-out effort to discover what caused the problem, and taking steps to prevent reoccurrences. It also means interacting with the media by being accessible and open to questions without inappropriately accepting responsibility or admitting guilt until all the information has been collected. Once responsibility has been sorted out, it is important for the company to "do the right thing."

Effective media relations coupled with reputation-building advertising can position a company as a leader in its industry. This proactive approach ensures that company leaders and its experts are in a reporters' Rolodex as the people to call both for industry information and company information. A reporter with a strong relationship with a company will often call that company first if he or she has questions about the industry.

Since it is impossible to prevent employees from talking about their work experiences, it becomes important to make sure the work experience is positive. Internal marketing is an important first step in informing employees and helping them feel more involved. Another is having a focused company mission which employees can participate in and support, one which enriches a company's overall culture and builds employee's pride in their affiliation with the company.

Internally, the employee grapevines and rumor mills can play havoc if left unchecked. One way to track such potentially negative messages is through electronic employee bulletin boards. These public discussions can be monitored, and negative messages that appear can be addressed and influenced. Sophisticated employee communication managers have techniques to manage the "grapevine," and these should be coordinated with the marketing communication planning.

One of the most important things a company can do to influence potentially disastrous unplanned messages is to have communication plans for the most likely crises. The bottom line of *crisis communication* is damage control when a major disaster hits a company, such as a multiple murder on the property, a deadly explosion, product tampering, or charges of an environmental crime. In this day of instant news, the world soon learns of any major crisis. Most of these are anticipated in the CEO's nightmares, but the question is, how well are they planned for?

Scripts for different types of anticipated crisis should be outlined. Airlines, for example, presume it's not a question *if* one of their airplanes will crash, but *when*. Oil companies know that they will have some type of major oil leak or spill some day. Drug companies know that someday one of their medicines will suddenly be cited as causing certain negative side effects or reactions in a certain group of people. These can be anticipated and planned for.

The focus of most crisis plans is on how to deal with the media—who speaks to them and about what—and how to set up and manage media relations. When a company chooses to make "no comment," it completely abdicates content of a story (e.g., brand messages) to someone outside the company. Just as customers integrate all brand messages whether a company does or not, the story is going to be written whether the company cooperates or not. And just as a company is taking a chance when it does nothing to influence the way customers integrate brand messages, it takes a chance when it does nothing to influence (through cooperation) the way a media story plays out.

A crisis management plan also contains internal communication plans that detail which executives and other key stakeholders are to be notified, by whom, and how (e.g., a phone tree, e-mail posting, faxes). It also includes a method for informing employees as well as other people, such as relatives of those affected. Finally it has plans for dealing with victims and families. All of these tasks are assigned to various managers who know exactly what they are to handle and how to go about it the moment a crisis hits. Some companies seed these plans by developing worst-case scenario workshops for their managers in which they practice taking responsibility for their assigned function in a fast-breaking crisis.

THE INTEGRATION TRIANGLE

The *integration triangle* is a simple way of illustrating how perceptions are created from the various brand message sources. From the customer's perspective, integration exists when a brand does what its maker says it will do and then receives confirmation from others that it in fact delivers on its promises. A simple model can identify inconsistency in a brand's communications and can alert a company to potential relationship problems—when it doesn't do what it promises to do and/or others say the brand hasn't done what it promised. In other words, the "say" messages delivered by marketing communication must be consistent with the "do" messages of how products and services perform as well as be consistent with what others "confirm" about the brand. (See Figure 5–3) Confirmation, or lack there of, should be used in managing both "say" and "do" messages.

Gaps or disconnects between any of these three communication sources create inconsistencies and threaten the brand relationships. The greater the inconsistencies and gaps, the greater the potential relationship damage.

Southwest Airlines is a good example of a company that does what it says. It promises low prices and no luxury seating or gourmet food. And its product and supporting service messages deliver just that. Not only do passengers keep using the airline, but it has received positive media coverage, and confirmation that its fares are low and its operations reliable.

Relative to its competition, Southwest Airlines has spent far less per passenger mile on advertising and promotion and yet has been profitable every year since it started in the 1970s. Also it has become the number one carrier on the majority of routes it serves. It has been able to do this because it consistently does what it says it will do and has this confirmed not only by its customers but the media and other stakeholders.

An example of communication integration not working often occurs when an airline places "special handling" tags on the baggage of its frequent flyers. If at the end of the trip the bags arrive no sooner than

FIGURE 5-3

The Integration Triangle

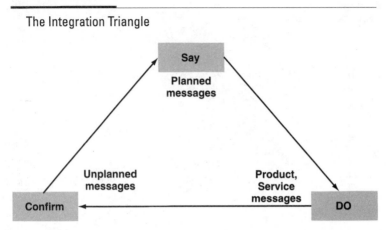

they ever did, the frequent flyers have received inconsistent messages. Their expectations were raised, but operations didn't deliver, and therefore there is a disconnect between saying and doing.

MESSAGE IMPACT VARIES BY SOURCE OF MESSAGE

The type or source of a brand message greatly affects its level of impact. As shown in Figure 5–4, this impact is generally inversely related to the degree of control a company has over the message type. Of the four message types, planned messages generally have the least impact *per message*. Customers know ads and other MC messages are self-serving and frequently over promise. Commercial message clutter is another reason for this.

In one of our agency workshops, we were discussing the claim—"long lasting aroma"—of a brand which this agency handled in several different countries. One of the participants from a country which had just introduced the brand said they had to change the claim to "the aroma that lasts forever" because the other claim was already being used in that country by a competing brand. When another workshop participant questioned this revised claim, pointing out that it was untrue because the aroma did not last forever, the response was, "Oh that doesn't make any difference, no one believes advertising anyway."

FIGURE 5–4

Message Control vs Impact

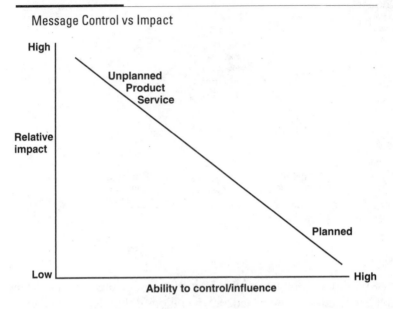

Other factors minimizing the impact of planned messages include the growing distrust of business and increasing irritation with intrusive commercial messages. Although these are not new problems, they are intensifying as media-savvy consumers zip and zap TV commercials and condition themselves to psychologically ignore most print messages. (Zapping is changing channels when a commercial comes on; zipping is fast forwarding through commercials on programs that have been videotaped.)

Another challenge in consistency planning is the increasing emphasis on mass customization of products and messages. Customized products, in particular, challenge consistency. If your company distributes products through powerful retailers like Wal-Mart, you may have found yourself being asked to revise your product line to fit into Wal-Mart's categories. What does that do to your product consistency?

That's another dimension of the consistency problem that Pepsi confronted in its "Project Blue" effort. Not only were the marketing communication efforts inconsistent from country to country, but consumers were also complaining that the cola tasted different in different countries. To address this problem, Pepsi had to revamp its manufacturing and distribution systems, as well as its marketing communication, in order to achieve strategic brand consistency worldwide.

Yankelovich Partners has found that people want more structure but also more change. On the surface, this is a paradox. However, meeting this paradox is the essence of strategic consistency. By changing the product but maintaining brand integrity, a customer can have it both ways.

Making Consistency Strategic

Consistency begins with brand positioning, which is based on core values, selling promises, and distinctive features. All messages—planned, product, service, and unplanned—must complement and reinforce this position. A consistency strategy addresses the problem of overlapping stakeholders and the tendency of people to automatically integrate the wide range of brand messages they continually receive. The principle of consistency, however, must also operate from the customer's or stakeholder's viewpoint in order to accomplish something other than a system that controls, or perhaps over controls, the creative elements of business.

> **Consistency begins with brand positioning, which is based on core values, selling promises, and distinctive features.**

Managing strategic consistency across all four message types creates an added value for a brand because consistency helps build long-lasting brand relationships by increasing trust, increasing message synergy, and eliminating contradictory messages. The effort to align (i.e., consistently integrate) the entire operation is what must be done with brand messages to ensure they are working toward the single, long-term purpose of effectively building the relationships that drive brand equity. An IM consistency strategy calls for a systems-based approach that integrates the established core values, a customer-first philosophy of doing business, brand identity, brand reputation, brand positioning, and planned messages. When strategic consistency is in place, it is then possible for the company to achieve communication harmony.

ENDNOTES

1. "Seeing Red Abroad, Pepsi rolls out a New Blue Can," *The Wall Street Journal*, April 2, 1996, p. 31.

2. Lynn Sharp Paine, "Managing for Organizational Integrity," *Harvard Business Review*, March–April 1994, pp. 106-117.
3. William Taylor, "Message and Muscle: An Interview with Swatch Titan Nicolas Hayek," *Harvard Business Review*, March–April, 1993, p. 103.
4. "Printing Money," *Sales & Marketing Management*, February 1995, pp. 64-69.
5. Peter Sealey, press conference, March 1993, Atlanta, Georgia.
6. "'Always' Brand Building," *Advertising Age*, August 1, 1994, p. 20; Association for Education in Journalism and Mass Communication presentation, August 12, 1994, Atlanta, Georgia.
7. Mike Haggerty and Wallace Rasmussen, *The Headlines vs. The Bottom Line*, Freedom Forum First Amendment Center, Vanderbilt University (nd), p. 89.

6

Make Interactivity Purposeful

Ironically, one company that doesn't understand the balance between talking and listening is one of the U.S. regional phone companies. When interviewed about what his company was doing to build better customer relationships, its new marketing manager mentioned only examples of "talking at" customers—none involved listening or soliciting feedback. Getting access into the home through direct-response advertising, he said, was the key method the company used to inform customers about its various products and new services. Although the interview was about building better customer relationships, he never discussed how his company provided easier recourse when customers had a problem, complaint, or inquiry. This company, which makes its living selling two-way communication, claims it is building stronger relationships by merely using more ways to *reach* its customers rather than by interacting with them.

From a customer's perspective, interactivity means accessibility, recognition, responsiveness, and accountability—all the things people require in a relationship, whether personal or commercial. From a brand perspective, it means the ability to listen as well as speak and then modify behavior as a result of the feedback.

Interactivity is the process by which customers are integrated into a company, made part of the product planning and development process, and dealt with individually. To be interactive, companies must put as much emphasis on receiving messages as they do on sending messages. The interactivity dimension of integrated marketing proposes that media can be used both to send messages efficiently and to receive and capture messages from customers (and other stakeholders) in order to create a long-term, purposeful dialogue. Purposeful dialogue is a type of communication that is mutually beneficial for the customer and the company.

One of the psychological barriers that prevents many companies from really listening is an attitude that customers don't have anything valid to say. Because many customer inquiries and complaints are redundant or trivial (in the eyes of the company), managers find it difficult to listen creatively for problems that can be fixed and ideas for new strategies. Also, when these interactions are not encouraged, recorded, and collectively examined, a company doesn't have an accurate reading of customer perceptions.

> One of the psychological barriers that prevents many companies from really listening is an attitude that customers don't have anything valid to say.

The extent to which computer and software programs are user friendly is determined by their interface complexity. The same thing is true for companies. Those with a customer focus are sensitive to the interface complexity that people must deal with when interacting with them—whether buying their products, requesting information, voicing a complaint, or ordering a repair. To what extent a company facilitates interactivity (i.e., has a user-friendly, company-customer interface) is critical in nourishing customer support. An interactivity strategy is the way companies and customers get to know and trust each other. It is also the basis on which companies can change to better serve customers and other stakeholders.

This chapter will discuss what we mean by interactivity—media menus, individualized messages, and purposeful dialogue—as well as the benefits of interactivity, such as relationship building and organizational memory. Before we look at interactivity, however, let's consider all the ways a customer comes in contact with a brand, since all of those points deliver messages and operate as part of a larger system of contact.

CREATED AND INTRINSIC BRAND CONTACT POINTS

Brand contact points are situations in which customers have the opportunity to be exposed, in some way, to a brand message. Brand contacts are the sources of brand messages and are either created or intrinsic.

Created contact points are, for the most part, planned messages such as advertising, promotions, and PR releases. *Intrinsic contact points* are those situations which automatically exist as part of the buying, performing, and servicing processes and include most product and service messages, as well as packaging (a planned message). For example, when a person decides to take an airline trip, he/she must contact an airline or its representative to make a reservation, check in at the airport, interact with a flight attendant, and retrieve baggage. Each of these mini-experiences is an intrinsic brand contact point because the person cannot use the service without making these contacts.

Not only is it necessary to control or influence the brand messages coming from these intrinsic contact points, but also intrinsic brand contacts should be seen as "media" opportunities. Because companies are so departmentalized and budgets so functionalized, they will often continue to create messages (e.g., creating and placing mass media ads, running promotions) even when intrinsic contact points are sending more powerful negative messages that are in need of repair. That is what happened at U.S. West as advertising continued to promote services while customers and regulators were criticizing the company for its lack of service performance.

Another reason for making intrinsic messages a top priority is that they primarily reach current customers whose retention, as we have said, is more economical than acquiring new customers. Finally, to be most cost effective, intrinsic message points need to be fully leveraged, maximizing not only their ability to supply information, but also their ability to listen to and gather information from customers.

MANAGING BRAND CONTACTS

The communication management of brand contact points requires: (1) identifying them, (2) prioritizing them based on their potential impact, (3) determining which are most suited for capturing customer feedback, (4) determining the cost of controlling messages being sent and collecting customer data at each contact point, and (5) determining which contact points can be used to carry additional brand messages and facilitate purposeful dialogue.

Intrinsic brand contact points must be handled with care. They need to be managed to ensure that messages are positive and consistent and, not overly commercialized. It is easy to misuse these communication opportunities, especially in service businesses such as airline travel, car rental, and restaurants where customers are a captive audience. Some companies use brand contact-point analysis merely as a way to find more opportunities to send customers and potential customers more brand messages. Such contacts may not make a positive contribution to a relationship, however, if they are perceived as irritating.

The contact point concept was first recognized by Scandinavian Airlines' former CEO, Jan Carlzon, as "moments of truth." Carlzon's definition of moments of truth meant doing the best job you can in all those areas that most impress customers.[1] Key contacts, in other words, are opportunities to make negative or positive impressions. He didn't develop the notion of contact points as a way to increase brand message bombardment.

According to one ad agency president "The better we are at understanding and responding to the consumer's decision points, the more it throws us into integrated communications. Likewise, separate programs can be developed to locate and manage information provided to key influencers, identifying who they are and how they affect the ultimate consumer. If that means the right way to reach consumers and influencers is putting signage up in 7-11 stores as opposed to doing a 30-second TV spot, we'll do it."[2] For example, one of the alternative media being used to reach the fast-growing "senior" market (which in the United States in 1996 had over one trillion in assets) is a network of wallboards, called Senior Network, which are in 4,500 senior community centers throughout the United States, places where this 55 plus group comes for fitness classes, language lessons, and just to gather and socialize.

Another aspect of brand contact-point management, especially in business-to-business marketing, is recognizing when several different departments are reaching a customer at the same contact point. Integrated marketing, through cross-functional monitoring and planning, brings these departments together to maximize the synergistic benefits of multiple contacts. A good example is how 3M responded when it realized that one of its intrinsic brand contact points with its customer, Boise Cascade, was Boise Cascade's warehouse.

A 3M cross-functional team made up of representatives from sales, MIS, and logistics brainstormed and came up with a way Boise Cascade could reduce its inventory and warehouse operation costs by $500,000. One of the ideas suggested by the 3M team was logistics label maps showing appropriate slot locations for 3M products in the warehouse, making it easier and faster for warehouse employees to place 3M products into inventory. As one of 3M's executives explained, the integrated culture at 3M that makes employees sensitive to the importance of customer contact points made this happen.[3]

MAXIMIZING VALUE-ADDED INTERACTIVITY

In order to have the type of interactivity that supports integrated marketing, a company must: (1) balance its media menu of mass, interactive, and addressable media that carry mass and individualized messages; (2) build databases that track customers' interactions (not just transactions) as well as their wants, needs, and concerns; (3) use and facilitate purposeful dialogue with customers; and (4) ensure that organizational memory and learning produces the necessary changes in corporate behavior.

Balancing the Media Menu

Everyone, companies and customers alike, has a media menu—a list of media used for sending and receiving messages to and from other people and organizations. Most companies, however, make limited strategic use of the media menu for sending messages to, let alone for receiving feedback from, customers. The advertising industry, for example, has conditioned us to think of media as a one-way street by which messages are sent to customers and potential customers. Little attention has been paid to two-way media that carry messages back from customers and other stakeholders. Although some marketers will argue that market research studies and 800 numbers provide feedback, this is only token communication in most organizations. (Other sources of feedback exist, such as sales records, orders placed, returned warranty cards, and customer comment cards, but these are seldom combined to construct a customer/potential customer profile.)

The *media menu* concept recognizes that because of media fragmentation, customers have more media from which to choose. When John Malone, CEO of TCI, first talked about someday having 500 channels, he used the number merely to emphasize that the choices would be much greater than we have today. The reality of our future media choices is, however, much, much greater than a mere 500 channels. Once computers, TVs, and telephones converge, the number of channels will become virtually infinite. Add to all the telephone numbers in the world the growing number of e-mail addresses, World Wide Web sites, and other informational databases that we will be able to easily access, and the "channel" options are unimaginable. Even today, there are more TV channels, more magazine titles, more radio stations, and more businesses and brands than ever in our history. Meanwhile, people are going on-line and visiting web sites 24 hours a day, 7 days a week to retrieve whatever bits and pieces of information they find most interesting, including information about brands and companies.

In integrated marketing, media includes everything that carries a message both to and/or from customers and other stakeholders. The proliferation of toll-free telephone numbers, faxes, and most importantly, the Internet and company Web sites, makes it easier and more cost effective to facilitate customer feedback. Add to this the combinations of mass media, place-based media (e.g., kiosks, in-store/in-office closed circuit video-casts, event signage), and the willingness of stores to tie into promotions. The result is the ability to become extremely creative in designing message sending and receiving systems.

As Mark Goldstein, president, Integrated Marketing at Fallon McElligott, explains, "media is no longer planned and bought; instead it's created, aggregated, and partnered." Companies and agencies need to think in terms of "message handling," being as responsible for *receiving* as for sending messages. The media department of the future may be better named the *Connect Department*.

Time to Spell Media Backwards: "Aid'em."

Media should aid customers by being two-way and providing value added information. Only when companies do this can they begin to really listen to what customers (and other stakeholders) want and don't want. For too long media have been used only as a tool for delivering sales messages.

This does not mean mass media are dead or will soon die, as some are predicting. To borrow a phrase, the death of mass media has been greatly exaggerated. Nevertheless the CEO of a global ad agency has stated that mass media are going to die because: (1) retail scanner data can show which items sell best in which stores, (2) databases now have individual household profiles, (3) companies can now mass customize products, and (4) there is a proliferation of media alternatives.[4] Although these four situations certainly exist, they are by no means sufficient to kill mass media; they merely open up new ways of communicating with customers.

Mass media are still cost effective for delivering certain types of messages, such as awareness, announcements, images, and brand reinforcement information to large, defined audiences. And as explained above, mass media are also a cost-effective way (in certain product categories) to qualify customers and generate trial to replace those who have been lost, as well as to expand a customer base.

One of the main challenges of planned messages, in addition to getting people to respond, is managing *who* responds in order to aggregate only the most qualified prospects and learn from them. This is true whether selling consumer or industrial products, because the cost-per-thousand (CPM) of addressable media is significantly more than mass media CPMs, as the following shows:

	CPM
Mass media messages	$10—$50
Direct-mail messages	250—5,000
Telemarketing calls	8,000—24,000
Field sales calls	40,000—400,000[5]

Smart companies are finding ways to leverage their media by using one media buy to open up another opportunity for contact. For example, an ad announcing a new shampoo for people going through chemotherapy can include a coupon that invites those specific people to get in touch with the company. What is often overlooked is that mass media can be used for this type of prospecting within a niche market, e.g., inviting people who are really interested in your company and its products to identify themselves for a dialogue and self-select themselves into a database. Furthermore, for megabrands, mass media can be a cost-effective way to not only reach current and potential customers but also other stakeholders with messages that are important to all of these groups. When a company such as Coke sponsors the Olympics, for example, it wants all customers and potential customers, as well as other stakeholders (employees, investors, the media, suppliers, and distributors) to be aware of this sponsorship.

Determining the Mix of Mass, Interactive, and Addressable Media

Commercial relationship strategies demand a new set of communication objectives. A brand must deliver more than expected, treat customers with respect, and most of all, reward profitable customers for their loyalty. To create and sustain long-term relationships with profitable customers, a company needs to take six steps:

1. Create awareness.
2. Qualify prospects.
3. Generate trial (and learn from those that don't respond).
4. Motivate repeat purchases.
5. Motivate purchases in additional brand/company categories.
6. Re-acquire those who have defected or at least learn why they defected.

For most consumer products (as well as industrial products), mass (or niche) media can be used to economically prospect for, qualify, and attract customers. Interactive media are good for stimulating a response and encouraging people who are interested to self-select themselves into a relevant database. Building awareness and creating a response are the steps used to *acquire* customers. Once a customer has been acquired, addressable media then becomes, in most cases, the most economical way of connecting, retaining, and reacquiring—the steps needed to *manage* customer dialogue.

Because of the new media alternatives, the term media mix takes on a whole new meaning. No more will it refer to merely a mix of mass media alternatives, but rather a mix of mass, interactive, and addressable media. This is what we mean by using a media menu strategy to execute integrated marketing. As Figure 6–1 shows, the relationship begins with mass media creating awareness. It strengthens the relationship as interactive media facilitate responses. The relationship is further strengthened and sustained by using addressable media to create an ongoing personal dialogue.

For example, when Procter & Gamble introduced Cheer Free, a detergent for people who are sensitive to detergents, mass media ad-

FIGURE 6–1

Menu Media and Relationships

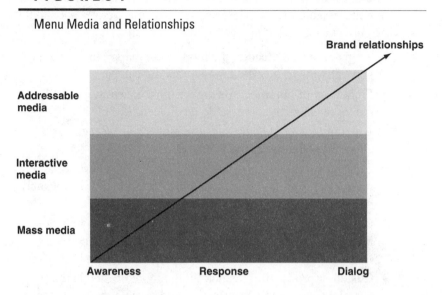

vertising announced the new formula (which prospected and qualified readers and viewers) and contained a reply device (attracting
those with allergies who were potential customers). The replies were
then collected into a database of prospects who were sent coupons
(for connecting) and additional brand information (for retaining and
reacquiring).

In product categories where each transaction is significant (e.g.,
cars, insurance, industrial products) or where the purchase frequency is
relatively high and the prospects are relatively few and easy to identify
and reach, addressable media, rather than mass media, can and should
be used for prospecting, qualifying, and attracting. In the same manner,
the lower the margin, the less frequent the purchase, and the more diverse the user groups, the more mass media should be used for connecting, retaining, and reacquiring. For example, in consumer
package-goods marketing, mass media, by carrying strong image advertising, can develop and nourish psychological relationships that will
not only connect consumers to brands but sustain the relationship.
Many luxury beer, tobacco, and sporting goods brands have done an
exceptional job of this.

The question is: What should be the mix between mass, interactive, and addressable media? Here are some of the factors that should be taken into consideration in making that decision:

- Target audience breadth: the more mass market the category, generally the more efficient mass media can be.
- Frequency of purchase: the higher the frequency, generally the more efficient addressable media can be.
- Amount of average purchase: the higher the average, generally the more efficient addressable media is.
- Churn level (brand switching): the greater the churn (of a mass market product such as cable TV), both addressable and mass media can be used efficiently.
- Current share of customer's category buying: if share is low, interactive media may provide an added value to increase customer share.
- Customer profitability: generally the more profitable the customer, the more cost effective addressable media can be.

LEVERAGING INTERACTIVE MEDIA

One thing that will increase the use of interactive media is the same thing that increased the use of sales promotion and direct response marketing over the last several decades—measurability and accountability. Interactive channels such as web sites, kiosks, and 800 numbers can record the number of hits or inquires and to a certain extent even measure the quality of these interactions (e.g., did the person go on to buy or request additional information?).

Interactive media are of two basic types, passive and active. *Passive* interactive media are such things as World Wide Web sites, kiosks, and CD-ROMs that allow a person to choose and configure information as desired. Also, some of these media allow a customer to leave a message requesting more information, a sample, or whatever. *Active* interactive media have the capability to send and receive messages in real time. Examples are 800 numbers, telemarketing and online sites that are actively monitored. The advantage of active or real-time, two-way dialogues is that individualized questions can be answered and objections can be addressed. With active interactive media, purchases can be made without causing a disconnect such as occurs when a customer must go from watching a TV commercial with an 800 number to a phone in order to respond.

Although the new media (as interactive media is sometime referred to), especially the Internet, give companies alternative ways to interact with customers, more importantly they also give customers the ability to be selective in what brand messages they receive, to talk back to companies, and to talk about companies and brands to other people all over the world. For example, McDonald's ran a trivia contest in 1996 with a $1 million top prize. Within days after the contest started, there were over a dozen WWW sites carrying answers to the trivia questions. One site alone had answers to over 3,500 of the 6,000 questions being asked. This shows how the new media is affecting old marketing tools.

Another example of the impact of the new media comes from the work of an American Association of Retired People (AARP) staffer attending a Congressional Committee meeting and taking notes on a laptop computer. AARP very much wanted the bill under discussion to make it out of committee. When the committee broke for lunch, the staff member used his laptop to compose an "issue" alert. He made a quick modem call to AARP headquarters, which selected the names of 100 key issue advocates from its membership database, merged the names with his message to create personalized memos, and simultaneously faxed the customized alerts to the AARP advocates. Within minutes, the committee members' offices were flooded with phone calls and faxes.[6]

> Companies are slowly learning that the Internet is not a direct selling tool for most products, but rather a supplemental channel of information that can be accessed and manipulated at the customer's convenience.

The Internet's Viability as a Marketing Tool

Much has been written about the Internet and the role it will play in marketing. The rush to set up homepages, however, reminds us of the 1848 gold rush. Many mining claims were staked, but for the most part those who made money were selling eggs and mining supplies. To date, those designing the Web sites are making more than

most sites are producing for their owners. Companies are slowly learning that the Internet is not a direct selling tool for most products, but
rather a supplemental channel of information that can be accessed and
manipulated at the customer's convenience.

Many who visit Web sites are just curious net surfers. Desert Rose
Foods, an Arizona manufacturer of salsa, set up a web site offering a catalogue and brochure and the ability to order its salsa direct from the fac-
tory. Although the company received numerous hits and information
requests from all over the world, in one year it received only one order
over the Internet.[7] Obviously people are not very interested in buying
salsa via the Internet. On the other hand, Power Express, a company that
sells computer, cellular, and camcorder batteries direct, receives over 30
percent of its orders via the Internet. And half of these orders are ac-
companied by the buyer's credit card number, which is sent unsecured.

Charles Schwab Corp., a major discount stockbroker, receives
over a quarter of its trading orders either by computer modem or from
customers entering their trades on a touch-tone telephone.[8] The importance of timely information needed for buying stocks versus its importance for buying salsa demonstrates that interactive media should be
used to make a transaction only when it makes the most sense.

Desert Rose also learned that site hits are not a good predictor of
sales. One way to qualify potential customers is to see if they are willing
to provide information about themselves that pertains to your product category. Because a relationship requires investment from both parties, a
truly interested customer should not be opposed to supplying information
that will help a company serve him or her better. How the information is
requested, however, is critical. The request must make clear why the information is being requested and how it will be used by the company.

Lynn Upshaw, former head of Ketchum Interactive, advises his
consulting clients to think of their homepages as "media properties,"
not as advertising. Jane's Cosmetics, for example, has a site on Prodigy
called Jane's Brain, which is aimed at 12- to 18-year-old females. By
providing a program "atmosphere," this vehicle has become the single
most effective marketing effort the company has used. The Jane
Company owns the whole program, which is similar to the early TV
soap operas (which were produced by the soap companies), and has designed content specifically for on-line use. It is easier to nurture a relationship via a proprietary program than via traditional advertising.

Another area in which the Internet can play an important role in managing relationships is the monitoring of unplanned messages. Up to now, a customer mistreated by a company has only been able to talk to family, friends, and co-workers. Using the Internet, however, a bad experience can be shared literally with millions. The ability of a single individual to have such reach will be extremely critical in narrow niche markets whose users have their own on-line interest groups. An example is Intel's experience in 1995 when one Prof. Nicely went on-line saying he had discovered a slight flaw in Intel's Pentium chip. Within hours of the first Internet posting, news of Intel's "bad" chip was known by computer operators all over the world. As the Internet discussion grew, it soon attracted the attention of CNN, which began a mass media discussion of the story at an eventual cost to Intel of millions of dollars.

Although Intel reacted slowly to this problem, it learned fast. The company eventually set up a $400 million contingency fund to handle such emergencies in the future. But more importantly, it also hired several people full time to monitor all the Internet conferences that deal with computers in order to have an early warning of any future discussions, especially negative ones, about Intel and its products.

The Internet will mature more quickly as a tool for interacting with other businesses than with consumers simply because there is a greater penetration of computers in the business world and in most cases a greater need for buying information. Also, companies can more easily justify the cost of responding to a business customer than a consumer (especially those buying low margin goods and services). When electronic commerce does become popular with consumers, one of the major elements will be shopping agents which are already being used by some businesses. These are online software programs that can be asked to electronically search for information about a certain product— its price, availability, and other pertinent data.

A concern of those companies selling online is to what extent will they be able to build relationships with customers? If customers are strictly shopping on price, relationships will be thin. As with regular retailing, we believe the supporting services—credit, delivery time, return policy, customer service availability—will continue to play a role and define the relationship. When it comes to searching for the best price, a software agent is merely a faster way of having your computer do the walking rather than your fingers through the Yellow Pages.

Variables Affecting the Internet's Marketing Role

Although the Internet's growth has been significantly faster than other media, it still has a way to go before it will rival radio, TV, newspapers, magazines and the mail service as a marketing communication channel. Unlike these media, the Internet's ability to provide both passive and active interactivity will continue to speed its adoption and use. However, several barriers still must be overcome.

- *Content:* a commonly heard statement is that the Internet is a technological solution waiting for a problem. The content of most commercial Web sites, other than those that supply specification catalogues, inventory and pricing information, is basic print advertising. Not only is most content not very creative, it is a copy of material available in other forms.

- *Speed of operation:* the infrastructure—primarily bandwidth—of the Internet was designed to carry only text, but is now being asked (and expected) to transport graphics, video, and voice. These new demands, plus the skyrocketing increase in users and old equipment, often makes reception of information very slow.

- *Penetration of use:* there are two types of penetration barriers. One is physical. The majority of customers, especially consumers, simply do not have the computers and modems that allow access. The second is psychological. Many who do have the hardware have not learned to navigate the Internet and some of those who have have not found the experience worthwhile.

- *Security:* although several transaction security systems were being tested at the time this book was printed, once a system is proven to work it will still take months or even years for the majority of customers to be convinced it is safe to make financial transactions over the Internet.

- *Strategic use:* with few exceptions (e.g., highly niched) the Internet should be used as a marketing communication support medium. Marketers are still struggling to figure out exactly how to do this. As explained above, broadly soliciting questions is often not cost effective. Marketers need to start with the Internet's strengths—"open" 24 hours a day, 7 days a week;

capable of storing and providing access to enormous depths of information; can screen Web site visitors by requiring them to answer questions; Web site information can be instantly changed on a global basis. When the security issues are solved the Internet will become a major direct marketing tool.

The Costs Considerations of Using Interactive Media

Interactive systems are relationship-building investments and do not come cheap. When companies make the decision to "go interactive," they are sometimes surprised by the hurdles they confront. If you advertise an 800 number and invite people to call, what happens when they actually do call *en masse*? Microsoft was overwhelmed with 40,000 phone calls a day when it introduced Windows '95.

Similarly, when Ford introduced the redesigned 1996 Taurus, it ran an 8-page color newspaper ad and invited people to make contact with the company via an 800 number, the World Wide Web, or through Prodigy or CompuServe. The inducement was, "We'll send you the book on the all-new Ford Taurus." The day the ad broke, at least one person's search of the WWW for Ford's homepage ended in an hour wait for downloaded graphics to finally produce a single, poorly-designed page that told users how to get the "book." CompuServe, meanwhile, responded that it had no address for "Taurus 96."

Another cost consideration is that the more knowledgeable and articulate a company representative is in an interactive situation, generally the more expensive that person's time will be. Add to this the cost of installing and maintaining an 800 number, designing and maintaining homepages, and setting up the MIS system and hardware to capture customer data and manage the database, and the costs can easily be several hundred thousand dollars a year. Finally, to answer some of the questions and inquiries that come in will require involving other people in the company and their time, which is an additional cost. The alternative to foregoing the investment in interactivity, however, may be not only the loss of customer support, but the generation of a brand-basher as disappointed customers find no one to talk to except other customers.

Before implementing an interactive program, a company should evaluate what it can realistically handle with the resources it is willing to commit. GTE found that it was more cost effective to focus on ways to reduce complaints for its cellular phone service than to maintain an elaborate response system for handling complaints. A survey had found that, after calling to complain, customers were still likely to cancel.[9] This, of course, is a basic principle of TQM—fix the process so you don't have to waste time and money correcting a mistake—that also makes it possible to avoid the negative message sent when a product fails. Evaluating feasibility involves systemic and cross-functional thinking in order to accurately assess the costs and benefits.

A good interactivity system ensures that the company is easily accessible to customers and provides an economical way for it to listen and respond, giving the customers a sense of empowerment by letting them know that their ideas and comments matter. It also provides a way to rapidly respond to customer complaints and inquires.

Maximizing the use of addressable media with individualized messages requires building and managing customer databases, which is discussed later in this chapter.

LEVERAGING ADDRESSABLE MEDIA

These are the media—direct mail, email, telemarketing, fax—that carry messages to individual geographical and electronic addresses. Addressable media should not be confused with personalized messages. Merely because a medium can be individually addressed doesn't mean the message being delivered is personalized. As a matter of fact, the majority of direct mail and telemarketing, although personally addressed, contain *mass* rather than personalized messages. Merely dropping a person's name several times within a direct mail piece, for example, does not fool many people into believing it is a personal message.

Although there has been a great deal of discussion about the virtues of one-to-one marketing, the challenge is to find a cost-effective way of practicing it. Unfortunately, most companies that are building databases and enhancing them with database overlays are using this enriched data only for media targeting, not for individualizing message content. In other words, they are using addressable media to carry mass messages. This is because the cost of doing individualized messages is prohibitive in many product categories.

Developing closer and stronger relationships with customers, however, requires personalized or value-added messages. Although addressable media guarantee a higher degree of message attention relative to those delivered by mass media, addressability has become so common it is quickly losing its impact. Personalized messages, however, have more impact, especially when the customer's past buying or some other personal behavior or trait (relevant to the product and/or its use) is referred to so that the receiver knows it is meant just for him or her.

For example, a company in San Francisco, 2 Market, provides direct-mail catalogues on-line. It also offers a gift expert who will suggest gifts once provided with certain profile information about the person for whom the gift is needed. In this way, the company is offering a value-added service to customers. Designing individualized messages also allows it to build a rich, relational database that can be used to contact the gift giver a year later (for the next birthday) and on other gift-giving occasions reminding customers of their previous gift selections.[10]

ROLE OF DATABASES IN INTERACTIVITY

Databases are the engines that drive interactivity. Simply put, data-driven marketing is identifying customers, listening to them, and tracking interactions with them. Up to now, most executives have felt that tracking customer behavior and attitudes could only be justified for business-to-business products or high-ticket consumer products. But as the cost of database use continues to fall, this is changing. Donnelley Marketing has found that over half of the major packaged-goods companies are building consumer databases.[11] But this still doesn't mean every business can cost-justify tracking every end user. As a matter of fact, very few packaged goods companies can but that doesn't mean they can't make use of data-driven marketing.

Take a company such as Colgate. Although it cannot justify individually capturing and responding to every purchase of one of its many products, it can, through retail store scanner data, identify and respond to heavy users of its toothpaste and other Colgate products, which could amount to $200–300 a year per household. With this type of customer information, it now becomes cost effective to mass customize messages to these high-volume Colgate customers with offers that reward them and encourage them to buy even more Colgate brands. These are also the customers whose feedback is most valuable.

Chapter 10 will present an expanded discussion of how to build and use databases, but the following discussion will explain why marketing and marketing communications should be data-driven.

MASS CUSTOMIZATION OF BRAND MESSAGES

The ability to mass customize products has limited value if a company can't mass customize (that is, individualize) its brand messages. Just as knowing a customer's individual needs is necessary before a product can be customized for added value, the same is true for customizing communication. Customized messages are based on knowing customers' past interactions, their attitudes towards the brand and company, their lifestyle and demographics, and knowing what the company has said to them before and how they have reacted.

Knowing who your profitable customers are and how, when, and in what way they have interacted and want to interact with your company, depends on collecting this information in accessible databases. With *transaction and attitude memory*, a company can differentiate its customers just as it does its products. The concept of segmentation and the wisdom of focusing marketing efforts on heavy users is nothing new. The problem has always been identifying these customers and then tracking their purchase and other brand behavior to accurately identify those who are more profitable and most receptive to other product offerings.

Building profiles of customers (and other key stakeholders) makes it possible for companies to *recognize* these individuals and treat them as individuals rather than as members of a mass market or even a niche group. This is a significant step toward the creation of long-term customer relationships, the value of which was seen by a professional baseball team, the San Diego Padres, which was having attendance problems. When baseball fans in its area were asked what would attract them back to the ballpark, a key finding was that they wanted recognition for being fans and supporting the team. When asked how they wanted to be recognized, the answer was: "Allowing us [loyal fans] to talk to and with the team and its players in some way." In other words, they wanted some type of interactive, personal link to the team. The team responded by setting up a variety of programs in which the database of loyal fans was used to send out invitations to these affairs.

Another example of a company using computers and databases for consumer goods is Domino's Pizza. Using caller ID tied into a customer database, a repeat customer's order history immediately comes up on a screen along with his or her address and phone number. A customer in a hurry has only to say "The usual" and hang up because on the screen is the customer's usual order as well as her or his name, address, and telephone number. A software program instantly identifies the source (name and phone number) and integrates that into a database containing the caller's purchase history. (For first-time callers, a company that has subscribed to a white pages database can have the caller's name and address on the screen in less than four rings.) Domino's has installed this system in all of its 700 company owned and operated stores and close to half of its franchised stores.

Similar combinations of databases and software improve customer service several ways. For one, it can route a call to a particular sales representative or department. A utility company can route incoming calls from a business customer to the same company representative who has handled calls from that customer in the past. Such systems eliminate name, address, and phone number recording errors because this has only to be done once (and if a mistake is initially made, it is corrected for all future transactions). They are also more efficient for both the customer and the company, allowing shorter phone conversations because the information can be automatically printed on order forms or invoices.

FedEx, which handles over a quarter million customer phone calls a day, has been able to significantly reduce labor cost and time on the phone by having the calling customer's record automatically retrieved, saving the time it takes to ask and record all the basic identification information.[12] Just as important as saving the company money, it saves the customer time and, more importantly, recognizes the caller as a customer.

To address an individual's requirements requires dealing with customers individually and convincing them to take the time and effort to inform the company of their wants, needs, and concerns. Once a company has this information, it has the obligation to use it appropriately, by sending messages that have added value for customers. Integrated marketing must be collaborative, not adversarial or manipulative.

In addition to relationship building, databases also provide a *continuous feedback loop*. Information obtained from these individual contacts is captured and fed back into the planning process, providing immediate, real-time information about product and marketing communication successes and problems. In addition to capturing useful feedback, these tools also make it possible to empower employees to make better decisions in their contacts with customers and other stakeholders.

Databases in contemporary marketing are more than just tools for targeting. Today, information in the form of extensive customer databases is becoming more valuable than land, labor, and capital.

THE "5 Rs" OF PURPOSEFUL DIALOGUE

Integrated marketing does *not* mean collecting customers' names and addresses in order to just send them more and more brand messages. It *does* mean learning about customers in order to have a *purposeful dialogue* with them. While corporate executives and marketing managers pay lip service to the idea of creating a dialogue with customers, in too many cases they don't understand the difference between purposeful and diabolical dialogue. Diabolical dialogue is intrusive, irritating, and perceived by customers as having no added value.

The criteria for purposeful dialogue are the 5 Rs: *recourse, recognition, responsiveness, respect*, and *reinforcement*. Customers are looking for recourse, recognition, and responsiveness—and companies must conduct their dialogue with respect and to reinforce customer support.

1. **Recourse.** A major concern of most customers is how to avoid risk when buying a product. What are their options if they don't like the product, if it doesn't work properly, or it breaks? An essential aspect of recourse is making it easy for customers to contact a company with their problems. A company's willingness to replace a product is negated if customers must fill out numerous forms, find receipts, send in the product at their own expense, and then wait weeks for a decision on the replacement.

   For example, one global appliance manufacturer's policy for handling problems with its brand of phones is for the customer to mail the phone back to the company (at the customer's expense) and agree to a $35 service/handling charge up front. Think of the implied negative messages this policy sends. First of all the product broke, so it did not meet performance expectations. Second, customers are told they must go to a lot of trouble and expense. Finally, there is no information on the product itself concerning what to do or where to send it. Situations like this make the customer feel commercially impotent rather than important.

   The recourse problem begins with ease of contact. In a focus group on computers and customer service, one of the participants asked: How do you call IBM? Trying to call a company, particularly a large, multinational company, is a discouraging thought for most people. The easier it is for a customer to get questions answered and problems dealt with, the easier it will be for that customer to develop a supporting relationship with that company. Easy accessibility to an organization, particularly when there is a problem, is an added value to customers.

One reason brand loyalty has become less important to consumers of most packaged goods is because they no longer have to depend on the manufacturer to stand behind a brand. Retailers with no-questions-asked return policies have taken over this important role, making exchanges and then demanding credit from their suppliers. A form of brand loyalty migration, this is one of the situations that is transferring brand loyalty from manufacturers to retailers and making the latter so powerful. In other words, retailers are reducing risk for consumers and consumers, in return, are transferring their loyalty to the retailer brand rather than the manufacturer's brand. Since manufacturers ultimately take responsibility for these returns, they should be getting more benefit for standing behind their products. This can be done through planned messages, by telling customers to make returns to their retailers and, if customers do not receive satisfaction, to contact the manufacturer.

2. **Recognition.** Customers and other stakeholders like to be personally recognized—that's one of the first steps in a relationship. On cold-call solicitations by mail and phone, for instance, companies often address a potential customer by name. If the company has had no relationship with the customer, however, the person being contacted will recognize this as a ploy. However, when a customer has given a company its business (or buys stock in a company), he or she feels a relationship has been established, even if the company sees it as an "acquisition." If the company fails to recognize this "connect," then the customer or investor sees the relationship as weak.

Companies must be able to match customers' transaction memory in those product categories where the customer has direct contact with the company. Person's who most frequently rents cars from Hertz have a good feel for the number of annual rentals plus the specific problems they have had with Hertz. If Hertz is able to acknowledge this interaction history when the customer makes a reservation or picks up a car, the brand relationship is strengthened and the customers are more likely to feel they are getting a return on their brand investment.

Nieman Marcus discovered how starved even affluent customers are for attention. The retailer rewards its most important customers (those spending more than two million dollars a year) with a trip around the world and lunch with the local store manager. In its ongoing customer-satisfaction research with these big spenders, lunch with the store manager, not the trip around the world, is mentioned first. As rich as they are, they still crave personal recognition, which the lunch with the manager provides.

One way Sears is rebuilding its customer franchise and strengthening relationships with its top customers is a very simple, low-cost recognition program. The chain sends top customers a small, pressure-sensitive "Best Customer" label to put on their Sears charge cards. Employees have been instructed to give these customers special attention, such as calling over the department or store manager and introducing these customers or making a special effort to point out items on sale. Sears research has shown the technique is well appreciated.[13]

3. **Responsiveness.** Merely providing customers an 800 number or an e-mail address so they can easily reach the company is only the first step in being responsive. Responsiveness consists of a company representative listening to the customer, putting the conversation into a context of the customer's profile and history, and staying with the customer until the problem is solved or next steps are agreed to. The elapsed time between when a customer places an order, complains, or asks for help and is satisfied is a strong service message and an indication of how responsive the company really is.

There is also an emotional aspect of responsiveness that should not be overlooked. For example, when a direct-response customer calls in to order from a catalogue, the person is generally excited about making the purchase. However, because companies are so internally focused, they structure this buying process according to what is best for them. Instead of immediately discussing what the customer wants to discuss—the items being purchased—many direct-response companies require customers to first talk about what is most important to the company—"Give me your customer number, the one printed on the front of the catalogue above your name. Now give me your current address, etc. etc." They proceed to turn a pleasant experience into a tangle of red-tape.

The question for managers is whether their company is ready for the effort and cost necessary to be responsive. It is critical to avoid creating customer expectations that can't be filled. (That's one of the problems faced by US West and discussed in the story at the beginning of Chapter 1).

4. **Respect.** Customers aren't interested in having their lives interrupted with corporate messages, being interrupted by non-relevant telemarketing offers, or continually being offered another product or line extension that they don't need. They resent intrusive messages and are creating more and more defense mechanisms against them. They are more willing to be part of a commercial relationship if it is clear that the company respects them and their time. All brand contact points should be labeled "Handle with Care"! The way most companies send brand messages brings to mind the old movie images of a doctor chasing a patient around the office to administer a shot with a large needle. The more self-serving the brand message, the longer the customer perceives the needle to be.

Marketers have messed their own relationship bed. According to Mike Green, President of Direct Marketing Research Associates, the company has to mail out three times as many surveys as they did a decade ago in order to get the same number of responses. In other words, the average customer is so tired of being surveyed and solicited that the response rate has fallen two-thirds. Although the average response rate to direct-mail promotional offers has on the surface not dropped that significantly, it needs to be kept in mind that direct-response methods and targeting have greatly improved over the last decade, yet the average response rate is still around 2 percent. This can only mean that the improved methods are simply balancing out the overall resistance (as explained elsewhere, companies that do an exceptional job of targeting can generate response rates as high as 50 percent). Because there is such a great concern about intrusive media in Europe, the European Union is working on legislation to heavily regulate telemarketing and direct-mail solicitations.

Companies and communication agencies have become quite proficient at being intrusive. In response, customers have become proficient at blocking, dodging, and avoiding these commercial messages. To take advantage of the growing criticism of intrusive advertising on TV, Thompson Electronics is now selling VCRs that automatically zip viewers through commercial pods when watching a video replay.

In a focus group of business customers that we conducted for a major computer company which had recently discovered traditional database marketing, it was pointed out just how intrusive commercial messages can become. Each of the company's divisions had been bombarding the same customers with surveys, customer satisfaction checks, new product information, and "courtesy calls" not to mention regular sales calls. When this company was mentioned in the focus group one of the respondents said he had both its software and hardware, but if he received one more disruptive call from that company he would move to a completely different system, no matter how much the cost. He was just plain tired and disgusted, he said, of being bothered by this company.

Fifteen minutes later in this same discussion respondents were asked if they would attend a half-day seminar sponsored by this particular computer company. One of the first people to say "yes" was the person who had threatened to drop the company. When asked why the change in attitude, he explained that he could schedule the seminar at his convenience. In other words, he was willing to give the company a half-day of his time on *his* schedule, but not two minutes on *the company's* schedule.

When commercial messages become intrusive, they build up customer avoidance and ultimately hurt the industry as a whole, as well as the brand. To avoid being considered intrusive (or "junk mail"), a message must have an added value for the recipient and be received when, where, and in the form preferred by the customer or potential customer. Unless the message contains something a person feels is of value (e.g., either entertainment or relevant information), chances are it will be rejected. To find out what information customers value (and when, where, and in what form they want that information), they simply need to be asked. Companies are willing to spend on testing new products but not on testing relationship building techniques.

The director of marketing for one of the largest retailers in the United States believes that his company must talk to customers six to eight times a year to maintain relationships and convince customers that the company thinks they are important. The question most companies never ask is: Do customers want to hear from them six to eight times a year, especially by way of another mass mailing? It's not even a message problem, it's the contact itself.

An example of showing respect for customers was a Citibank direct-mail offer to current customers. The purpose of the mailing was to motivate customers to schedule a personal interview with a Citibank financial planner. On the reply device (which promised the customer a free copy of Price-Waterhouse's *Investor's Tax Guide* for meeting with a bank representative) the customer was asked to name the day and time and provide a phone number that would be most convenient for the financial planner to call to set up an appointment.

5. **Reinforcement.** One of the important benefits of mass-media and addressable advertising is reinforcement for people who have already purchased the product. In fact, studies have shown that in many cases the majority of ad readers are current customers. For someone who has just spent $25,000 on a new car, for example, an intelligent, attractive ad about the new vehicle can be seen as very purposeful communication because it reinforces the $25,000 buying decision. If it contains an

interactive device for feedback, the ad can start a dialog that will reap referrals and repeat business for years to come if the dealer selling the car maintains its records. Saturn does this for its owners.

Reinforcement of a purchase decision, especially on high-ticket items, should be part of a company's communication strategy. The more expensive the item, the more likely "buyer's remorse" (cognitive dissonance) may set in. Car dealers, for example, often call new buyers to make sure everything is working properly and to answer any questions customers might have about their new car's operation. It is also a way to collect information, not only about customers' perceptions, but also about product performance.

Companies can also find ways to respond with more sincerity. A phone call from a mechanical-sounding voice thanking customers for their business, may insult rather than flatter. The unimaginative, scripted message carries the same level of personalized sincerity as the "thank you" that comes from those 1980s cars when you fastened your seatbelt.

USING INTERACTIVITY TO CREATE A LEARNING ORGANIZATION

Capturing customer (and other stakeholder) data makes it possible to individualize messages and have a purposeful dialogue. But if this collected data is used only for that, a company is not getting full value from its database and database management system (DBMS). With proper monitoring and capturing of customers' attitudes and interactions, interactivity programs can add to, if not replace, many traditional marketing research efforts.

Capturing customer interactions provides an ongoing read of the market rather than periodic customer satisfaction surveys, plus a closer working relationship with customers. For example, if the brand group comes up with a particular question, it can be given to the customer service center, and/or the telemarketing team (if the brand uses this tool) to reach nonusers as well as brand users. A continuous feedback program has three dimensions: (1) ongoing data collection, (2) continuous aggregation, and (3) periodic trend analysis. In other words, the data is collected and aggregated continuously, but the analysis step is as frequent as the company sees fit and can afford. The trend analysis looks for a "critical mass" of comments or behaviors that suggest problems or opportunities. In addition to knowledge building, internally publicizing customer feedback also keeps a customer focus a top priority of employees.

In business-to-business marketing, as well as consumer service marketing, much of the customer information is stored in employees' heads. Salespeople who have developed a long-term relationships with clients often know their clients' needs but never take time to record them (in most companies there is no incentive for doing so). In an ad agency, for example, a particular client's likes and dislikes are seldom recorded by the account managers who service the account. Thus, when a new person takes over the account, the client is forced to endure a learning curve as the new account manager gets up to speed. In the case of manufacturers, when a new sales representative takes over an account without the benefit of a recorded client history, for some period she is unable to efficiently service the account and loses potential sales because she doesn't know the customer's history well enough to up-sell and cross-sell. The value tied up in future purchasing is probably considerable. A sales and service, customer-contact database, collected as a byproduct of doing business, (not from just filling orders), is needed.

Companies learn from past experiences, but only if there is an institutional memory system that makes it possible to record, store, aggregate, and share customer and other stakeholder information. In customer-driven marketing, companies can't just ask customers what they want or need. Often customers (both consumer and business) can't articulate what they really want or need. This is because they are not by nature creative, especially in the area in which their suppliers work. Also, they have been conditioned by the products they are currently using. By collecting

> **Companies learn from past experiences, but only if there is an institutional memory system that makes it possible to record, store, aggregate, and share customer and other stakeholder information.**

information on how they use a product and listening to them explain the situation in which the product is used and why it is used, companies can be more creative in designing new solutions, products, and brand message strategies to present these innovations. The challenge is to capture the kind of qualitative information that drives this type of creativity.

Oftentimes it is as simple as developing a listening program for interactions that are already going on. Although many companies have 800 numbers, few use them to engage customers in strategic feedback. Yet the opportunity is there, and most customers are not only willing but feel complimented when they are asked for their experiences and opinions. Such programs are win-win: The company sends an important message of "You are important," plus it learns more about customer perceptions and the product category in general. In most cases, it's simply a matter of setting up a system to ask and record such information when a customer interaction occurs.

Another advantage to real-time customer feedback is reducing the time between designing a program and testing it. This instant feedback loop can significantly shorten time-to-market. To reduce time-to-market involves the whole organization and demands integration. The Mervyn's department store chain captures conversations with 50,000 to 70,000 customers a year in its stores. Survey responses are entered on computers and tallied the next day. An example of how Mervyn's has benefited from this data collection effort is what it was able to do in some of its Texas stores right before Christmas a couple years ago. When shoppers in several of these stores said they had started listening to a radio station that had recently switched to country-and-western music, Mervyn's was able to instantly revise its radio buy to include this station and more effectively drive its Christmas business. In the past, an outside firm took six weeks to tabulate data, and Mervyn's would not have known that its customers' radio listening habits had changed until after Christmas.[14]

Another element of interactivity that is often overlooked is learning from disgruntled customers. For example, according to one study, only 18.9 percent of the marketers surveyed who used direct mail made an effort to interview nonresponders and defectors.[15]

Customer complaints are especially valuable information. They provide both upstream and downstream related messages from consumers. The upstream message is generally a production or operations concern. Something may be wrong in the production process or in the way a service was provided. The downstream message that a customer is unhappy must be addressed for two reasons. The first is customer retention. The fact the customer has taken the trouble to contact the company may be an indication he is willing to be saved. The second reason is that this customer can either become a brand basher or brand endorser. Either way, the person has credibility because of brand use, so others will listen.

Customer complaints offer a valuable opportunity for learning about the customer as well as about the company's product category. Frederick Webster says it very well: "When customers complain, they are telling us how they define value and why, in their judgment, we are not delivering it. They may help us to identify a process or a product feature that needs improvement. They may be telling us something we didn't know about our competitors. They also are telling us that they care about our products and our company and want us to do a better job."[16]

The value of being a learning organization is that it helps counterbalance what Noriaki Kano calls the "natural effect of gravity pulling down the innovative performance into the competitive area of performance and then into the basic area of performance."[17] In other words, without continually listening and anticipating the needs and desires of customers, the gap between a company's performance and its customers' expectations will widen.

A learning organization is also a continuously adaptive organization. Information and strategy are shared throughout the system. Such a system, however, can't work unless it is an integrated system.

MAKING INTERACTIVITY PURPOSEFUL

An interactivity strategy highlights another important difference between traditional marketing, which is focused primarily on sending messages, and integrated marketing, which supplements mass and niche media messages with purposeful dialogue. Listening not only demonstrates respect for the customer's views and concerns, it also provides a mechanism to get continuous, real-time feedback that can be used strategically to monitor and modify products, services, and programs as they are being developed and delivered.

By taking advantage of new computer and communication technologies and having a corporate commitment to listening to customers, companies can cost-effectively gather information that will enable them to mass customize messages, just as they are beginning to mass customize products. And as we know from personal selling, the more individualized a message is, the greater its impact.

E N D N O T E S

1. Jan Carlzon, Moments of Truth (New York: Harper & Row, 1987), p. 3.
2. Personal Interview, January, 1995 in Chicago.
3. Rahul Jacob, "Why Some Customers Are More Equal Than Others," *Fortune*, September 19, 1994, p. 218
4. Rick Fizdale, "Integrated Communications: The Whole Picture," *The Advertiser*, Summer, 1992, p. 58.
5. Vic Hunter, "Increasing Sales Productivity," presentation at High-Tech Direct Conference, Santa Clara, California, February 27–March 1, 1995.
6. David Kirk, "State of the Dream: How American Corporations Are Using Technology to Support Key Relationships," file on CompuServe, *Tech Benchmark Study*, March 7, 1994.
7. Joan E. Rigdon, "For Some, the Web Is Just a Slow Crawl To a Splattered Cat," *The Wall Street Journal*, January 25, 1996, p. A14.
8. Allan J. Magrath, *How to Achieve Zero-Defect Marketing*, (New York: AMACOM, 1993), p. 138.
9. David Greising, "Quality: How to Make It Pay," *Business Week*, August 8, 1994, p. 58.
10. Gene Koprowski, "The Electronic Watchdog," *Marketing Tools*, (July/August, 1995), p. 6.
11. "Using Databases to Build Brands; Consumer Database Marketing Requires a Long-Term Focus and Retailer Input," *Potentials in Marketing*, 26:8, (September 1993), p. 20.
12. Rodney J. Moore, "Hold the Phone!," *Marketing Tools*, January/February 1996, p. 68.
13. Fred Newell, presentation to National Direct Marketing Institute for Professors, sponsored by the Direct Marketing Educational Foundation, San Francisco, March 20, 1996.
14. William Bulkeley, "More Market Researchers Swear by PCs," *The Wall Street Journal* March 15, 1993, p. B7.

15. "What's in Store? *DIRECT's* Second Annual Reader Survey Tracks Where Marketers Are Putting Their Money. Database Development Is a Top Priority," *DIRECT* 4:12 (December 1992), p. 26.
16. Frederick E. Webster, Jr. *Market-Driven Management* (New York: John Wiley & Sons, 1994), p. 277.
17. Gregory H. Watson, *Strategic Benchmarking* (New York: John Wiley & Sons, 1993), p. 12.

7 CHAPTER

Market the Mission

The majority of today's adults have grown up in a commercial message cocoon and know how to deal with it. They are smarter and more demanding than ever, but also more distrusting. Trust of businesses (and most other public and private organizations) is lower than it has been for decades. And this is true in Europe as well as in the United States. As former Yankelovich partner Watts Wacker has put it: "We all operate from the premise of being, or having just been, screwed."[1]

In 1995 when Carl Sagan was asked what invention he would best like to see, he answered: "A baloney detection kit, so that every citizen can tell when he or she is being lied to by those in power." Although this comment was specifically directed at U.S. politicians, the idea that those in a position of authority can't be trusted is a popular perception that carries over to business. A report from Roper Starch Worldwide found that Americans: (1) have lower expectations of society, (2) have more personal long-term uncertainty and insecurity, (3) are increasingly distrustful of elites and institutions, and (4) are increasingly disillusioned with their work.[2]

One reason these attitudes exist is that although companies have made significant strides in lowering product defects, the same progress has not been made in lowering relationship defects. There are still too many instances of taking customers for granted, misleading them about what products will do, failing to listen and respond when customers complain or ask questions, and putting profits before everything else including the welfare of employees, customers, and the environment.

Attitudes of customer disrespect, disgust, and distrust create new marketplace challenges. The bottom line for many stakeholders is that most businesses have little integrity. Therefore, if a company wants to shed this stereotype and increase its integrity among customers and other stakeholders, it must prove that it is a good corporate citizen, accepting the privileges *and responsibilities* of functioning within an economic and social community whether local, national, or global. It can do this by practicing mission marketing, which adds value and trust to brand relationships.

There are two basic levels of mission marketing. The first is having a mission or purpose for existing in addition to creating shareholder value and profits. This requires a corporate culture and discipline to ensure the mission is visibly practiced and is more than merely fancy words framed on the boardroom wall.

The second level of mission marketing is more executional and applies to those companies who are involved in a broad range of philanthropic activities. This requires changing the way they handle their social outreach and cause marketing programs. Interestingly, when we have found companies with these programs, they have been doing little to maximize their return on being good corporate citizens. Most companies, in an attempt to maximize their social outreach, are spreading their philanthropic support so thin it makes little impact and the company receives little benefit. Also, most who do cause marketing are failing to generate long-term benefits from these programs. The attractiveness of mission marketing at this level is that it requires little investment because the budgets already exist. It's merely a case of integrating the efforts and concentrating them.

To maximize the benefits of mission marketing a company should do both—have and promote its mission as well as concentrate its philanthropic programs into an activity that reinforces the mission and has a presence. We'll first discuss the benefits of mission marketing and its role both internally and externally. That will be followed by an explanation of how to get a better ROI from corporate philanthropy and cause marketing activities. At the end of this chapter is a description of how to manage a mission.

BENEFITS OF MISSION MARKETING

Having a mission that is integrated into a company's marketing effort can generate many benefits. These benefits will vary, however, depending to what extent a company's mission is focused, pervasive, long-term, relevant, and communicated. The more these criteria are met, the more mission marketing:

- ◆ Builds integrity and trust. A study on corporate equity done by *Fortune* and Yankelovich Partners found that the two most important linkages to determining whether people like a company are 1) to what extent the company can be trusted, and 2) to what extent it conducts business in a human, caring way. These two criteria also affect the extent to which a customer recommends a company's product.

- ◆ Helps reach customers and other stakeholders more economically than mass media advertising and traditional sales promotion activities.

- ◆ Provides source credibility. When a company with a recognized and respected mission sends out a brand message, it is more likely to be believed.

- ◆ Helps integrate and psychologically bind employees together, which enhances internal communication and the exchange of ideas.

- ◆ Provides an added value for customers and other stakeholders to support a company/brand since so few companies have a real mission, and of those that do, most are failing to market and leverage it.

- ◆ Generates "confirmation" types of brand messages. A mission that stakeholders can believe in helps creates positive, "confirm" messages.

- ◆ Helps counter social activism that may be harmful to the company. According to a study by the Social Investment Forum, shareholder activism is on the rise and influencing $450 billion of corporate assets. Religious and labor groups, as well as employee pension funds, are becoming more sophisticated in the way they try to influence corporations.

Sometimes these causes create rather unexpected coalitions, such as women's groups joining with the Catholic Church to put pressure on companies doing biotech research.[3] As these groups become more sophisticated in applying economic pressure on companies both directly and through investors, executives will come to realize that being socially responsible is no longer an expense but rather a worthy investment.

- Leverages money already being spent.
- Enriches brand awareness by associating brand/company with social responsibility.
- Can positively impact all stakeholders, not just customers.
- Attracts higher quality employees.
- Reduces employee turnover.
- Helps keep employees focused on the company's fundamental objective of growing profitable relationships. As companies flatten out by removing layers of management, and as decision making is pushed lower in the corporate hierarchy, a danger grows. Empowering managers when there is not a clear mission and no clear objectives can create negative tension, infighting, and segregation rather than integration. Within an organization, empowerment must go hand and hand with overall objectives and a common mission to keep it on course.
- Works as an emotional lever in people's decision-making processes. The idea that human emotion affects business decisions is not new. Robert Lucas, who won the 1995 Nobel Prize for his economic theory, which he began working on 20 years ago, has successfully pointed out that the "human factor" needs to be given more weight in economic models that predict behavior.

A viable mission heavily influences a company's corporate culture, which is a combination of the behavior patterns ("the way we do things around here"), tone and style of the organization, and core values. There has been much discussion in recent years about the need to move away from command and control management. Mission marketing offers a way to help replace the militaristic model by creating core values and corporate cultures that enable employees to direct themselves because they understand where the company wants to go and how it's getting there.

According to Martin Sorrell, CEO of WPP (holding company of J. Walter Thompson, Ogilvy & Mather, Carl Byoir, and Hill & Knowlton, among many others), helping companies enhance their corporate identity is one of the two fastest growing areas in WPP. A mission creates an integrity platform and helps define and humanize a company. Simon Mottram, Director of London-based Interbrand, says: "Successful corporate identity today is about . . . expressing the vision, purpose, values and personality of a company, in essence, the corporate brand." What Sorrell and Mottram are talking about is what we mean by mission marketing—providing your company with an essence and integrity.

> **A mission creates an integrity platform and helps define and humanize a company.**

A recent article in *Sales and Marketing Strategy News*, a trade journal that prides itself on carrying real-world, practical articles, pointed out why executives must begin thinking about more than just making a profit:

> Everybody's business is everybody's business these days.
> Organizations are beginning to realize that far from being exempt, they're being called upon to rise to the occasion of improving the world. Responsibility has taken on a whole new meaning—but rising to the challenge also holds opportunity . . . Some call it mission marketing; many call it cause-related marketing. In fact, it's the ultimate brand contact, the manifestation of the company's mission and philosophy. It can drive communication campaigns and even strategy.[4]

THE CORPORATE MISSION'S ROLE IN IM

Food conglomerate ConAgra, which had a rather innocuous mission of "We build on basics," changed its mission a few years ago to "Feeding people better." This change to a more humanitarian focus was made by CEO Mike Harper after he suffered a heart attack. His personal experience caused him to realize the serious problem of cholesterol in diets and the opportunity it presented to his company. One

of the first major results of this new mission was ConAgra's development and launch of its highly successful Healthy Choice line of frozen
foods designed to appeal to both men and women concerned about
their health. ConAgra developed a mission and then marketed it both
internally (which created Healthy Choice) and externally (by promoting Healthy Choice, among other things).

For mission marketing to work, a company must first have a realistic, applicable mission that is incorporated at all levels. It cannot be just
a superficial PR effort to get more media attention and sell more products. Mission marketing adds value for customers and other stakeholders
because it gives them something to believe in, something beyond the
company's internalized objective of making a profit. A mission should
not be confused with corporate financial objectives such as profit and
ROI. Both are needed. Making a profit, however, is an objective that
means a great deal more to shareholders and corporate executives than to
other stakeholders such as customers, suppliers, and channel members
who can sometimes feel that a company's profit comes at their expense.

Mission marketing means not only having a mission but making
stakeholders and potential stakeholders aware of it, and ideally, involving them in it, like McDonald's has done with its Ronald McDonald
houses, which are operated by local volunteer groups. When this happens, it makes stakeholders feel good about a company and gives them
an extra reason to support the company. A good mission can generate
comments such as: "I want to work for that company . . . buy its products . . . buy its stock . . . be its neighbor because this company
does/supports/is responsible for XYZ." A known mission strengthens
the relationship between a company and its various stakeholders.

Some companies fail to recognize the value of making stakeholders aware of their good deeds and the relationship-building potential of
these deeds. Peter Coors, CEO of Coors beer, said his company has for
years had a mission of being socially responsible, but his grandfather,
who founded the company, also had a strong philosophy that you
"don't blow your own horn." That was fine until charges of racism and
sexism started to fly in the 1970s. In *Business Ethics* (which recently
named Coors as one of its 100 Best Corporate Citizens) Peter Coors explained why it's wise to do mission marketing: "The fact we didn't
have a base as being seen as a good corporate citizen meant we didn't
have a lot of credibility when accusations started to fly. Today, we don't
broadcast all the things we do, but we don't hide them either."[5]

A mission shows that a company has a purpose *in addition to* generating sales and making a profit. For many executives, however, not having shareholder value or profit as the organization's only corporate objective is scary. Frequently in seminars and speeches this mission marketing strategy is challenged because it makes the mission just as important as profits. What these challengers fail to understand is that we are not talking about charity or de-emphasizing profits, but rather about engaging in activities that positively impact relationships and profits by positioning the company as "giving something back" to society—a win-win situation.

According to former Ford CEO Don Petersen, "Putting profits after people and products was magical at Ford" and was key to the company's turnaround in the mid-1980s. John Young, former CEO of Hewlett-Packard, says that at his company it has "always remained clear that profit—as important as it is—is not why the Hewlett-Packard Company exists; it exists for more fundamental reasons."[6]

As Collins and Porras point out in their excellent book, *Built to Last*, companies do not have to choose between being socially responsible and making a profit. Many of the most successful companies have done both. Nike's *mission*, for example, is not to sell athletic shoes, but rather to help athletes maximize their performance. Nike has very successfully turned this performance mission into a well-promoted brand position which has produced enormous profits and brand equity.

The ideal mission creates and reinforces a brand positioning. The ultimate in marketing strategy is when the positioning and the mission work together in concert, as in the case of Nike. In other words, the mission is not just a warm-fuzzy statement in the annual report but becomes operationalized in all aspects of the company's business practices and operations. The synergistic benefit of mission-based positioning can drive the relationships that produce bottom-line results.

Hallmark's mission is not to sell cards but to provide people with a high-quality means of communicating emotions. Hallmark's dedication to quality communications comes alive not only in the design and production of its products, but also in its sponsorship of quality TV programming such as the "Hallmark Hall of Fame." Its employee relation's program is also of high quality, which is why Hallmark has never become a union shop. Hallmark has made its quality—an abstract concept—real and believable because it has made it actionable throughout its operations. Like Nike, its brand positioning has been a natural extension of its mission.

Apple had a mission to build a computer "for the rest of us," liberating nontechies from the need to know a lot about computers in order to benefit from them. That mission—computer literacy—also drove Apple into the educational market, which it has always dominated. Apple's mission to be user-friendly was a viable business platform that guided the development of its products and helped position the brand to create brand equity. (Unfortunately, Apple seems to have lost sight of this mission in recent years, resulting in management and marketing decisions that have reduced its brand equity.)

Southwest Airlines operates with a mission that expresses both its corporate culture and its values. Its mission is to transport people in a low-cost but fun and relaxing environment. Having fun is an important part of Southwest Airline's philosophy, and that is proclaimed and driven by its president, Herb Kelleher, who has been seen walking through airports wearing a bunny custom, among other things. Surprisingly, Southwest has chosen to use only the low-cost part of its mission in its positioning. As low-cost competition increases, however, Southwest may find it needs to market the rest of its mission.

MISSIONS WITH DIRECT SOCIAL RESPONSIBILITY

Some companies have missions that directly take on a social responsibility such as Ben & Jerry's buying all its dairy products from local Vermont farmers, The Body Shop sourcing from third-world countries in order to support these economies, Hannah Andersson offering its customers a 20 percent trade-in discount on outgrown children's clothes and then giving these trade-ins to needy families, and Tom's of Maine, who gives 10 percent of pretax profits to charities.

Few people support a company *only* because it is doing something socially responsible. The good or service must be acceptable, the after-sale service must be acceptable, the price must translate into a value, and the availability must be convenient. These socially responsible activities have helped each of these companies receive a premium price for their products, which helps account for their profitable track records.

In 1995 Eastman Kodak began tying a portion of its CEO's compensation package to social responsibility. In 1996 legislators proposed a bill in the U.S. Congress that would reward corporations for investing in employees and communities rather than just pursuing relentless downsizing to boost short-term profits.[7] Similarly, former U.S. Labor

Secretary Robert Reich, trying to promote better relationships between companies and their employees, observed that, "There's no way we can sustain recovery and the economy if workers don't have enough pay in their pockets, and if their hearts and minds aren't engaged."[8] People's hearts and minds are engaged when they work for companies they respect.

As explained earlier in this book, one of the major changes in the marketplace is the increasing difficulty of creating brand differentiation. As goods and services become more similar, people look for a point of difference. According to Avon CEO James Preston, his company's efforts to support breast-cancer research has been beneficial because it has enabled Avon to differentiate itself. "When there is parity in product and price, consumers go for what's relevant," he explains.

Ryka, Inc., founded in 1987 by Sheri Poe, produced a line of aerobic shoes designed especially for women. By the time Poe sold the company in 1995, it had grown into a multimillion dollar enterprise, driven primarily by its strong mission—helping battered and raped women—which also drove its positioning. What made Poe's mission different from other socially responsible missions is that it stemmed from a tragic personal incident: Poe was raped when she was a freshman in college.

Ryka's initial competitive advantage was selling an aerobic shoe with a narrow heel and high arch, which conforms to the contour of women's feet. As competitors picked up on this idea, however, Poe had to find other ways to differentiate her brand. After hearing Oprah Winfrey testify before a Senate committee on child abuse, she decided to go public with her own story. Also, she recalled that physical workouts had helped her recover from all the emotional problems resulting from her rape. She realized and promoted the idea that women need to be supported physically *and* mentally, and that a woman can't be emotionally healthy if she isn't physically healthy. Poe manifested her company's mission by pledging to give 7 percent of her company's profits to the ROSE Foundation (ROSE is an acronym for "regaining one's self-esteem"). In explaining the success of Ryka Inc., Jennifer Groves, an athletic apparel analyst with Black & Company says: "Sure, Ryka's got a good, unique line of shoes. But what built Ryka is Sheri Poe and her story."

Likewise, Anita Roddick built The Body Shop on a platform of social responsibility. The company, which boasts 1,000 stores worldwide, promoted itself through its good works, as did Sheri Poe and

Ben & Jerry, not through advertising or sales promotions. However, in Fall 1994, *Business Ethics* magazine, in an article called "The Shattered Image," called The Body Shop hypocritical and raised questions about its environmental dedication and the level of its ingredient sourcing from third-world countries. The article also called attention to the large number of complaints that the House Committee on Small Business has received from disgusted franchisees. The main danger of mission marketing is that you have to walk the talk. Companies that proclaim more than they do will be in trouble with their stakeholders.

Being socially responsible is not something that only relatively small, owner-driven companies can do. Merck, the multibillion dollar international pharmaceutical company, is a good example of a large company with a socially responsible mission. According to its Management Guide: "We are in the business of preserving and improving human life. All of our actions must be measured by our success in achieving this goal." Merck's work in curing river blindness along the Amazon river and helping eliminate the tuberculosis epidemic that broke out in Japan after WW II—neither of which were profitable ventures—are examples of a socially responsible mission.[9] Notice Merck's mission statement says nothing about making a profit, and yet Merck has been quite profitable over the years.

IMPORTANCE OF CONSOLIDATING PHILANTHROPIC ACTIVITIES

The easiest, quickest, and generally the least costly way to begin practicing mission marketing is to consolidate and concentrate current philanthropic activities. We have found most companies make little or no effort to strategically manage their philanthropic investments and market their good deeds. Most of the companies we have audited have been providing financial support to many different groups, but because these efforts are spread so thin, few, including their own executives, are aware of most of them. When top

> The easiest, quickest, and generally the least costly way to begin practicing mission marketing is to consolidate and concentrate current philanthropic activities.

management is not aware of what is being done, it's a sure bet neither are customers and other stakeholders.

When companies unify their philanthropies and strategically focus them on something that reinforces their mission and business, their involvement is generally large enough to have a presence and to make a real difference, thus making it more likely to gain stakeholder attention and appreciation. Concentration of effort creates impact. Focusing philanthropic activities follows a basic principle of marketing communications—being single-minded. When a company focuses its philanthropy, it not only increases its opportunity to get additional publicity for "really doing something," but also begins to be associated with this effort—which is why the efforts should be related to the company's business mission. For example, McDonald's is closely associated with Ronald McDonald's Houses even though individual McDonald's units have no financial or managerial responsibility for them.

According to Craig Smith, president of Corporate Citizen, a think tank focusing on the social role of international corporations, companies are discovering the value of being more strategic in their philanthropic activities: "For the first time, businesses are backing philanthropic initiatives with real corporate muscle. In addition to cash, they are providing nonprofits with managerial advice, technological and communication support, and teams of employee volunteers. And they are funding those initiatives not only from philanthropy budgets but also from business units, such as marketing and human resources."[10]

In an IM audit of a sporting goods chain (which was providing minimal support to numerous, unrelated community groups) we recommended that it consolidate these efforts and have a mission of "bringing the experience of athletic activities to all people, regardless of age, income, or physical limitations." One way to operationalize this mission would be setting up an ongoing athletic equipment trade-in program. The used equipment would be repaired and given (or sold at a minimal price) to those who could not afford new equipment.

Such a program could set up a large advisory board of school coaches who would actually administer the distribution of the used equipment, creating a strong relationship between the chain and the coaches. And because coaches are in a key position to affect what and where people buy sports equipment, sales should be positively influenced. Such a program could also involve suppliers who could supply parts for the used equipment. It could also involve customers and potential customers who would come into the stores to help repair the trade-ins. This type of strategic philanthropy is good mission marketing because it can be integrated into the total operation of the business operation.

Not only would this program provide customers, employees, and other stakeholders an additional reason for supporting the chain, it would provide many media photo and story opportunities to help keep brand awareness top-of-mind and the chain's reputation positive.

LIMITATIONS OF CAUSE MARKETING

Many companies, in an effort to exploit the average customer's social consciousness, do cause marketing. Cause marketing is offering to support a community or nonprofit activity when a customer makes a purchase. In other words, cause marketing is sales promotion with a PR spin. Cause marketing generates positive publicity both for itself and the cause it is supporting. As nonprofits find it more difficult to raise funds, they have become more willing to work with companies and "commercialize" themselves. In a 1996 special issue, *Promo* magazine carried six pages of causes that were looking for corporate sponsorships.[11]

What really gave cause marketing a boost was marketers' realization that cause-marketing programs can generate sales increases for less investment than required by traditional sales promotions. One reason for this is that cause marketing programs are clutter-busters, distinctive from other promotions because they offer an emotional "reward." The power of affiliation with a good cause was documented by findings from a national survey of 2,000 U.S. adults conducted by Roper Starch Worldwide and Cone Communications. When given a choice between two brands of equal price and quality:

- ◆ 78 percent said they would be more likely to buy the one that supported a cause they cared about.
- ◆ 66 percent said they would switch or would be likely to switch brands to support a cause.
- ◆ 62 percent would switch retailers.
- ◆ 54 percent said they would pay more for a brand that supported a cause they cared about.[12]

Despite its successes, however, cause marketing has limitations. It is often not strategic and very seldom is it well integrated into a company's overall marketing program, let alone the total business operation. As practiced by most companies, it is relatively short term, often seen as self-serving and exploitive, and generally done on an opportunistic, ad-hoc basis. In other words, it does little to create and nourish long-term relationships.

The Roper Starch/Cone study found that 58 percent of consumers think cause marketing promotions are done "just to improve the company's self-image"[13] (i.e., seen as self-serving) or to pump up the bottom line. The exploitation perception can occur when a cause is not closely linked to the sponsoring company's mission or product category.

An example is the American Express program to feed the homeless. While one can say that food and shelter are linked to American Express' business, the connection to homelessness is tenuous given the social elitism of the card. American Express began running print and broadcast advertising in 1993 stating "Every time you use the American Express Card, you'll help provide a meal for someone who is hungry." The TV spot had shots of homeless people on the street interspersed with interior shots of an upscale restaurant. What the ads said in the small type was that American Express would donate *two cents* for each credit card transaction, and that only up to a certain amount during a specified time period.

This campaign is estimated to have helped increase AmEx charge card transactions during its 1993 fourth quarter by 9.4 percent. Although the sales results appear to be impressive, at least in the short term, one must question the long-term wisdom of a campaign that prompts people to give two cents to the homeless by charging a $95 Polo shirt or a $150 lunch at a luxury restaurant. Given that American Express has the most upscale membership of any major credit card, reminding cardholders of the homeless every time they indulge in one of their upscale purchases seems like it could eventually create more guilt than satisfaction.

Trendiness is also a problem because it contributes to the cause-of-the-month mentality: Companies sometimes jump on the latest cause with little regard to its life span or their own communication goals. Says Lesa Ukman, editor of *International Events Group Sponsorship Report*, "Companies are just desperate to find something to tether their brands. Cutting prices didn't work. What's left?" Carol Cone, president of

Cone/Coughlin, a New York ad agency that matches companies with nonprofits, says, "Some marketers do what I call a 'cause du jour' that looks like a promotion" but they're in and out of it too fast for the cause to do anything substantive for the company's reputation.

Another problem comes from negotiating the details of the relationship with the nonprofit organization. Express, a retail division of Limited, Inc., got itself in trouble by running a promotion whereby it would donate used jeans to a women's charity without checking with the charity. Express promoted the event and gave customers a discount on new jeans in exchange for their old ones. But the charity, Women in Community Service, didn't authorize the use of its name and didn't want the jeans.

Another drawback to cause marketing is that companies can get burned when new information comes to light. Miller Brewing Company's $1 million/year sponsorship of the Special Olympics, for example, was ended by the charity a few years ago when research started linking alcohol consumption during pregnancy with mental retardation.[14]

Finally, because cause marketing is generally just a public relations or promotion department activity, it doesn't involve and motivate the other customer-contact employees in the company. For all the effort, there is no attempt to build on cause marketing contacts and turn them into long-term relationships. The emotional connection is, in effect, thrown away.

DIFFERENCES BETWEEN CAUSE AND MISSION MARKETING

The only way to add a long-term dimension to cause marketing is to make it a corporate activity with companywide buy-in. Add the goal of developing long-term relationships to cause marketing, and you have mission marketing. Some may argue that mission marketing is nothing more than a sophisticated version of cause marketing. As Table 7–1 shows, however, the two practices vary in many ways.

Mission marketing that is based on being socially responsible is broader and deeper than cause marketing. It is broader because it is pervasive—stakeholders of all kinds care about it. It is deeper because it is more relevant and long term.

T A B L E 7–1

A Comparison of Cause Marketing and Mission Marketing

Characteristics	Cause Marketing	Mission Marketing
Long term (more than 12 months)	Seldom	Always
Has bottom-line objectives	Often	No
Adds value for all stakeholders	Seldom	Yes
Controversial	Rarely	Rarely
Hot media topics	Often	Seldom
Related to organization's expertise	Seldom	Yes
Provides organization/brand a competitive advantage	Short term	Long term
Integrity (i.e., isn't seen as self serving)	No	Yes
Supported throughout the organization	No	Yes
Senior executive championing	No	Yes
Outside advisory board	No	Often
Can be globally applied	Seldom	Usually
Easy to set up and execute	Yes	No
Easy to measure, determine payout	Yes	No
Enriches corporate culture	No	Yes

THE FIVE CRITERIA OF MISSION MARKETING

In order to fully benefit from mission marketing, a company must strategically manage social programs. When these activities are strategically managed, they will be: 1) focused, 2) pervasive, 3) long term, 4) relevant, and 5) communicated.

Be Focused   As explained above, most companies have myriad unrelated causes that they support. In mission marketing all of these efforts are focused and coordinated to create a strong presence and higher level of visibility for the company and strongly establish an association with a socially responsible program.

One company we audited was giving as much money away as it was spending on mass media advertising and promotion. Not only were its own executives unaware of where the philanthropic monies were going, they had no system for measuring to what extent its stakeholders were aware of, or cared about, all the support the company was providing.

Be Pervasive When a mission is pervasive, it is present in all aspects of a company's operations. A good example is The Disney Company. Disney's mission is to provide quality entertainment for families—adults as well as children. This mission is so pervasive that the company has become its own message, product, and media—the ultimate example of corporate integration of communication and marketing.

Many cutting-edge companies—Disney, Marriott, Southwest Airlines—have leaders with a strong vision and a sense of mission which they have been able to get their stakeholders—especially employees—to accept and endorse. Companies such as Apple, Komatsu, and Canon went from obscurity to rivaling their key competitors (IBM, Caterpillar, and Xerox) in less than two decades because, according to Peter Senge, their leader's vision was shared by employees, and it focused their energies, creating a common identity among diverse people.

Although having a charismatic corporate leader—such as Philip Knight, Herb Kelleher, Michael Eisner, Steve Jobs, Anita Roddick, or Sheri Poe—helps in solidly seeding a mission into business practices, it can also be done in an organization that doesn't have a charismatic leader if the mission is made part of the integrated marketing process. As we have seen, Saturn is a good example of how this can be done.

Another example of making a mission pervasive is REI (Recreation Equipment Inc.). Started in 1938 by a group of Seattle climbers who founded the company as a consumer cooperative, the original mission was to provide high-quality climbing gear for members. Since then the company has expanded its merchandise to include sales and rentals of a broad spectrum of outdoor gear and clothing. With 1.3 million members and an annual revenue approaching $450 million, REI is the largest consumer cooperative in the United States. The company's mission has evolved, however, to one of protecting the environment for recreational use. REI began its conservation program in 1976 and since then has had an annual donation level of $760,000.

Over two decades REI has contributed more than $4.4 million to grassroots environmental organizations. But its program involves more than just donations. The conservation effort is focused on local REI stores, their communities, and the store's employees, who volunteer to help with the conservation programs. In addition, the company has founded various organizations, created alliances with other outdoor recreation retailers and suppliers, and given grants to worthy organizations involved in conservation. By putting together coalitions with national environmental groups and outdoor product stores as well as local community leaders and groups, the company makes its mission visible to stakeholders who are important to its business as well as its cause.

Plan Long Term   There are several reasons it is strategically sound to have a long-term mission. The first, and hopefully the most obvious, is that a genuine mission is a direct extension of a company's core values, as has been the case with Merck and Hewlett-Packard. These do not change, so consequently neither should the mission.

Seeding a mission into the culture of an organization takes time and the energy and effort of top management. Therefore, it makes sense to maintain the mission long term in order to get a return on this investment of time and effort. Along the same lines, the longer a company practices a mission, the higher the awareness of its mission will be. When this association has been constant over a period of years, as in the case of Ben & Jerry's and The Body Shop, it can be enough to drive the business itself. Only recently have Ben & Jerry's and The Body Shop, for example, felt the need to use advertising.

Some companies are concerned about the long-term commitment that mission marketing requires. They feel that "evergreen" causes can get old and less motivating and yet because of the investment, both financially and emotionally, which the company has made, it cannot make a change. The way to eliminate this concern is to carefully pick a mission that is not based on a social fad or fashion. For example, Merck's mission of improving human lives is definitely long-term. When it is no longer motivated to improve human lives, Merck will be out of business anyway, regardless of its mission. The same is true for Disney's mission of providing wholesome entertainment and Apple's mission of "making a computer for the rest of us."

Be Relevant   Companies should tie their contributions to an area that is relevant to their business expertise. Good examples are Binney & Smith, the makers of Crayola crayons, which supports arts education; Dalton Books, which supports literacy programs; and Church & Dwight Co. (maker of Arm & Hammer baking soda products, long considered environmentally friendly), which sponsors environmental causes.

Heinz's relevant mission of supporting children's hospitals is its primary marketing effort. For every Heinz baby food label mailed back to the company, six cents is donated to a children's hospital. "Our share of the baby food market is up and this is the only program we do," according to a company spokesperson: "We don't do advertising. We don't do print. We don't do TV." Petsmart, which has developed an adopt-a-pet program, works in conjunction with local animal shelters. Abandoned animals find homes, and Petsmart gains goodwill and potential customers. Owens Corning, which makes building materials, works closely with Habitat for Humanity, a network of community-based volunteers that build homes for those who can't afford them. Owens-Corning provides building supplies and volunteers as well as direct financial support. According to the company, the program has had a positive impact on all the company's corporate audiences.

The first clue that a program may be exploitative is when it is completely unrelated to a company's area of expertise. Some might argue the opposite, saying if it *is* closely related, then it is obvious the company is promoting something that will benefit it. If mission marketing is done correctly, however, this will not be the case for several reasons. First, it will be made clear by the company's actual behavior that the company is socially responsible. Second, even though the average consumer's trust in business is low, there is no evidence consumers are against companies being successful.

Another benefit of having a relevant mission is that the company has more expertise in this area and therefore can make an intellectual as well as financial contribution. Also, when the company is supporting an area in which it does business, participating employees have the opportunity of getting new ideas by seeing their industry from a different perspective.

A relevant mission can also create and build relationships with important stakeholders other than customers. In Eastern Europe, for example, American Express's mission is to help develop tourism in countries struggling to find ways to attract hard currency. To accomplish this, it has loaned executives to the Hungarian government to work with its tourism staff, set up a foundation financing university research projects on ways to promote the areas' museums to foreigners, and funded educational programs in 23 secondary schools to prepare students to work in tourism and travel-related businesses.

One of the smartest strategies of these programs was enlisting help from government officials and local airline, hotel, and restaurant managers. Not only did this provide necessary staffing, it also, and more importantly, provided American Express in Budapest an opportunity to develop personal relationships with the major players in Hungary's growing travel industry. This type of strategic planning makes mission marketing very valuable to a company from a cost-value perspective.

In the execution of its mission, American Express has built stronger relationships with the government, which regulates travel; hotel and travel executives, who decide what credit cards they will accept; and young people, who are potential employees and cardholders. Probably most important, it has made the American Express employees working in Hungary (and other parts of the world) proud of their role in the economic progress of Eastern Europe.

Another good example of the benefit of having a relevant mission is illustrated by the success of Arco as compared to Exxon in dealing with environmental crises. By choice, Exxon for years kept its foundation work directed toward education, which has no direct relationship to oil exploration and refinement. Consequently, when the Exxon Valdez incident occurred in the late 1980s, the company had little support from any of the environmental groups. In contrast, Arco has used the majority of its social dollars to support environmental groups, and as a result these groups have worked with Arco rather than against it, even in environmentally sensitive situations.

Finally, supporting efforts that are business related means that whenever the company expands, it will more likely be able to also expand its mission, no matter what countries are involved. The reasoning is, if there is a need and desire for the company's products, there should be a need and desire for a related mission. This saves the company from having to find and develop another mission, which may not in the long run return to the company what it has come to expect from its current philanthropic programs.

Communicate   A mission is of little value if no one knows about it. It can't produce the motivational benefit that comes with stakeholder buy-in. Although individuals may find it rewarding to support a good cause and keep it secret, that's not an effective practice for most businesses who need the visibility of the effort in order to justify their activities to investors and other ROI-minded managers. It is also a critical part of the say → do → confirm triangle. Good deeds provide a platform for marketing communication and a reason for referrals by friends.

HOW TO ESTABLISH AND MANAGE MISSION MARKETING

Before a company can fully benefit from mission marketing it must make two tough decisions. The first is hiring qualified staff to set up and manage "mission" activities. Second is to involve the total organization in the mission marketing activities. Mission marketing should not be run as a separate foundation any more than any other program should function in isolation within an organization.

One of the questions we are most frequently asked by executives is: "Can a large company which doesn't have a charismatic leader really have integrated communications and a strong image?" The answer is yes, but it takes more work and planning.

All big ideas need a leader, a champion. This champion has to be high in the organization and be able to put in time and effort to make it work. It's more important to have a vision czar than a communication czar. If you capture the spirit, the actions will follow. Strong entrepreneurial spirits like Henry Ford, Tom Watson, Walt Disney, Bill Gates, and Herb Kelleher have provided not only product ideas but a culture for their companies. As companies grow, diversify, and spread out, the energy and inspiration of these original strong personalities can easily become dissipated. A company can guard against this by doing the following:

1. *Institutionalize the mission:* This means having staffing and infrastructure that will allow the mission to continue to be executed.

2. *Measure its contribution to the organization:* One way to guarantee that a portion of an organization's energy and resources are used for a certain program is to measure that program's performance. In the case of a mission, there are several ways to evaluate the performance of the people assigned to run the program:

   ◆ Awareness of the organization's mission activities among key stakeholders.

   ◆ Evaluation by key stakeholders of the program's benefits to society in relation to other, similar corporate sponsorships and involvements.

   ◆ Evaluation of news clips taking into consideration where
     they ran, audiences reached, and their degree of positive-
     link to the organization.

3. *Make it a top management responsibility:* Mission marketing
   must be directed by a top executive.

4. *Appoint a representational executive committee:* Establish an
   executive committee made up of representatives from all
   levels of the company to ensure the effort doesn't have an
   internal, elitist image. Make membership on this committee a
   prestigious assignment by providing members "executive
   perks" such as special dinners and trips.

5. *Incorporate the mission's essence into all departmental plans:*
   For example, the sporting goods company mentioned above. If
   it adopts a mission of "ensuring that the fun and excitement of
   sports is available to everyone," should include in its marketing
   plan certain events which provide underprivileged youth and
   adults an opportunity to participate in something more than
   backyard basketball. It might also set up a volunteer coaches
   workshop which would supplement these special events. The
   coaches who participated would be rewarded with extra
   discounts and parties put on by the sporting goods retailer.

Mission marketing has all the advantages of cause marketing and
much more, because it leverages the power of respect. It strengthens
your company and brand images, helps in working with government
regulators, reduces R&D costs, and motivates the sales force and other
employees. In addition, it lubricates the integrated marketing processes
because it fosters associations and thus synergy among business units
and outside stakeholder groups. In sum, it can increase the *cultural
capital* of your company.

ENDNOTES

1. Watts Wacker, "The Information Highway: The Road to a New
   Paradigm for Consumer Decision-Making," Presentation to Creative Research International Group, May 17, 1994.
2. Patrick Jackson, *pr reporter* (January 23, 1995).

3. Susan Gaines, "Growing Pains," *Business Ethics*, January/February 1996, p. 22.
4. Gina Bonar, "Mission Marketing: Whose Business Is It, Anyway?" *Sales and Marketing Strategies & News*, (March, 1996), p. 31.
5. Dale Kurschner, "The 100 Best Corporate Citizens," *Business Ethics*, May/June 1996, pp. 24-35.
6. As quoted by James Collins and Jerry Porras in *Built to Last*, (New York: Harper Business, 1994), p. 48.
7. Robert Kuttner, "Rewarding Corporations That Really Invest in America," *Business Week*, February 26, 1996, p. 22.
8. Robert C. Yafie, "Pass the 10Q, Partner," *Journal of Business Strategy* 17:1 (January/February 1996), pp. 53-56.
9. As quoted by James Collins and Jerry Porras in *Built to Last*, (New York: Harper Business, 1994), p. 48.
10. Craig Smith, "The New Corporate Philanthropy," *Harvard Business Review*, May-June, 1994, p. 105.
11. Daniel Shannon, "Doing Well By Doing Good: Special Report on Cause Marketing," *Promo*, February 1996, pp. 29-38.
12. Paul Carringer, "Not Just A Worthy Cause," *American Advertiser*, Spring, 1994, p. 17.
13. Geoffery Smith and Ron Stodghill, "Are Good Causes Good Marketing?" *Business Week*, March 21, 1994, p. 64.
14. *The Alcoholism Report*, "Alcohol dollars readily available to health-related charities," December 1993, 21:12, p. 3.

8

C H A P T E R

Use Zero-Based Planning Strategy

When MCI executed its successful "Friends and Family" promotion, it moved dollars from the sales division into sales promotion. This was done because the company found that rewarding current MCI customers for "selling" their friends and family members on joining MCI was more cost-effective than many of its traditional customer acquisition programs, such as heavy emphasis on telemarketing. Being able to reallocate based on strategic need is fundamental to integrated planning.

IM campaign planning is more complex than traditional planning because it takes into consideration more target audiences, makes more use of addressable media and messages, and uses more two-way communication. IM also uses a customer perspective (rather than just internal judgments) to analyze the company, brand, and competitive situation.

This chapter discusses how to use an IM analysis and planning process to develop an integrated campaign aimed at customers, although the model applies to all stakeholder groups. At the heart of the planning process is *zero-based planning*, the idea that tools are used based on an assessment of what needs to be done now and not based on last year's budget allocations. The IM planning process includes the following:

1. SWOT analysis and prioritization
2. Relationship analysis
3. Using prioritized SWOTs to determine the MC mix

4. Integrating messages

5. Integrating media

SWOT ANALYSIS AND PRIORITIZATION

Most marketing plans in the United States are based on an annual *situation analysis*, which is basically a look at everything that could affect a company's marketing effort, brand equity, and profitability in the coming year. The problem with this type of analysis is that it doesn't provide a standardized way to evaluate all the collected information and draw conclusions about what should be done. Also, it isn't designed to specifically analyze the strengths of the company's relationships with customers (and other stakeholders).

A SWOT analysis covers all the areas of a situation analysis and provides a more systematic way to organize data and draw conclusions. SWOT is an acronym for Strengths, Weaknesses, Opportunities, and Threats. The strengths and weaknesses are internal factors under the company's control; the opportunities and threats are external elements over which the company has no control (but on occasion can influence). A SWOT analysis is used in IM because it logically leads to zero-based planning.

External Factors

External conditions will be discussed first. Opportunities and threats are conditions and situations that can directly or indirectly affect a company and how it does business, such as laws and regulations, changes in technology, industry trends, socioeconomic conditions, and changes in the marketplace.

Opportunities

These are social and economic conditions and situations in the marketplace that can make the company's products more attractive. For example, in the early 90s when consumers in developed countries became concerned about fat levels in products, all those products which were naturally low-fat or contained no fat, such as yogurt, suddenly acquired an extra value. As reports have come in about possible problems with tap water, bottled water companies have leveraged this concern to greatly expand the beverage category.

Threats

The opposite of opportunities, these are marketplace conditions that reduce the perceived value or attractiveness of a product or result in it being more costly to make or provide. For example, new or tougher
pollution regulations can increase the cost of manufacturing, or an increase in postage rates can make direct-response marketing more
costly. By definition threats can't be controlled, but sometimes they
can be anticipated and actions taken to minimize their impact.

Internal Factors

The *internal* strengths and weaknesses include a wide range of variables,
such as the company's expertise in R&D, the value of the patents it holds,
its distribution system and product availability, product cost to customers,
depth and breadth of its sales force, brand positioning, extent and condition of physical facilities, brand share, and its overall financial strength.

Strengths

These are the competitive advantages, resources that allow the company
to offer benefits which competitors cannot offer or not offer at the same
level of quality or as economically. For instance, Disney's heritage of
quality gives it an advantage when offering new entertainment products.

Weaknesses

These are competitive disadvantages or areas in which customers perceive competitors to have an advantage. A company that has all its production in a developed country may find itself at a cost disadvantage
when competitors increase their production facilities in countries with
significantly lower wages; or just the opposite, if it has all its production in developing countries it may be in trouble with consumer groups
if there is evidence that child labor is being used.

  The strength and weakness analysis should be done from the perspective of both management and customers. Customer perceptions need
to be compared to those of brand and marketing managers, whose views
may be protective. A key SWOT finding is the gap between these internal and external perceptions of the company, its products, and its operations. We have found in our audits that not only do mangers' perspectives
differ from customer's, but the managers themselves are not always in
agreement on the company's strengths and weaknesses.

In an audit of a service company, for example, we found that top management believed one of the company's key strengths was its employees; however, the company's marketing managers did not. As for customers, they perceived the employees to be no better or worse than those in competing companies. Such perception gaps need to be reconciled so there is either agreement or an explanation of why the gaps exist. Although customer perspectives are most important, the perspective of managers must also be given consideration for they can identify strengths that customers are not aware of or have misunderstood.

One way to ensure that the SWOT analysis has a customer focus is to think in terms of Bob Lauterborn's 4Cs rather than the traditional 4Ps.[1] Figure 8–1 illustrates the difference in perspective.

Rather than focusing on the product, focus on the customer. Rather than just doing internal competitive product lab tests, ask *customers* how the brand compares to the competition. Rather than just comparing prices to competitors, ask customers how the *cost* of buying and using the product compares. Rather than just doing store checks to determine brand penetration, ask customers how *convenient* it is for them to find and buy the brand. And finally, rather than just looking at promotional redemption figures and doing brand tracking studies, ask customers if they are receiving the kinds of information they need to make their buying decisions and if the company is accessible and responsive to their complaints and inquiries, e.g., is the company *communicating* with them.

FIGURE 8–1

The Customer-Focused Approach to Analysis

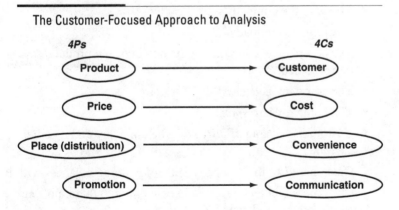

In addition to asking customers to list the brand's strengths and weaknesses, it is important to determine the basis for these perceptions. What brand contact points lead customers to believe the brand is better or worse than competing brands? Only by knowing the source of the negative messages can they be changed or influenced, and only by knowing the sources of the positive brand messages can they be leveraged.

RELATIONSHIP ANALYSIS

Although the SWOT analysis will provide a good basis for communication planning, that analysis can be enriched by adding another research dimension that profiles the various types of relationships on which brand equity is built.

Each stakeholder group generally has a different set of perspectives about a company's strengths and weaknesses. Investors, for example, are much more interested in the expertise of management than are most customers; employees are more interested in the conditions of the company's facilities than are customers (unless it's a retail business). Therefore, each internal group or department that is responsible for managing the relationships with a particular stakeholder group needs to analyze how the company is perceived by its stakeholders and how strong the relationship is between that stakeholder group and the company.

Based on continuous customer feedback tracking and specific customer studies, the strengths of customer (and other stakeholder) relationships should be determined. Recall from Chapter 3 that there are eight major constructs that determine the strength of relationships:

- *Knowing* the company.
- *Trusting* the company.
- The company is *consistent* in its dealings and product performance.
- The company is *accessible*.
- The company is *responsive*.
- Customers have an *affinity* with the company and its other customers.
- Customers *like* the company and enjoy doing business with it.
- Customers feel the company is *committed* to them, putting their interests and needs first.

Just as important as how a brand or company scores on these constructs is *why* it scores high or low. For example, if a brand scores low on trust, little can be done to correct that perception until the source of the distrust is determined (e.g., poor customer service, over promising in planned messages, poor product performance). Once the "whys" are identified, they can be compared to the findings of the perceived brand strengths and weaknesses to make sure none of them has been overlooked. For example, if it is found that customers have scored the company low on trust and the reason is that products don't meet expectations, this can mean there is either a weakness in the planned messages (e.g., over promising) or in the product quality (e.g., low performance).

An example of a communication strategy built on a better understanding of stakeholders comes from Nike's experience when it realized in the late 1980s and early 1990s that women made up a small percentage of its customer base, only about 5 percent. One reason for this was that women were not finding the Michael Jordan and other male endorsement advertising messages appealing because they didn't talk to women. As a result of this analysis, a new campaign was created with advertising copy that addressed how women feel about their bodies and themselves, with lines like, "Did you ever wish you were a boy?" to "You were born a daughter," and "A woman is often measured by the things she cannot control." One result of this targeted campaign has been that women now account for 15 percent of Nike's sales.[2]

Once the SWOTs are identified they need to be prioritized. Although many things can be taken into consideration when prioritizing SWOTS, the following set of criteria can be applied to almost every SWOT list regardless of product category. Each of the criteria should be weighted depending on the product category and the individual company's long-term objectives:

1. Realistic damage to brand equity if a weakness or threat is *not* addressed.

2. Realistic benefit if a strength or opportunity is leveraged.

3. Realistic ability to address/leverage each SWOT.

4. Cost of addressing/leveraging each SWOT.

5. Length of time company has to leverage/address each SWOT.

Once SWOTs have been prioritized, a cross-functional team needs to determine the best strategy for leveraging the top strengths and opportunities and addressing the most serious weaknesses and threats. This prioritizing provides a blueprint for allocating corporate resources. Using a scoring system based on the above five criteria, the relative importance of each SWOT can be presented graphically as shown in Figure 8–2.

In determining the best strategies for leveraging and addressing the key SWOTs, the cross-functional team will establish objectives for the various departments, depending on which message types need to be changed. For example, if a product is perceived by customers as being low in quality, yet blind tests show it is equal to competing brands, the cross-functional team needs to determine the source of the misperception. The cause may be that the product is sold in a discount store, unlike its competitors, requiring a change in distribution strategy. Or, if the advertising is focused on price, then maybe the marketing communications are sending the low-quality message and need to be revised to focus on quality.

An example of how one company reconfigured its marketing communication based on a better understanding of an external threat comes from the wine industry. Retailing in the wine and liquor industry is moving from small, family stores to larger, self-service stores.

FIGURE 8–2

Hypothetical SWOT Prioritization for an Automobile Company

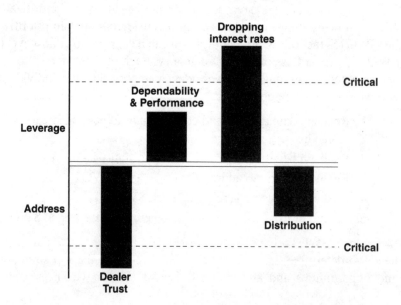

Because of this, customers must make their own selections without the help of an informed salesperson. Wineries such as Robert Mondavi had depended on retail clerks to sell its products, and the loss of this support was a threat to the brand. To make this condition even worse, the number of wine choices is increasing, making it even more difficult for a single brand to be noticed.

To address this external threat, Mondavi and its agency, Ketchum, San Francisco, put together a relationship-building campaign that included not only advertising in specialty magazines (which Mondavi had used very little over the years) but also sending a newsletter and direct-mail pieces to people who had visited the Mondavi winery or talked to the winery via its Internet site (which receives about 5,000 visits a month).[3] By using addressable media aimed at customers who have initiated contact with the brand, Mondavi is hoping to at least partially replace the personal attention its buyers once received in the family owned stores.

The difficult budget allocation or reallocation decisions are best made by a cross-functional team. The team's objective is to ensure that the most impactful negative messages are being changed and that the most impactful positive messages are being reinforced and leveraged. The budget must be zero-based, meaning the moneys are to be allocated on the basis of greatest need and, greatest opportunity, rather than by historical precedent. This can require changes in product and service messages, as well as planned messages.

The strategy should begin first by ensuring that the key product and service messages are positive and that strategies are in place to handle unplanned messages as positively as possible. Then the planning can focus on the planned messages. Such strategic planning and budget re-allocation led Ukrop's to invest in employee communication and training which it had found to have the greatest impact on customer perceptions and behavior. The lack of such planning is what, in part, led U.S. West to pay more than five million dollars in fines due to its poor customer service (while also receiving a ton of negative publicity).

USING PRIORITIZED SWOTS TO DETERMINE MC MIX

Although more companies are using a SWOT analysis to help better understand their market situation, once the SWOT analysis is done few have a structured process for using that information to determine their MC mix.

The SWOT analysis leads directly to marketing communication objectives which can be summed up as: 1) leveraging the key strengths and opportunities and 2) addressing the key weaknesses and threats. These objectives then determine which MC areas should be employed.

Most companies with multimillion-dollar MC budgets fall into the trap of setting up individual MC functions and then supporting each of these with a relatively fixed portion of the MC budget year after year, regardless of the company's overall communication needs. The essence of zero-based campaign planning, however, is being neutral regarding each MC function and media alternative rather than using historical precedent to drive the function choices and MC mix.

As explained in Chapter 5, planned messages can create and nourish customer relationships in a variety of ways, such as increasing brand awareness and brand knowledge, increasing the credibility of brand claims, generating trial, increasing purchase frequency and quantity, creating and facilitating purposeful dialogue, and providing useful product information. Often there are several different MC tools that can solve the same problem. The challenge is to select the ones that can be used most cost effectively and efficiently. Following is a brief list of typical MC objectives and the most effective and efficient MC tool for achieving each objective:

MC OBJECTIVE	MOST EFFECTIVE TOOL
Establish credibility and build trust	PR
Create lifestyle associations	advertising, events
Establish awareness and create images	advertising
Stimulate repeat purchases	sales promotion
Stimulate trade participation	trade promotion
Reward frequency and loyalty	frequency program
Create a sense of involvement	events
Reach a tightly targeted audience	addressable media
Leverage social responsibility	mission marketing
Stimulate referrals	club or affinity group
Stimulate trial	sales promotion
Make a news announcement	PR

Although the big campaign idea can come from any MC function, it is logical to search for it primarily within the MC function that is most appropriate to address or leverage the situation. Once the big idea is selected and it is determined how the lead MC function will be used, other MC tools should be selected to round out the support.

For example, Black Gold is a Swedish premium beer that found that its user base was aging and declining. The brand realized it needed to reposition itself as a more youthful product, but at the same time it wanted to maintain its premium image. The problem, therefore, was credibility—how to convince younger beer drinkers that Black Gold, which had an "older drinker" image—was the beer for them.

A traditional solution would have been to create image advertising that showed Black Gold being enjoyed by younger beer drinkers. Traditional, but not very believable or creative. The big idea developed by DDB Needham was found in the PR/event arena—have Black Gold sponsor, and therefore associate itself with a stylish art form, *film noir*. The campaign's objectives were to establish the association, make it credible, and make it relevant to the target audience.

A *film noir* festival held in three cities anchored the campaign and created involvement. The festival was supported with mass media advertising, PR releases, premiums such as posters and postcards showing some dramatic scenes, plus a specially made film trailer that was shown at the beginning of each of the festivals. Targeted customers responded by attending one or more of the showings, reading about it, and/or collecting the posters and postcards. The event provided a behavioral dimension to the brand's new positioning as well as a basis for an attitudinal change regarding the brand.

As in the case of Black Gold, a big idea must have the ability to work and be integrated in a variety of MC functions. It also should be evaluated in terms of its impact on all key stakeholders, not just customers. Is the campaign idea counter to messages being sent to other stakeholders? Does it contain messages that other stakeholders would find offensive, irritating, or unbelievable?

The timing of campaign activities is a critical dimension of integration. For example, when advertising and PR are used for the introduction of a new product or any kind of major announcement, PR is more effective when it is used before the advertising. If ads have already run announcing the product launch or improvement, any good editor will refuse to use PR releases because they are no longer "news." Likewise, when mass media advertising is used to reinforce a direct-response mail campaign, timing of the mass media advertising is critical—too far in advance and it will be forgotten; too long after the mailing hits and the response device will have been lost or discarded. In this case, the mass media advertising should run one-to-two weeks before the mail drop, and if telemarketing is part of the plan, follow-up phoning should be done one to three days after the mail is received.

INTEGRATING MESSAGES

Because planned message are the "say" messages, the first guideline in designing these is not to over promise. This is difficult if not impossible for most brand managers and copywriters. Their rationale goes like this: Conventional wisdom says most customers automatically discount brand promises because they don't believe advertising. Therefore, to compensate for this automatic discount, it's necessary to over promise so that after the claim is discounted, customers are still motivated to respond. The end of this road is scary and many think we have already gotten there.

As explained in chapter 5, all planned messages should be integrated so they have strategic consistency. A truly big idea is one that can be used successfully with each of the MC tools to create and deliver the message synergy that IM is designed to do. The content analysis which is explained in the last chapter is a method for helping ensure that planned messages are integrated and consistent.

In cases such as Coke, where the brand has distinct customer segments which require different executional voices and looks, there still should be a set of brand identifying elements that appear in all brand messages. Just as the acid test of a good salesperson is to recommend a customer not buy when a product is not right for that customer, the true test of an integrated agency is to reject a clever, creative execution idea when it is off strategy.

Every planned message should be designed to increase brand awareness, knowledge, image and/or generate behavior of some kind—try, request more information, visit the showroom, buy, buy in larger quantities, buy more frequently. Having said this, however, these behavior decisions should not be made internally. Unfortunately, most copy platforms are designed on the basis of what the company wants customers to know about the brand and how the company wants customers to respond. Customers should be asked not only what information they want, but in what form, when and where as mentioned earlier, and what steps they want to go through in making a buying decision. Do they want to take the time to make a store visit for your type of product or would they rather order it from a catalogue?

In most cases, of course, there will be a segment of customers who want to visit a store and another which prefers buying from a catalogue. This is why it is necessary to facilitate letting customers self aggregate and indicate which type of information and behavior they prefer.

One criteria for evaluating all advertising, packaging, and PR messages is to determine to what extent they say or reinforce one or more of the relationship constructs. Every planned message should be designed to either create or strengthen the relationship with the target audience. What relationship drivers (constructs) do these messages communicate? What consistency elements link them together? Finally, consider how well they support the brand positioning. A message matrix can help in doing this analysis. (See Figure 8–3.)

It needs to be decided what portion of mass messages are designed to acquire new customers and what portion are designed to reinforce current relationships. A new or expanding company will have a higher proportion of "acquire" messages vs that of a more established company with a profitable established customer base.

FIGURE 8–3

Message Matrix

Target audience	Message content	Reinforcement of relationship constructs	Brand consistency elements	Interactivity motivator/ facilitator
1. _____	1. _____	1. _____	1. _____	1. _____
2. _____	2. _____	2. _____	2. _____	2. _____
3. _____	3. _____	3. _____	3. _____	3. _____
4. _____	4. _____	4. _____	4. _____	4. _____

For those messages designed to acquire customers, especially for industrial products, executions need to help potential profitable customers self-select and identify themselves. Because so much has already been written on lead generation, screening and managing, we are not going to go deeply into the subject other than to say that ads and other planned messages can be designed to discourage response from those who don't meet a company's customer criteria. Some of the ways this can be done are:

Describing in the ad the company's typical customer.

Requiring interested customers to supply certain profile information.

Stating the characteristics, situation, or facilities that customers must have in order to benefit from using the product.

Saying what the brand will not do along with its benefits.

The more high priced/high margin a brand is, the more messages should be designed to lead the customer and potential customer through the buying process. This, of course, can only be done with the support of a customer/lead tracking database. The more service sensitive a product is, the more important it is to include in planned messages how customers can reach the company. When we talk about facilitating dialogue, this does not mean just having an 800 number and e-mail address or Web site, but actively and continuously providing and promoting these numbers and electronic addresses so whenever a customer wants to make a brand contact, it is easy for them to do so.

When addressable media are used, the relatively high cost of these media can be leveraged by personalizing the messages. The reason 97–98 percent of all direct mail offers quickly end up in the waste basket is because they contain a mass message. Personalization can be done on two levels. The first, and less costly, is categorizing those with like behaviors, purchase record, lifestyle, and relate the offer to the needs and wants normally associated with the life style/behavior of this segment. The more effective (and costly) message will refer to something that is obviously personal, e.g., "your purchase of a Toyota Camery last week," "now that your youngest child, Ted, is leaving for college," etc.

There is a potential downside to this more effective personalization, however, and that is a perceived invasion of privacy. The perception of privacy invasion will vary by product category and how relevant to the product such personalization is (generally, the more relevant, the less it's seen as an invasion). To minimize negative reactions, the individualized message should clearly explain how and why the individualization is being used (e.g., "Although we have a lot of new products this year, based on our records of what you have bought, Mr. Smith, the only one we thought you might have a real interest in is XYZ.").

INTEGRATING MEDIA

The first step in developing a media strategy is to identify the points where customers come in contact with the brand or company. Using the contact point matrix analysis shown in Figure 8–4, these contact points should be prioritized based on which have the highest impact, which are intrinsic vs created (e.g. media buys), and what specific messages are currently being delivered at each brand contact point. It should also be determined if unintended messages are being delivered at these contact points. For example, check-in/check-out counters are intrinsic contact points and generally an opportunity to provide a cost effective brand message. However, if understaffing results in long lines, such messages as "Customers are our first concern" become laughable and negative in their contrast to reality (the say–do messages are out of sync).

F I G U R E 8–4

Contract Point Matrix Analysis

Intrinsic contact Points	Primary message delivered	Impact on buying decision (lo, mod, hi)	Relationship impact (lo, mod, hi)
1. _____	_____	_____	_____
2. _____	_____	_____	_____
3. _____	_____	_____	_____
4. _____	_____	_____	_____
Created contact points			
1. _____	_____	_____	_____
2. _____	_____	_____	_____
3. _____	_____	_____	_____
4. _____	_____	_____	_____

The media strategy needs to be developed essentially at the same time as the message strategy because the decisions are interdependent. The media analysis should be neutral as to specific tools, but broad in scope. The objective is to use the most cost effective and efficient mix of message delivery systems based on:

- Reaching targeted customers at optimum points of brand contact.
- Matching media to customer's point in the decision/buying process.
- Matching media to acquisition and retention situations.
- Maximizing messages delivered at intrinsic contact points.
- Maximizing opportunities to generate purposeful dialogue.
- Strategically balancing the integration of mass and addressable media.

Media mix decisions should also be based on answers to customer behavior and attitude questions such as:

- What are their media behaviors and patterns?
- What are their buying behaviors and patterns?
- When and where are the best times and places to reach them?
- What alternative media, as well as traditional media, do they use?

A good example of integrating mass and addressable media is the integrated campaign Johnson & Johnson used when it introduced its Acuvue disposable contact lenses, a product that required an eye examination and needed to be distributed by eyecare professionals.

The launch of Acuvue illustrates the use of leveraged media in a fully integrated campaign.[4] Coordination was achieved through the use of a customer and trade database to manage a 3-way relationship keeping J&J in constant touch with both potential customers and local eyecare professionals. Because it was a new product, the primary objective of the campaign was to generate trial. Mass media advertising with a heavy pull strategy was used to stimulate potential customers to self-identify themselves to J&J. The company then directed them to their local provider and provided incentives to drive trail. J&J knew that users of contact lenses would not switch to disposable lenses without the support of an eye-care professional.

FIGURE 8–5

Acuvue Interactive Campaign

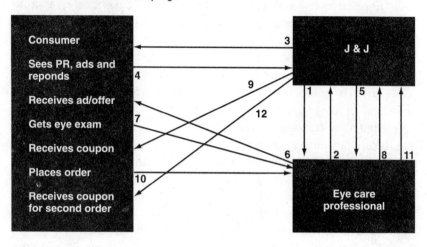

The functional areas used were mass media advertising for announcing the new product, public relations for delivering the credibility message—i.e., "it's safe,"—telemarketing to the trade, direct-response mailings to trade and consumers to keep them informed and heighten their interest, and sales promotion which used coupons to drive both trial and repeat business.

The campaign was made up of a series of strategically integrated activities as shown in Figure 8-5. In the first activity (step 1) J&J used trade advertising and PR to help create awareness of Acuvue among eyecare professionals and request those who were interested in selling Acuvue to contact J&J (step 2). Using a database of eyecare professionals, a telemarketing effort was used to maximize the number of retail distribution points. While building its database of Acuvue retailers, J&J ran a series of mass media ads (step 3) with a mail-in card for more information on this new contact lens product. In this way, mass messages in mass media were used to motivate potential customers to identify themselves and self aggregate (step 4).

So the second database was built, this one of end-users. Rather than J&J responding to potential customers, however, their names were sent (step 5) to the eyecare professional closest to each customer who had requested more information. This was done by overlaying the customer

database on the eyecare professional database and using a software program that did geographical proximity matching.

Eyecare professionals then sent (step 6) to each name received from
J&J an Acuvue information kit supplied to them by J&J but personalized
for their eyecare office. To motivate customers to give serious consideration to using the Acuvue systems, this mass-customized mailing included
a free eye examine offer from the local eyecare professional.

When customers came in (step 7) for their free eye exam, J&J was
informed (step 8) so it could send (step 9) a first-time coupon offer direct to potential customers who had further qualified themselves by having taken advantage of the free Acuvue eye examine. When the
customer showed up in the eye-care professionals office to use the J&J
coupon and order his/her first set of lenses (step 10), J&J was again informed (step 11) so it could send the new customer a follow-up offer
(step 12). (Because the lenses were disposable, the strategy was to get
customers hooked on the convenience of using the product.)

The integration of the promotional efforts from both J&J and the
local eyecare professionals made this a cost effective campaign because each brand contact was designed to further qualify and screen
prospects. This minimized the media waste. Also each contact led to
another message opportunity until the customer was finally a loyal user
of the Acuvue system.

By linking two databases—one of eyecare professionals and the
other one, which was developed through this campaign, of contact lens
users—prospective customers were individually tracked as they moved
from expressions of initial interest through trial and repeat purchases.
Each step of the process was monitored by J&J's database.

One of J&J's business objectives of this campaign was to build
and own the database of customers rather than leaving it in the hands of
each local retailer. This not only allowed J&J to use this database for
other product offers, but also allowed it not to lose contact with a group
of customers when an eyecare center decided to no longer carry and fit
Acuvue lenses. The integrated strategy also provided a way to monitor
and evaluate how the product was handled at retail. From this campaign, J&J learned which optometrists were doing the best job of working with customers.

An example of a situation where message leveraging did not occur
was found in the case of a public utility gas company that wanted its
customers to fully insulate their homes in order to conserve energy. The

company's campaign of mass media ads, brochures and bill stuffers was directed totally at its residential customers, failing to integrate other key stakeholders. Although the insulation had to be bought from lumber yards or hardware stores, and in many cases installed by a carpenter, these retailers and installers—who could have been sources of additional messages—were ignored. Also ignored was the media, which are generally interested in stories on energy conservation. They could have not only delivered some of the "selling" message for the utility, but added credibility to the utility company's offer. By not integrating and leveraging the media opportunities of these other groups (who would have distributed the "insulation" message at their own expense), the utility company bore all the costs. The final omission was in not working with insulation manufacturers and asking them to co-sponsor the campaign and set up special displays in retail locations.

MANAGING COMPLEXITY

Integrated marketing is about managing complexity. A prioritized SWOT analysis should be built on an understanding of stakeholder perceptions. That means coordinated campaign plans may be needed for several different key stakeholder groups as well as several customer segments. A zero-based planning strategy maximizes integration effectiveness by giving equal consideration to all marketing communication functions—advertising, public relations, sales promotion, events, packaging, direct response, sponsorships. Keep in mind that each of these functions has the potential to anchor a MC campaign. Figure 8–6 illustrates how the SWOT analysis leads ultimately to the marketing communication mix dimensions.

> Integrated marketing is about managing complexity.

In multi-message campaign plans that speak to and with several different stakeholder groups and customer segments, different tools and mixtures of messages will be needed. As more stakeholders are addressed, as more functional areas are used in support of the big idea, as more message delivery systems are added to the media mix, both planning and monitoring for consistency becomes more complex and demands more attention from the cross-functional brand equity team.

F I G U R E 8–6

Zero-Base Communication Planning

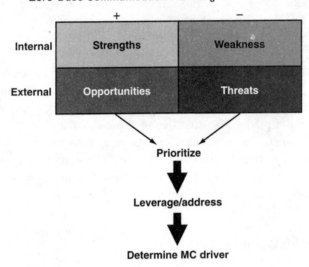

ENDNOTES

1. Don Schultz, Stanley Tannenbaum, and Robert Lauterborn, *Integrated Marketing Communications* (Lincolnwood, IL: NTC, 1993), p. 12.
2. Allan J. Magrath, *How to Achieve Zero-Defect Marketing* (New York: American Management Association, 1993), p. 14.
3. Gerry Khermouch, "Mondavi Seeks ID Above Wine Glut," *Brandweek*, September 11, 1995, p. 14.
4. John Deighton, "Features of Good Integration: Two Cases and Some Generalizations," *Integrated Communication: Synergy of Persuasive Voices*, Esther Thorson and Jeri Moore (Eds.), (Mahway NJ: Lawrence Erlbaum, 1996): 243-258.

PART FOUR

IM INFRASTRUCTURE

9

CHAPTER

Use Cross-Functional Planning and Monitoring

Although a cross-functional structure alone does not guarantee integration, the lack of one almost always guarantees disintegration. Metropolitan Life Insurance Company (Met Life), the second largest insurance company in the United States, is a good example of what can happen when a strong, cross-functional management system is not in place and one department is allowed to operate unilaterally. Because its agents were allowed to use questionable sales practices between 1989 and 1993, over 40 states have levied fines against Met Life, totaling $20 million. It is also expected that the company will have to issue refunds of over $75 million. For the first nine months of 1994, the company's life insurance sales were down 25 percent versus the same period the year before. Finally, because of all the lawsuits and legal problems, the company's credit rating was reduced from AAA to AA by Standard & Poor's.

> Although a cross-functional structure alone does not guarantee integration, the lack of one almost always guarantees disintegration.

According to a Met Life spokesperson, the company failed to enforce its own stated policies for sales messages. The Met Life auditors "would give a warning, lawyers would go down there [Florida, where much of the trouble was centered] and say 'This has to stop,' but there wasn't follow through."[1] The internal pressure for sales performance drowned out the wiser voices. If a cross-functional brand equity team had been in place, then perhaps the voices of those who were more concerned with the long-term impact would have been heard. Regardless of who was to blame, it was a marketing communication nightmare both internally and externally for Met Life.

Integrated marketing is organizationally dependent. As one divisional manager told us during an IM audit of her company: "I'm concerned about structure. There is no central person. We need a central mechanism. Senior management may set goals, but these are not communicated. We need someone or a team to identify these goals and make sure they are being addressed, and figure out a way to make the team work without creating barriers or being too much of a gatekeeper."

THE CROSS-FUNCTIONAL BRAND EQUITY TEAM

Organizational structure is one of the most critical challenges most companies face when trying to impliment IM. What is needed is a cross-functional brand equity team which basically acts as a brand board of directors.

Hallmark benefited in its speed-to-market when it integrated its planning and physical organizational structure for developing a new line of cards. According to Bob Spark, president of Hallmark's Personal Communication Group:

> In the summer of 1991 we developed a new line of cards in an entirely different way [previously the company had been using a system that required 25 hand-offs for developing a new line]. We grouped people together who had been separated by disciplines, departments, floors, and even buildings to cut down on the queue time, spur creativity, and end the throw-it-over-the-wall-it's-their-problem cycle. These experiments in integrated teams worked so well that half of the line hit the stores . . . eight months ahead of schedule . . . We think the teams worked because by bringing a group of people together like that, they got focused and [had] direct communication linkages.[2]

He goes on to explain that a reorganization of this nature, because it involves multiple functions and different departments, "had to be driven top-down." In other words, people and departments did not have a choice of not participating in the integrated planning.

The responsibility for planning and monitoring relationships that drive brand equity must be put into the hands of a corporate (or brand) wide cross-functional team that includes key members of every major department and division from which the planned, product, and service messages originate, as well as all units that can influence unplanned messages. Cross-functional teams are the horizontal woof that crosses the vertical warp (departments and divisions) to create a strong fabric (e.g., relationships).

At the corporate level, cross-functional teams are being used to manage a number of horizontal processes, such as customer relationships. To strengthen its trade relationships, Pillsbury restructured in the early 1990s, forming 13 different business teams, each of which included sales, marketing, R&D, operations, and finance. Each team was built around a category with individual sales teams sub-grouped by major customers. Pillsbury has also taken this concept to the local level and set up cross-functional teams for major accounts. Now when a retailer has a question about deliveries, pricing, promotions, or whatever, there is a specific logistics person on the local retail account team who can quickly find the answer, saving the retailer the time and the frustration of calling the company and being transferred to half a dozen different departments. Other companies using similar cross-functional teams are Quaker Oats, General Motors, Kimberly-Clark, Kellogg, and Kraft.

A study of the role of integration in quality programs found that "cross-functional management is the most cutting-edge quality system today."[3] Figure 9–1 shows a corporate cross-functional approach similar

FIGURE 9–1

Cross-Functional Chart

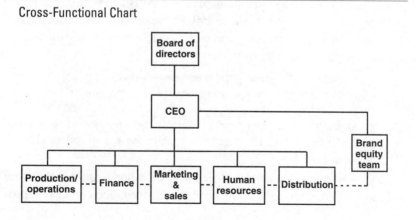

to what Texas Instruments uses. Such teams consist of managers from production/operations, sales, marketing, customer service, human resources, finance, and any other major department that impacts on the company's image and reputation.

An inherent problem with a cross-functional team is that it is corporate or brand based rather than customer-based. On the surface this seems to be the antithesis of IM. For example, Kraft has 36 different business teams, each with a representative from brand management, sales, logistics, information technology, and finance. At the same time, Kraft, like many packaged goods companies, is moving toward having one sales representative handle all Kraft products for each key account. This means that each key account cannot be directly represented on each brand team unless the sales representative for an account wants to be a member of 36 different teams, which of course is not practical.

This situation means it is more important than ever that members of the sales force be made aware of, understand and reinforce the strategic consistency guidelines for each Kraft brand. Although they want to work individually with each key account, what they do with each account should be consistent with each brand's positioning and the brands' and company's core values.

In 1995 the CEO of Harrah's Entertainment asked his operating and functional group directors to write an annual report for the company for the year 2000 based on realistic predictions of what they thought the company could accomplish by that time. The result was that many good marketing ideas came from other areas, just as marketing came up with good ideas for operations, human resources, and other major divisions in the company. Using an annual report format, this is an example of a very creative way of doing cross-functional planning. As Brad Morgan, senior VP of marketing, pointed out when describing the process, it revealed where there was executive consensus and where there were gaps regarding corporate objectives. According to Morgan:

> "It is helping us to identify those programs and efforts which are most important to our future, including identifying some which are not in place now. This is helping to prioritize our development and testing programs for the coming years . . . Interestingly, it is also having a very positive effect on the morale of the organization and on communications between groups."[4]

Cross-functional integration works best when team members are in place for an extended period rather than assembled for ad hoc projects. Not only is integration an ongoing process, but it takes time to develop team expertise and learn how to resolve group conflicts. By reforming cross-functional teams on a task basis, the group is always in the learning curve of group dynamics, taking unnecessary amounts of time to test and learn to trust each other rather than focusing on managing stakeholder relationships.

In order to more deeply integrate customers into operations, some companies have created organizational structures that include the customers in cross-company teams. At General Electric, cross-company teams include GE representatives and major business customers. For example, GE and Southern California Edison, which owns two 750-megawatt GE steam turbine generators, used cross-company teams involving 140 people to cut outage time (when the turbine is shut down for maintenance) and costs by more than half. GE contributed about 60 people; the rest were from SCE. As one SCE executive explained: "You have to go beyond customer surveys. Working as a single entity enhanced communication." GE and SCE executives jointly attend management seminars. If SCE beats its goals on cost, scheduling, and safety, GE earns a bonus.

In larger organizations where finance, marketing, and all the other major corporate areas are so large that they are made up of many departments, it is necessary to have a second level of cross-functional team that is responsible for following through on directives from the brand equity team to ensure that the messages being sent by each division are strategically consistent and integrated. This second-tier cross-functional team is especially important to have in marketing in order to integrate the communication planning and execution of messages produced by the brand group, marketing services, sales, and customer service. (The marketing communications cross-functional team is discussed in more detail later in this chapter.)

Some companies have found that assigning a cross-functional team its own work space makes sense. When General Motors integrated its corporate communication program, it established a "war room" where team members could meet and where the joint projects were posted and their progress tracked. Frequent meetings are also important; however, if groupware is available, members can keep in constant contact and minimize the number of face-to-face meetings.

Although a charismatic leader may be the best person to initiate IM, he or she may not be the best person to head the cross-functional brand equity team on an ongoing basis. Instead, the team should establish itself within the organization on its own, so that if and when the charismatic leader departs, IM doesn't depart also.

Some may argue that a marketing representative should head the cross-functional brand equity team. This could be a mistake if it merely reinforces the antiquated idea that managing brand equity is marketing's responsibility. The best approach is rotating the leadership as long as the designated leader has a customer focus, understands that customer perceptions are reality, and that everything a company does has a communication dimension. It is also important that the leader have the support of, and direct access to, the CEO.

Many good executives intuitively understand integration. Examples are IBM's former CEO Tom Watson Sr., Microsoft's Bill Gates, Disney's Michael Eisner, and Nike's Phil Knight. These people have been able to integrate their organizations to create a strategic consistency that has produced enviable brand equities.

RESPONSIBILITIES OF THE CROSS-FUNCTIONAL BRAND EQUITY TEAM

One of the primary objectives of cross-functional managing is to minimize the isolation and narrow perspective that is a natural by-product of departmentalization and specialization, while at the same time preserving and reinforcing the expertise of the various specialist areas. Harvard's Frank Cespedes calls this "concurrent engineering" which he defines as "better integration among the marketing groups that must interact more often, more quickly, and in more depth across more products, markets, and accounts."[5] Cross-functional management is also similar to matrix management systems where there is both vertical and horizontal responsibilities.

A cross-functional brand equity team has four basic responsibilities: (1) monitoring the company's brand equity, (2) planning across divisions, (3) allocating budgets to leverage positive messages and address conditions responsible for sending negative messages, and (4) resolving the conflicts that are barriers to integrated efforts.

Monitoring

The monitoring function is critical because, as the old management adage states, what is measured is what gets attention. When an organization agrees to monitor its reputation and the strength of its relationships as indicators of its brand equity, then its brand messages will be managed in a way that maximizes the synergy of its communication efforts. To what extent relationships are measured determines to what extent a company has a stakeholder focus. By agreeing to measure the perceptions of customers and other stakeholders, a company has taken the first step towards making an external customer focus a reality.

When managing integration, it is not only critical to know the perceptions of customers and other stakeholders, but also those of management. Most managers have two perceptions of the company, one being what the company is, the other being what they desire it to be. Seldom do these two perceptions match the stakeholders' perceptions. The following are three potential sources of perception gaps:

1. What the company's reputation actually is (e.g., stakeholder perceptions).
2. What management perceives (and desires) the reputation to be.
3. What stakeholders desire the reputation to be.

These three perceptions are seldom identical. The challenge is to bring the first two in line with the perception desired by stakeholders (or else change the stakeholders' perceptions if they are unrealistic). Stakeholder perceptions can be obtained from an analysis of their interactions with the company (taken from tracking and profiling databases) and supplemented with traditional marketing research surveys; management perceptions come from the IM audit described in the last chapter.

Once the perception gaps are identified (and there will always be gaps), the cross-functional team needs to identify the most serious and the reasons for them. This means identifying the source(s) of the messages causing the gaps. For example, if a company learns its products are perceived as being of only average quality although they are premium priced, it may find the product design is perceived as being out of date, its product distribution is in low-image outlets (as was the case with Montblanc pens in the early 1980s), or the products are not performing as the planned messages have promised.

The cross-functional brand equity team's job is to plan strategic corrections for these problems and assign the execution responsibility to one or more of the company's functional areas. Through ongoing monitoring of stakeholder dialogue and behavior, the cross-functional team will be able to determine to what extent the problems have been corrected. At the same time the team is monitoring and addressing the gaps, it also needs to look for strengths that can be leveraged. When these are identified, they too need to be prioritized and strategies determined for those that will provide the greatest return. When Montblanc discovered that the number one reason for buying its pens was for gift giving, it was able to leverage this "endorsement" of its quality and status.

Periodically the brand equity team needs to also pay close attention to all critical customer/brand interface functions such as customer service, order entry, billing, distribution as well as the obvious—sales and marketing. These functional areas will obviously change by product category. Because each transaction is an opportunity to either reinforce a strong relationship or strengthen a weak one, each of these functions should be proactively managed. To do this, requires that each of these functions have access to each customer's complete file (assuming it is a type of business that is able to track customers). Also, employees in these areas need to be knowledgeable and trained to genuinely help customers while suggesting other company products. Finally, these people need to have the authority to make decisions so customers are not passed around or told to call back later.

Monitoring also requires monthly stakeholder feedback reports. Although much of the feedback will come from the stakeholder databases, the team should have the authority and budget to call for special research when ongoing data collection is not adequate to explain why certain perceptions are being formed.

Another benefit of continuous relationship monitoring is that it maintains a corporate sensitivity to focusing on relationships. The more every employee can be given some responsibility for measuring relationships, the more successful will be a company's customer focus. At paper manufacturer Weyerhaeuser, for example, hourly employees regularly visit customers' plants to better understand their needs—even sites as far away as Japan. They work for the customer for a week in order to get better insights into their customers' business.

One employee interviewed by *Fortune* was getting ready for his third trip to Japan. He and three team members would spend two nights videotaping newspaper presses, working between 10 p.m. and 2 a.m., followed by meetings with managers and staff throughout the conventional workday. On returning, he would have to give presentations for two or three weeks to co-workers. He observed, "I have a huge responsibility to do a tremendous amount of recording and note taking and to share that information when I get back . . . It's very uplifting." he said.

Weyerhaeuser used to put a small bar code label on the newsprint rolls it shipped to printing presses. At one customer location, the company representative discovered the bar-code label was sticking to the presses. By simply relocating the bar code a few inches, the problem was solved. Other customers experienced the same problem, but none had complained, although it was occasionally causing down-time.[6]

This kind of personal involvement can be a better guide to strategy than simply sizing up competitors or taking routine customer surveys. Says Gimini Consultant Francis Gouillart, "If you work with one customer at a time, you can invent recipes that escape the commodity trap. If you define yourself in relation to your competition, you are commoditizing your product. You are already in the copycat mode."[7]

Planning Across Divisions

Although the planning of brand position and branding strategies should remain with marketing, these need to be approved and endorsed by the cross-functional team. The "reputation" objectives which drive relationships are generally not articulated in most companies. These objectives should be stated in terms that are measurable for each key stakeholder group. For example:

> 80 percent of customers rate the company good or very good on product quality.

> 90 percent of customers rate the company good or very good on quick response.

> 85 percent of all stakeholders agree/strongly agree the company is socially responsible.

> 95 percent of all stakeholders agree/strongly agree the company can be trusted.

> 85 percent of the investment community agree/strongly agree the company is a good investment.

> 80 percent of suppliers agree/strongly agree the company considers them to be important players in the company's success.

This list, of course, will vary by company and product category. The important point is that the objectives are measurable so future monitoring will have a benchmark against which to compare results.

Based on findings from its formal and informal monitoring of its stakeholder contacts, the cross-functional team must determine what can be done to correct messages that are weakening relationships, as well as determine how to leverage those messages that are strengthening relationships. For example, when Marlboro found its pricing was beginning to send the message "overpriced" rather than "premium brand," it reduced the price in order to avoid further negative messages. The price decrease minimized the number of customers who were terminating their relationship with the brand because they were no longer convinced the price spread was worth the difference. Another approach is to send fewer price-focused messages through sales promotion and spend more on advertising, which sells branding benefits.

Any major changes in product design, service, financing, or promotional offerings should be reviewed by the cross-functional team in order to determine what messages these changes will send to stakeholder groups other than the specific group for which the changes are intended.

Finally, a cross-functional team should ensure that the information that is driving one department's recommendations and actions is available to all other departments. This provides managers and staff with access to all the available information they need to make the best decisions. Such information provides insights into the consequences of their actions and inactions. In other words, people need to know how and where they fit into the big picture—how they can add or detract from brand value.

Here's an example of what can happen when internal departments are not integrated in their planning, which we found in one of our audits. Marketing was responsible for putting together the marketing plan with input from operations. Results of the audit showed that operations wasn't following the marketing plan, continuing to produce their own *pamphlets* and brochures with off-strategy brand messages. When operations was asked why, its managers claimed it wasn't a good plan and that they had no input. Marketing's story, however, was that they had asked operations for input but didn't get a response because operations people were too busy to give the marketing plan serious attention.

Although both the operations and marketing people were smart and genuinely interested in the overall success of the organization, the planning process was not integrated and the whole organization suffered. The reason for the breakdown was *allowing* the operations people to remain uninvolved. A cross-functional planning process, where all parties discuss and sign off on the agreed upon objectives, is central to integration. People and departments who interact with customers and other stakeholders do not have the option *not* to participate.

Budget Reallocations

If one area of a company needs budget and financial help in correcting negative messages or leveraging positive messages, the cross-functional team should make the budget reallocations or advise top management to do so. In other words, shifts in stakeholder priorities or changes in significant product or service messages almost always require extra spending, meaning the affected departments will need budget help. Strategic flexibility requires budget allocation flexibility.

Budget protectionism is, of course, a major barrier to IM. It can be a problem in annual planning when course corrections are needed. In annual planning, a zero-based approach helps the cross-functional team maneuver through this minefield.

Resolving Integration Conflicts

Turf battles are fueled by ignorance as well as negative attitudes. Downsizing, by its very nature, reduces the pool of resources and thus increases competition among departments for funds and staff and magnifies this turf problem. The problem with turf battles is they motivate each side to become more cohesive in the biases and stereotypes of their abilities and their "opponent's" lack of abilities. In marketing these battles frequently take place between sales and the brand groups, and in larger companies that departmentalize by MC function there are often battles between these groups. Unfortunately, that is not the extent of the turf wars. One that has intensified in recent years as computers and database usage has become more extensive is the battle between data processing (e.g., information systems) and marketing and sales.

A cross-functional team can help diffuse the organizational conflicts that result from misperceptions or just plain ignorance about what other departments and groups within the company do. A cross-functional team will not only enlighten each department about what other departments are doing to build stakeholder relationships, but also help each department have a more realistic perception of its own role within the organization.

DuPont is a company that embraces the idea of seamless communication management. "Our goal is to get everyone focused on the business as a system in which the functions are seamless . . . . Every time you have an organizational boundary, you get the potential for a disconnect. The bigger the organization, the bigger the functions, and the more disconnects you get," says Terry Ennis, head of a DuPont group implementing a horizontal organization.[8]

Finally, members must have the foresight to know when to seek advice from the team and when to ask it to review changes in unit plans. Bill Gore, founder of the company that bears his name and makes Gore-tex fabric, uses the "waterline" principle to help his people decide when a decision can be made within a department or division and when it deserves corporate approval. Those decisions that are above the waterline—e.g., if they are wrong they won't sink the corporate ship—can be made without corporate approval. However, managers are warned that decisions below the waterline—those that can potentially sink the corporate ship—should be approved by top management.[9] This is a good managerial approach for IM. If a decision can affect relationships with stakeholders other than the ones for which a particular department is directly responsible, then the program or activity should be reviewed by the cross-functional brand equity team.

Because integration brings together diverse groups with diverse sets of responsibilities, conflicts are inevitable. To help minimize these conflicts, the company should eliminate the hierarchical status of each group by equalizing compensation and rewards, minimizing the differences in allocated office space, and making sure all groups are represented on the brand equity team. Also, it has been found that the more various groups work together and better understand each others' expertise, the fewer the intergroup conflicts. Finally, rotating people from group to group will create personal relationships and give each group a more human dimension. This in turn will help people be more sensitive in dealing with the various specialists as well as making it easier because they personally "know someone they can call."

SUPPORTING THE CROSS-FUNCTION TEAM

To support the cross-functional brand equity team a company needs to do the following: a) open the corporate culture to change, b) revise compensation system, c) have top-down support of IM, d) set up a marketing communication cross-functional team, and f) ensure the internal communication system will facilitate cross-functional activities.

Opening the Corporate Culture to Change

In an analysis of reasons why companies fail, *Fortune* reported that a major problem is a corporate culture that is resistant to change. IM, by its very nature, demands change and openness, as closed corporate cultures can derail efforts to coordinate programs and communication. General Motors under Roger Smith has often been cited as an example of an organization that wasn't too bright. GM's problems in the 1970s and 1980s were not caused by corporate stupidity or self-serving leaders, however, but rather by the company "finding itself hopelessly tangled in a complex corporate culture that resisted change."[9]

AT&T former unit, Paradyne, which markets sophisticated telecommunications technology to corporate and governmental clients, is one company that has recognized that the success of IM depends on the corporate culture. Its marketing efforts involve everyone in the planning rather than placing the responsibility on a certain department, division, or person. As an example, one of its projects coordinated an 800-number response system, outbound telemarketing, direct mail, and direct and indirect sales channels—all of which were in different departments. It resulted in a reduction in sales-cycle time of 58 percent while increasing the closure rate 10 percent. And this was done making 46 percent fewer calls and cutting promotional expenses 28 percent.[10] The synergy that was created by integrating the expertise of the various departments was responsible for sharper targeting, which resulted in higher response rates with lower selling costs.

Revising Compensation Programs for IM

One of the greatest barriers to integration and cross-functional management is compensation. As we said in the discussion of monitoring, what is measured is what gets attention; we also know that behaviors that are rewarded are repeated. In other words, what is rewarded is what gets managed. In an IM cross-functional organization, people are rewarded not just for sales but for relationship-building activities and for activities that eliminate turf battles.

Reward systems unfortunately are often out of sync with business strategy because they tend to reward what is easy to measure. In an integrated program, employees are rewarded for building trust, customer longevity, relationship profitability, and for participating in cross-functional teamwork. One technique is career banding, which is the process of organizing jobs around broad, flexible career categories, and 360-degree feedback, using feedback from all internal customers, as well as supervisors, in evaluation.[12] The brand equity team should be assigned the responsibility for creating this type of reward system. Criteria for IM compensation should:

1. Emphasize profitability, not transactions.
2. Emphasize retention of good customers, not transactions.
3. Emphasize team performance rather than individual performance.

Successful cross-functional compensation systems put as much or more emphasis on team and corporate performance as on individual performance because the extent to which various stakeholders support a company is affected by more than one employee and by more than one department. Managers don't like giving up staff lines and chunks of their budgets to be used in some other area, in part because traditional compensation systems are based upon how much money and how many employees a manager controls.

> The most common element in successfully integrated organizational structures is the presence of a high-level executive who believes in integration and aggressively champions it within the organization.

Driving Integration From the Top Down

The most common element in successfully integrated organizational structures is the presence of a high-level executive who believes in integration and aggressively champions it within the organization. Top management must support the idea of cross-functional planning by providing the necessary support systems, such as flexible budgeting, compensation and rewards for teamwork and relationship building, and continuous monitoring of customer and other stakeholder perceptions.

The prevailing metaphor of the leader as captain-of-the-ship should be replaced by that of the leader as the designer of the ship. The "leader as designer" focuses on building organizational structures that facilitate integration across disciplines.[11]

There are two levels of integration in most companies that need cross-functional planning and monitoring. The first is the corporate or brand level (which we have been discussing) and the second is the marketing communication level. As we explained in the introduction, in companies with multi-tier branding such as General Motors, the brand equity team needs vertical representation from each "brand" (e.g., General Motors, Buick, and Park Avenue). Each brand's vote should be in proportion to what role its brand plays in the overall customer relationship. For example, if the average customer first thinks of his car as a Buick and secondly as a General Motors product, then the Buick people should have a greater say in the brand relationship. Such proportional brand links can be determined through customer interviews. The corporate level brand equity team is appointed by top management and the IMC team by the head of marketing. Obviously the head of the IMC team needs to also be part of the corporate brand equity team.

Setting Up the Cross-Functional Marketing Communication Team

Because marketing responsibilities are often assigned to various functional groups (e.g., sales, brand management, and marketing services, which may be further subdivided into advertising, marketing public relations, sales promotion, direct marketing, event marketing, packaging), there should also be a cross-functional team to manage *planned* messages. Such a team can ensure that planned messages don't contradict each other and are timed to deliver maximum impact. The more planned messages an organization produces, the more critical the need for a cross-functional MC team.

The purpose of this MC team is to ensure positioning consistency in all planned messages, see that big creative ideas are integrated, and coordinate the timing of various promotional activities to minimize overlap. When sales and distribution channel members are given more than one program at a time to sell-in to retailers and administer, it generally means one or more of the programs will receive minimal or no support. A cross-functional marketing communication team centralizes the strategic planning and monitoring of the communication activities, which helps increase synergy. According to the general manager of marketing services and communication at IBM:

> Experience has taught us that a centralized organization is the easiest path to achieving integration . . . all our U.S. marketing communications disciplines have been consolidated under a single management group, Marketing Services & Communications. It includes advertising, media relations, executive communications, direct marketing, trade shows, publications, employee communications, and more . . .[13]

As part of its efforts to integrate its planned messages, IBM has also consolidated much of its global marketing communication activities with one agency, Ogilvy & Mather.

Similarly, NEC Technologies (U.S. subsidiary of the $28 billion NEC Corp. of Japan and second largest computer company after IBM), invested $200 million in 1993 in a sweeping program to raise its brand profile as well as sales revenue, and restructured its organization. Going to a more focused marketing approach, it merged all of its communication elements together, integrating its advertising, packaging, logo and product design, and point-of-purchase activities.

One reason for having a breadth of communication expertise on the cross-functional team is that it's a good way to generate new ideas. Historically in consumer packaged goods, for example, it has been assumed that advertising was responsible for campaign ideas and that all the other supporting MC functions were to merely follow advertising's lead. Now, however, these "supporting" functions have developed their own expertise to the point that they can go head-to-head with advertising when it comes to producing creative ideas. Every marketing communication agency, whether marketing PR, sales promotion, direct response, or packaging, has case histories of successful programs which they initiated. The big idea can come from anyone in any of the marketing areas, both internally and externally.

In those companies where sales and/or customer service are separate from the marketing department, representatives from these areas should be on the team. Also on the team should be representatives from all outside communication agencies with which the company has an ongoing relationship. If the company is going public, refinancing, or merging with or acquiring another company, representatives from the company's outside accounting and legal firms should also be members of the team. These outsiders not only bring a more objective perspective, but also have insights into the experiences of other clients who have gone through similar situations.

An example of the role an outside agency can play in integrating planned messages is BBDO's work on Gillette. An agency account director played a key role in integrating the campaign elements that established Gillette's "Best a man can get" campaign. He worked with the client, his own agency, the public relations agency Porter Novelli, and direct marketing agency, Rapp and Collins, to keep all the work integrated and on strategy. Although Porter Novelli and Rapp and Collins are Omnicom sister agencies, they had to compete to work on the account and then operate as part of a cross-functional strategic team.

Nike's unified image and consistent messages are driven by the company's organization and management style, which one of its executives describes as "enforced teamwork." She says, "It's not so much a communications program as it is a way of operating day to day that ensures that everybody knows what's going on." This lets Nike launch new products with consistent success. For example, a year before the Air Huarache running shoe was introduced, a marketing communications team was developing point-of-purchase and trade-show displays, posters, a special logo, and video and other visuals, all reinforcing the message that a lighter shoe would improve performance.[14]

When it comes to selecting a leader of the MC cross-functional team, the most important criteria is not which MC area the person knows best, but rather his or her core competency in all MC areas as well as the ability to manage and lead.

The manager of the marketing communication function with the largest budget should not automatically be appointed leader. This may perpetuate the heavy use of this marketing communication function and make it more difficult for the team to be function-neutral when planning and making budget allocations. For example, a large packaged goods company that does a significant amount of mass media advertising should not feel that the head of advertising should lead the MC team. As a matter of fact, that could be counterproductive as that person will be conditioned to do things as he or she has always done them and will be less likely to look for more effective, efficient ways to build relationships. Leaders of the MC cross-functional team should have:

- A core competency of all the major marketing communication functions.
- Excellent leadership and managerial skills.
- An understanding of bottom-line realities.
- The respect of all the other marketing managers.
- Knowledge of the organization but willingness to change traditional ways.
- Resourcefulness and the ability to cut through bureaucracy when necessary.
- A strategic mind rather than a tactical one.

Setting Up an Internal IM Communication System

In a survey on internal communications in U.S. companies, half of the managers and front-line supervisors surveyed cited inadequate inter-departmental communication as the number one problem for poor customer service. Other researchers have found that compartmentalization within companies is a serious problem: "Each department builds walls around itself. Time to market is so critical in fast-paced organizations that seamless communication and responsibility sharing must become part of every business' culture. No one has a monopoly on a good idea or a better way of doing business."[15] Groupware, LANs (local area networks), and intranets are forms of internal communication systems that use computers and telecommunication networks to help break down these departmental walls.

For years one of the barriers to the kind of collaboration and computer integration that groupware provides, has been the fact that companies internally had hardware and software which weren't compatible. Only recently has software been developed which makes these differences transparent by providing a common protocol language.

If a company is to successfully build relationships with customers and other stakeholders, it first must build relationships internally. To do this employees must have access to customer information files along with all the other databases that affect servicing customers. The ability to collaborate on building databases and to collectively add, remove, and manipulate them, is what groupware provides. This collaboration allows an organization to create a body of timely knowledge that makes its communication with customers and other stakeholders more effective and productive.

Without some type of groupware, it is difficult if not impossible for medium- and large-sized companies to practice IM because integration must exist internally before it can exist externally. Groupware, in essence, is a technology for managing relationships.

If cross-functional teams constitute the head and heart of IM, and databases are the muscle, then groupware is the circulatory system that allows the head, heart, and muscles to function. Groupware is the infrastructure for capturing, sharing, and leveraging organizational information and knowledge. As Lotus, the manufacturer of Lotus Notes explains, groupware facilitates internal:

> **If a company is to successfully build relationships with customers and other stakeholders, it first must build relationships internally.**

- ◆ Communication (e-mail, messaging).
- ◆ Collaboration (shared databases, conferencing).
- ◆ Coordination of work flow (work flow applications that integrate messaging and databases).[16]

Groupware allows employees to continuously exchange and update information regardless of physical location or time. It is used internally for e-mail and remote access, group scheduling, conferencing, imaging and document management, task and work flow management, and database management.[17] As companies increasingly turn to sales force automation (SFA), groupware allows representatives to configure offers during sales calls, giving them instant access to current pricing, inventory status, and production and delivery schedules. All databases become accessible.

Groupware also helps employees become less myopic, which is one of the first steps in improving the relationship-building process. When people in an organization focus only on their own positions, they have little concern or sense of responsibility for the organization's collective

results. Such isolation is epitomized in the often-heard employee comment, "It's not my problem!" In a traditional organization it can be very
difficult to know why corporate objectives are not met. Because of their
isolation, employees just assume someone else screwed up.

One of the advantages of groupware is that it shifts more of the
burden of informing from the sender to the receiver. When doing the
IM audits we frequently hear managers say, "I'm always the last to
know." Because e-mail makes it so easy to originate and/or pass on
messages, it now becomes the responsibility of the receivers to assume
the responsibility for keeping themselves informed.

Employees need to be trained how to use the internal communication system. There are increasing complaints that employees are
drowning in information, with some managers receiving up to 200 e-
mail messages a day. Obviously, this is counterproductive and is an
indication that an organization does not have a good protocol for using e-mail. Often, as in the case of e-mail, the technology is easily
learned but the proper application is not. Just because e-mail instantly sends a message to hundreds of people doesn't mean that is
the way it should always be used. One of the critical aspects of e-
mail is properly and fully identifying the subject of the message.
This allows recipients to decide whether the message needs to be
read immediately or at all.

Banyan, a software developer in Westboro, Massachusetts, is an
example of how groupware systems can be used. Its geographically
dispersed 150-member sales force keeps in touch with headquarters,
and with each other, through a groupware system. Marketing notices,
technical notes, directories, press releases, pricing data, research results, and full product documentation are available to all Banyan sales
representatives through their laptop computers. They also receive full-
color product presentations, which they use at client locations on their
portable computers. The sales force can even print out product specifications or other information to leave customized product information
packets for their customers.

Although Lotus Notes is one of the most widely used groupware
programs, it and all similar programs, are being threatened by the
Internet, which offers many of the same groupware benefits at a much
lower cost (in late 1995, Lotus Notes cost per user was $69 versus
about $40 per user for intranet software). Following its successful ex-

perience of allowing customers to track their own packages by tapping into its database via the Internet, FedEx began looking for ways in which the Internet could be used internally. What it discovered was the "intranet."

Intranets are Web sites on the Internet that contain proprietary information and restricted access. Unauthorized people are prevented access through the use of firewalls. Thus, by providing employees Internet access and then creating restricted Web sites, a company has a ready-made, internal groupware program. The more databases they place within their restricted Web sites, the richer their intranet groupware program is. At the same time, however, employees still have access to the total Internet and the Web (firewalls are only one-way barriers). A study by Forrester Research in late 1995 found 22 percent of the largest corporations in the United States using some form of intranet.

Many companies are discovering that an intranet can be used cost effectively to eliminate tons of paper flow and at the same time place more accurate and timely information at everyone's finger tips. Some of the basic organizational communication and information resources that are now being distributed electronically are corporate telephone directories that are never more than 24 hours out of date, requisition forms, employee announcements, changes in procedures, and the distribution of training materials.

Unless an organization is willing to become more open and willing to trust employees with information, however, groupware is a waste of time and effort. As a matter of fact, in a closed corporate culture where the management style is strictly top down, groupware facilitates employee frustration and unrest because it increases awareness of what's happening in a company, encourages people to talk to each other, and provides more ways for employees to express their opinions and make them widely known.

THE ORGANIZATIONAL DIMENSIONS OF IM

Cross-functional management is the tool used to link specialists. As we have been told many times by our clients, it all comes down to organization. If the organization is calcified, with rigid walls between departments and a hierarchical communication system, then it will be impossible for people who need to work together to get together.

A basic premise of both reengineering and TQM is that critical processes such as managing customer relationships should not be restricted by functional walls and barriers. Others have found that companies most prepared to compete in the future "are typically companies with rich cross-currents of interfunctional and international dialogue and debate."[18] This can only happen, however, if a company has cross-functional links among its areas of expertise and specialization. Integrated marketing likewise requires an organizational structure that is open and has cross-functional management. These are requirements for IM strategy, and strategy should dictate structure.

Integration calls for more than new lines on an organizational chart. If it is to result in changed processes, it also demands new ways of thinking. G. Richard Thoman, the senior VP in charge of IBM's PC division, has made a crusade of going beyond product and image advertising and immersing himself in product development and operations. His goal is to change the consumer's "out-of-the-box experience with the computer."[19] Like Thoman, every marketing and marketing communication person needs to be involved in every aspect of the brand's business in order to understand how it all comes together. Understanding different functions other than one's own area of specialization is called *"core competency"* and is the focus of the next chapter.

ENDNOTES

1. Weld Royal, "Scapegoat," *Sales & Marketing Management,* January, 1995, p. 62.
2. Michael Hammer and James Champy, *Reengineering the Corporation,* (New York: HarperCollins, 1993), p. 167.
3. Anders Gronstedt, "Integrating Up, Down, and Horizontally: Lessons From America's Leading Total Quality Corporations," *IMC Research Journal,* 1:1 (Spring 1995), pp. 11-15.
4. Brad Morgan, "Corporate Planners Should Take a Look Back to the Future," *Brandweek,* July 31, 1995, p. 17.
5. Frank Cespedes, *Concurrent Marketing* (Boston: HBS Press, 1995), p. xvi.
6. Rahul Jacob, "Why Some Customers are More Equal Than Others," *Fortune,* September 19, 1994, pp. 215-224.

7. John A. Byrne, "The Horizontal Corporation," *Business Week*, December 20, 1993, p. 79.

8. Peter M. Senge, *The Fifth Discipline*, (New York: Doubleday Currency, 1990), p. 298.

9. Kenneth Labich, "Why Companies Fail," *Fortune*, November 14, 1994, pp. 52-68.

10. Mark Suchecki, "Integrated Marketing: Making It Pay," *Direct*, October 1993, pp. 43-49.

11. Anders Gronstedt and Esther Thorson, "In Search of Integrated Communications Excellence: Five Organizational Structures in Advertising Agencies," AEJMC, Kansas City, 1993.

12. Anita M. Pacheco, "Integrating Compensation into the IMC Process," *IMC Research Journal*, 2:1 (Spring 1996), pp. 37-41.

13. James Rielly, "The Role of Integrated Marketing Communications in Brand Management," *The Advertiser*, Fall, 1991, p. 32.

14. "The Great Communications: Successful Marketers Bring It All Together," *Enterprise*, April 1994, pp. 8-9.

15. Regis McKenna, *Relationship Marketing* (Reading, MA: Addison-Wesley, 1991), p. 148.

16. *Groupware: Communication, Collaboration, Coordination*, (Cambridge, MA: Lotus Development Corp., 1995), p. 9.

17. Vicki Gordon, "The Role of Groupware in IMC," *IMC Research Journal*, 2:1 (Spring 1996), pp. 32-36.

18. Gary Hamel and C.K. Prahalad, *Competing for the Future*, (Boston: Harvard Business School Press, 1994), p. 95.

19. John McManus, "Think Like a Peasant to Reap Regal Rewards," *Brandweek*, October 17, 1994, p. 16.

10
CHAPTER

Create Core Competencies

All doctors, regardless of their area, must have a basic understanding of medicine. It's for this reason they all take the same courses during the first three years of medical school. This ensures they know how the human body works and the basic causes and cures of the most common ailments. Only after achieving this core competency are they allowed to specialize and become pediatricians, gynecologists, orthopedics, and so on.

According to C.K. Prahalad and Gary Hamel, "Core competencies are the collective learning in the organization, especially how to coordinate diverse production skills and integrate multiple streams of technologies."[1] Although they were talking about manufacturing processes, the same logic applies to IM and managing brand relationships.

A marketing manager needs three levels of core competency. First is knowing what the brand's or company's core competencies are and then making sure his or her work supports these. The corporation's core competencies are what gives it its competitive edge. Therefore, if marketing managers are doing their jobs, they are continually ensuring these core competencies are properly "packaged" and interpreted for customers. (Other managers, of course, should be doing this for the stakeholders for which they are primarily responsible.) An important element of the corporate core competency should be an organization's mission. This should help determine how the core competencies are packaged and presented. It's up to marketing to integrate these competencies and keep them as a foundation in its relationship with customers.

The second level of core competency is understanding how the company "works," a deficiency in especially large companies. A study by Cooper and Lybrand found that marketing managers and marketing departments that lacked involvement with, and interest in, the "skills and techniques" in other areas of the company were at a disadvantage. This lack of involvement made it more difficult for these managers to internally network and position themselves and their programs as important.

In the larger companies we often find middle managers who have been with a company for only a couple of years, know few people outside their own area and consequently know little of what is going on in these other areas and don't know who to call when a question arises. A solution is to require all managers to get to know at least one other manager in every department which has an impact on customers. This can be accomplished by something as simple as designating one day a month as "Lunch with a Stranger" day. This gives managers (and other employees) license to call another manager they never met and set up a lunch. When we evaluate our workshops for companies, a positive that is always mentioned by participants is getting to know their co-workers, something that company picnics and other similar functions fail to really accomplish.

The third level, which applies specifically to marketing and which this chapter will focus on, is having a core competency in integrated marketing communication and managing stakeholder relationships. This applies not only to marketing and marketing communication managers, but also to outside communication agency executives. People are less likely to consider or agree to include public relations or telemarketing in a plan. For example, if they don't understand how they work together with the other MC tools. All managers involved in strategic communication planning need a basic understanding of, and a genuine respect for, the strengths of each major marketing communication tool—advertising, PR, direct response, personal selling, and so on. They need to know how these tools complement each other, and which can do what job with the most impact and greatest cost efficiency.

An IMC core competency also requires the understanding of the concept and process of integration explained in the first part of this book. If managers do not realize that all actions and inactions can send messages, that perception is reality, that stakeholders automatically integrate brand and company messages, that stakeholders overlap, and that focusing on relationships is more important than focusing on transactions, they do not understand the integration concept.

Also, if marketing and MC managers do not know how to ensure strategic consistency in all that a company does, use a balance of mass and one-to-one media to create purposeful dialogue, create and use databases that track stakeholder behavior, and focus on a mission that is more than making a profit, they do not have an integrated marketing core competency.

Finally, a core competency is incomplete without a sense of bottom-line realities, meaning managers must be able to demonstrate that maintaining strategic consistency, stimulating interactivity, and practicing mission marketing contribute to greater long-term profit than traditional, transaction-focused marketing.

Having a core competency, however, doesn't mean everyone should be a generalist. One of the major misconceptions about practicing IM and IMC is that everyone must be a generalist. This has no more logic than saying every doctor should be a general practitioner, and do away with all specialists. Generalist and specialists are needed in marketing and marketing communications just as they are needed in health care and many other fields.

> One of the major misconceptions about practicing IM and IMC is that everyone must be a generalist.

HOW TO CREATE MC CORE COMPETENCIES

One of the best ways to build MC core competencies is to have experts in one area work in another for at least three months. This is one of the things Dentsu did to build its expertise and become the largest advertising agency in the world. It originally had its people work in various departments for two to three years, which meant it took people 10 to 15 years to acquire the core competency that made them eligible for a managerial position. Because of this investment in developing core competencies, Dentsu was able to deliver on its slogan and promise of providing "communication excellence." (Dentsu has since shortened these assignments to several months rather than several years.)

In Canon's drive to "Beat Xerox," it used a similar long-term strategy to build core competencies. It went so far as to assign technicians in its camera division to work in its copier division and vise versa.

This, along with some other smart thinking, has enabled Canon to become a major global player in the copy business.

To have an IMC core competency requires: a) understanding customer behavior and b) understanding the strengths and weaknesses of the major marketing communication tools.

Understanding Customer Behavior

The first and most essential part of an IMC core competency is understanding the customer. Although this seems obvious, we have found in our audits that marketing managers frequently are so focused on their marketing communication tools and programs that they lose sight of whom they are selling to.

Four areas of customer behavior are especially important to understand: a) customers base their decisions on perceptions (not reality or how the company perceives things); b) buying decisions and brand choices, even for consumer products, are seldom made just by one person; c) customers make decisions with their heads and their hearts; and d) customer wants, needs, and concerns constantly change.

First, perceptions *are* reality: What customers perceive is what they believe, and what they believe drives their buying decisions. Since a basic premise of persuasion is starting your argument from the customer's frame of reference, this means it is important to know how the customer perceives your brand.

The importance of distinguishing between reality and customer perceptions is that often the two are different, and this can change the choice of MC tools that should be used. For example, it may be quite clear from an objective analysis of competitive products that your brand is much more durable and long-lasting than the competitor's. Based on this reality an obvious campaign for the brand will focus on its good value since it lasts so long. However, if the brand is not *perceived* as being more durable and longer lasting, the campaign focus that is really needed is one that *explains* and *proves* that the brand is more durable and lasts longer. The first plan would likely be heavy on mass media advertising while the latter would make more use of PR, as well as a different advertising strategy.

Second, few buying decisions and brand choices, especially for durables and other relatively high-price-point products, are made by just one person. Therefore, in order to plan an effective communication campaign requires identifying not only the actual decision makers, but also the users of the product and those who influence its purchase. Take office computers: The users are generally different from the buyers. Also, there are generally other employees, such as the chief financial officer, who will influence the brand choice out of concern for price and anticipated maintenance costs. A core competency means recognizing that there are often several different groups that must be targeted and with whom relationships must be built in order to create and maintain a customer.

Third, nearly all brand decision makers think with their heads and hearts. Even in industrial buying decisions, judgments have to be made regarding such things as how well a company will keep its word on delivery dates, service response, and using quality parts and ingredients that go into its products. Being sensitive to the balance of rational and emotional thinking used in a buying decision will influence the MC mix, the selling proposition, and the extent of purposeful dialogue that the customer will want to have with the company.

For example, when a customer is uncertain about a decision, emotional thinking is more likely to increase. This can be a signal that more dialogue is needed between the buyer and seller in order to identify and address the buyer's concerns.

Finally, in order for a manager to have a genuine, ongoing customer focus he or she must have a natural *customer curiosity*. In the academic world a characteristic of a good scholar is *intellectual curiosity*, meaning the scholar wants to know more and more about a subject and is never satisfied that he/she has learned or discovered everything there is to know about that subject. The corresponding characteristic of a good marketer is customer curiosity, the constant need and desire to learn more about customers' needs, wants, desires and what pleases and displeases them about the brand and company. A customer curiosity is manifested in the understanding and extensive use of research and other forms of feedback.

Understanding the Strengths and Weaknesses of Communication Tools

As discussed early in this book, each of the MC areas has developed its specific expertise to the point where it can individually drive a marketing communication program. Tom Harris' *The Marketer's Guide to PR*, for example, is filled with case histories where PR was the dominate tool used in introducing new products, increasing brand awareness, repositioning a brand, and increasing trial. *Promo* magazine every month has a special section highlighting promotion programs that have accomplished the same things. The success of direct response programs for such companies as L.L. Bean, Spiegel, and Land's End are legendary. And of course mass media advertising continues to be the MC tool of choice for many mass marketed packaged goods.

As explained in Chapter 8, the mix of MC tools that should be used at a particular time for a particular campaign should be based on the marketing communication objectives. As Figure 10-1 shows, certain MC tools are more suited and more cost-effective than others for accomplishing certain communication and behavioral objectives.

One of the measurements in an IM audit is determining the extent to which marketing managers understand the major strengths and weaknesses of the various MC functions. The majority of managers we have interviewed have not scored very well, generally only knowing the strengths and weaknesses of their own functional area and only a few of those in other areas.

Personal Sales

Personal selling is (or should be) the most effective MC tool a company has based on contact per customer. Good salespeople customize their presentations and offers for each customer. They also anticipate objections and immediately respond to questions, concerns, and unanticipated objections. With sales force automation systems, a salesperson is now capable of configuring or reconfiguring an offer on the spot. In order for salespeople to maximize their inherent advantage of being able to immediately respond and quickly reconfigure offers, however, they need the support of a database management system which is cross-functionally supported within the organization.

A characteristic of personal selling that is both a strength and a weakness is its measurability. On the surface, the number of orders a salesperson produces can be easily measured. Unlike marketing people, salespeople are seen as being more accountable because of this ability to tie orders to an individual. The weakness of this measurability, however, is its pressure to "make the sale," even when it's not in the best interest

F I G U R E 10–1

Primary Strengths and Weaknesses of MC Functions

MC Functions/Tools	Primary Strengths and Weaknesses
Mass media advertising	*Strengths* creates and maintains brand awareness, helps position brand, cost efficient for mass marketed products, controls content and timing *Weaknesses* low credibility, high percentage of reach is wasted, message clutter, often perceived as intrusive, effect difficult to measure.
Sales promotions	*Strengths* adds tangible value, gives sense of immediacy, stimulates behavior (e.g., trial, repeat, attend sales presentation), measurable *Weaknesses* conditions customers to buy on price, can set false retail, can significantly reduce margin
Product publicity	*Strengths* increases message credibility with third party endorsement, reaches hard to reach targets, relatively low cost (only for production and logistics—no media charges), can deliver claims that can't be presented in ads due to government regulations *Weaknesses* little control over content or timing, must go through media gatekeeper, effectiveness difficult to measure
Direct response marketing	*Strengths* very measurable, highly selective for audiences that can be individually identified, allows messages to be personalized, can efficiently and semi-confidentially test new products/offers, can be interactive *Weaknesses* high cost per impression, many consider direct mail junk mail and telemarketing intrusive, raises privacy issues
Events	*Strengths* involving and interactive, audience self selects, helps position brand, can add drama to brand *Weaknesses* low reach and frequency, relatively high cost per contact

Sponsorships	**S**trengths helps position brand, audience self-selects
	Weaknesses effectiveness difficult to measure, clutter
Personal selling	**Strengths** most effective selling tool, two-way communication allows immediate response to questions and objections, measurable
	Weaknesses extremely costly, brand messages sometimes difficult to control

of the customer. Also the sale may not be a profitable one. These are variables which IM addresses.

Another weakness of measuring sales performance is the validity of the measure itself. In actuality, to what extent is the salesperson responsible for making or losing a sale? As customer relationships become more important than individual transactions, and as relationships become more of a corporate responsibility (e.g., operating in the value field), the salesperson must become more of a team player in the total marketing process, making individual accountability more difficult to determine. This is why compensation systems are being changed to balance rewards for cross-functional teamwork as well as personal accomplishments.

Personal selling's biggest disadvantage is its cost since it is the most expensive per customer contact of all the MC functions. In an attempt to reduce sales cost, marketing is taking on more of the selling functions such as getting and qualifying leads, tracking prospects through their buying decision process, providing support materials at the right time to coincide with where prospects are in their buying process, and providing product databases that customers can access when and how they choose. Although these will not necessarily lower the cost-per-sales call, it should reduce the number of sales calls and help increase sales productivity of the calls made.

Since a salesperson is the primary contact most business/industrial customers have with a company, the sales representative epitomizes the company. Therefore, whatever the communication objectives are, the behavior of the sales representative will be a primary factor in determining if they are achieved. The sales representative must not only know and understand what the company's marketing communication objectives are, but buy into them and sincerely work towards achieving them. Because sales people work on their own, this MC function is one of the most difficult to control.

Traditionally most marketing departments have found it difficult to work smoothly with sales. Marketing people see themselves as the "creative ones" and criticize sales representatives for not wanting to try anything new. At the same time, salespeople feel marketing just doesn't get it, wasting time and money developing new ideas which the field says are "useless." In other words, the effectiveness of the sales force and marketing services can be increased the more the two departments integrate their planning and execution.

Mass Media Advertising

A primary strength of this tool is creating and maintaining brand awareness for mass marketed products. Because mass media advertising can be accurately placed and scheduled, its exposure can be fairly well estimated and its message content can be totally controlled. And because it is generally carried by mass media, its cost per thousand (CPM) is one of the lowest of all the MC tools (except packaging). However, when a *targeted* CPM is figured, the cost efficiencies often fall away.

(We are not distinguishing between mass and niche media because the differences are so subjective. There is no single media vehicle, for example, that reaches everyone—i.e., every media vehicle is a niche vehicle to some extent. Take the Super Bowl. Although it is considered by many to be one of the ultimate mass media buys, its audience has certain demographic skews. Niche media are often considered to have smaller circulations than mass media, however, such publications as *Modern Maturity* magazine whose circulation is nearly 20,000,000 shows that reach is not always a discriminating criteria.)

Another strength of mass/niche media advertising is maintaining brand awareness, keeping the brand top-of-mind. This is especially true for products that are frequently purchased and in highly competitive categories such as soft drinks, cigarettes, and rental cars.

Mass media advertising can also be used to efficiently and effectively position a brand or company and create an image. Also, because of advertising's relatively low CPM, it is an affordable way to send frequent messages, which are often required to create the desired image and level of awareness, especially for frequently purchased packaged goods and services.

The main weaknesses of mass media advertising are its low credibility and clutter. Because there are so many commercial messages customers have developed both physical and psychological ways of blocking them. Also customers apply a discount factor to most mass media ads merely because they are "advertising." And it's not just customers who say advertising stretches the truth. As we mentioned earlier, even some people working in mass media advertising feel that over promising and exaggerating shouldn't be a concern because "customers know better than to believe everything in an ad." Obviously such an attitude among a segment of those creating these messages perpetuates the declining credibility of advertising because they feel they have to exaggerate promises even more to make an impression. It becomes a self-feeding credibility cancer.

Product Publicity

More than any other tool, publicity can increase the credibility of a message. When a PR release, for example, produces a brand mention in a news or feature story, readers and viewers are more likely to believe what is being said about the brand because it is coming from someone who is not in a position to benefit from the sale of the brand. This is called source credibility.

Another strength of product publicity is its ability to get "free" brand exposure. Because legitimate media don't charge for writing about a brand or company, this exposure is extremely economical. Some trade and industrial magazines, as well as some cable channels that have editorial formats, do sell "editorial" space and time, although most customers recognize such stories as not being the most credible. Also, the free aspect is often misleading, however, as there is generally some amount of production cost involved. For example, sending a company spokesperson on a media tour to promote a new product can cost as much as $5,000 a visit because it requires creating the material and presentation the spokesperson will use, scheduling interviews, and paying travel expenses and the spokesperson.

In heavily regulated product categories, such as medicine, alcohol, and financial services, publicity can deliver messages that companies are not allowed to deliver through advertising. Stories about the introduction of Rogaine, a hair replacement product, were able to make more positive claims about the product than could the advertising, which was tightly controlled by the Federal Drug Administration.

The limitation of publicity is that there is virtually no control over most media releases. Not only is there no guarantee they will be used, there is no way of controlling when or how they are used. Finally, once a particular media vehicle does a story on a brand it is unlikely to do another for months or even years.

Sales Promotion

Because it adds tangible value to an offer, this is the best tool to use to directly affect behavior. By adding an incentive that is in addition to the benefits of the product itself, generally for a limited period, potential customers are given an additional reason to try a product, and current customers are given an additional reason to repeat or increase their frequency or quantity of purchases. Sales promotion offers are also used to motivate other pre- and post-sale behavior. For example, it can motivate a potential customer to visit a showroom or request more product information. Following a sale, it can motivate the purchase of service contracts or product peripherals. Increasingly, this tool is also being used to build databases by offering customers and potential customers an incentive to provide profile information.

Coupled with its unique ability to motivate behavior is the fact that it is measurable, a characteristic that has made it extremely popular during the recent decades of emphasis on accountability.

A potential disadvantage is that overuse can distort the perceived price of a product and condition customers to buy only when incentives are being offered, which results in reduced margins.

Direct Response

Although direct response—direct mail, telemarketing, fax, e-mail—is really a combination of several MC tools, most industry people treat it as a separate MC function. Its primary strengths are that it can be individually targeted, personalized, and is measurable. Because it has a relatively high CPM, it is generally best used to reach small, highly identifiable targets. Because of its success in industrial marketing and building retail businesses such as Spiegel, L.L. Bean, and Lands End, it is in danger of being over used. Recipients of "junk" mail and intrusive phone calls are learning how to ignore or avoid these messages just as they have with TV commercials.

Direct response media can be used to cost effectively generate leads and screen these leads. Frequently these are two- or three-step applications used to identify those most likely to buy and then take them through the buying process.

Sponsorships and Events

More than any other MC tool, this one has the ability to involve stakeholders. The events, however, vary in degree of participation. A person attending a seminar or workshop will be more involved than a person attending a sponsored stock car race. Another strength of events is that they are highly self-selective of their target audience. For example, those who choose to attend a seminar on computer networking are most likely to have a high interest in that subject, just as those attending a stock car race are most likely to enjoy racing and cars much more than the average person.

This tool is misused when marketers sponsor an event merely because it attracts a large number of people, paying little attention to content of the event and the type of crowd it is attracting.

Seminars create educational and brand involvement opportunities. They are also a good qualifier of prospects and allow sponsors to demonstrate and give a personal sales pitch to multiple prospects. Seminars are suited for more complex products or those that need to be demonstrated or tried. The advantages of seminars are that they have high impact because objections can be addressed and they generally have the undivided attention of participants. A disadvantage of seminars is their relatively high CPM. What makes them cost effective is proper screening and making sure only key influencers or decision makers attend. One way to reduce cost is to have a co-sponsor.

Packaging

In consumer goods, packaging is the last ad a person sees before deciding to buy or not buy in a particular category. The message can be highly targeted because, again, a person would not be looking at a product category section unless he or she had an interest in it. Often overlooked is packaging's extremely low CPM for delivering a brand message. Because packaging is an intrinsic (as well as created) contact point, the majority of the cost of delivering a message on it is covered.

In retail services, location is the "package" in which decor, ambiance, and functionality send powerful messages. When services are delivered off-premise by an individual, uniforms and the behavior of the service provider become the service package—what we call service messages.

Customer Service

Although not normally considered a MC function, customer service can be one of the most impactful communication tools. Because current customers are so valuable, it is essential that customer service be used strategically to ensure that profitable customers are retained. Also, in terms of relationship building, converting an unhappy experience into a positive one can turn a negative transaction into a long-term relationship.

From a strategic standpoint, it is important to realize that benefits can be gained from customer complaints. One obvious benefit is determining areas of the company's operation that need to be improved. Another is saving a customer and minimizing negative word-of-mouth about the brand. A good example of how to do this is what Peter Eckrich & Sons, a processed meat company which sold over 1,500,000 packages of hot dogs, bologna, and meat items each week, used to do (before it was acquired by Swift). Each complaint was answered within two working days of receipt. Most responses were sent by mail; however, the more serious were handled by telephone or a personal visit from a local salesperson.

At the end of the month, each person who had contacted the company with a complaint was sent a second letter, this one signed by the company president. In this he expressed his regret over their unsatisfactory experience and asked if their complaint had been properly handled. Enclosed with this letter was a business reply card on which he also asked if he could continue to count on them being loyal Eckrich customers. Over ninety percent of the returned cards said "yes." It was concluded by Eckrich's management that the promptness of the replies sent a much stronger message of caring than did the actual wording of the original response or even the coupon for a free replacement, which had also been enclosed.

Probably more important than retaining a high percentage of the complainers was the fact Eckrich significantly reduced the number of dissatisfied customers who told their friends about their negative experience. Through focus groups it was learned that many of those who had complained, but felt their complaint had been well handled, actually became extremely vocal about what a great company Eckrich was to have responded promptly and gone to so much trouble to make sure they were satisfied.

Customers don't expect companies to be perfect, but they do expect problems to be corrected quickly. When they are, customers generally stay loyal. Chrysler had four recalls in the spring of 1994 and yet its share went up, which observers contributed in part to the way Chrysler handled the recalls—quickly and honestly.[2]

> **Customers don't expect companies to be perfect, but they do expect problems to be corrected quickly.**

These examples point out the importance of a cross-functional MC team knowing how customer service operates and how complaints are handled. Customer service should be closely evaluated to determine what functions can be changed to make each customer contact as positive as possible. Responding to customers will grow more important as customers have more ways to talk back to companies.

Customer service sometimes can be a source of negative messages. When a company offers an 800 help line or service number, for example, but does not assign enough people to staff it, or the people are not knowledgeable, a negative message is sent. If the line is always busy or has such limited hours that it is inconvenient to use, it conveys a message of indifference. Offering customers the opportunity to respond and then not adequately handling the responses sends conflicting messages. Not only is there message conflict, the practice also contributes to distrust. As more companies go on-line with Web sites, the same problem may occur. This is what Toyota and the San Jose Mercury News found when they offered customers an e-mail address and then found they couldn't cost-justify handling all the responses. In late 1996 the *Wall Street Journal* picked a random number of companies that invited customers to contact their Web sites with questions. Not only did many of the companies take days and weeks to reply, many of the replies were not individualized or worse yet, told customers to contact another Web site or their local dealer.

Of course, good service does not come cheap. GE, whose Answer Center is one of the premier customer service groups in the world, hires only college graduates, trains these new hires five weeks before putting them on the phones, and then requires 100 hours of refresher training each year.[3] This center handles approximately three million calls a year at a cost of $10 million.[4]

For companies that can't afford to expand their staff, one solution is to give callers the option to leave messages for a call back. This would turn a negative maintenance message ("The company is too busy to talk to me") into a positive message ("The company cares enough to make an extra long distance call to help me").

The same thing is true for service representatives, particularly those like computer and copy machine repair people, who enter a client's place of business. Even some cable companies are training their service representatives to act like ambassadors and dress in business clothes.

BENEFITS OF A CORE COMPETENCY

For the last several decades, brand and product managers were taught to think of themselves as "presidents" of their brands. To many this role was the attraction to being in marketing. This position of leadership, however, is now being redefined. The real leader of a brand will be the person who has a core competency in all areas of marketing and promotes a cross-functional effort to build brand equity.[5]

A core competency allows people to be more creative in mixing and matching MC tools. Event marketing, for example, is a combination of advertising and PR. Cause marketing is sales promotion and public relations. By forcing people out of their experiential, psychological, and functional silos, companies have more opportunity to develop new ways to more effectively build relationships with customers.

A core competency also allows managers to be in more control. One of the problems of dis-integration is that many things are happening that directly affect customers and no one is in charge of all of them. Another benefit that will be realized is synergy—where messages reinforce each other and their strategic timing results in greater impact.

Specialists are needed in all areas of marketing and marketing communication to execute the programs outlined in the marketing plan. Generalists, however, are needed to manage cross-functional planning and monitoring. A core competency strategy is employed when you dedicate your company to the development of generalists at the management level who can apply strategy across functions and coordinate the work of the specialists.

Another area where generalists are needed is in the application of the new technologies and communication tools such as databases. Specialists deliver the database know-how, but good managers must know how to use such tools strategically to strengthen brand relationships.

ENDNOTES

1. C. K. Prahalad, "The Core Competence of the Corporation," *Harvard Business Review*, May-June, 1990, pp. 79-91.
2. Watts Wacker, "Cultural Schizophrenia," presentation to National Demographics & Lifestyle Summit '94, Denver, Colorado, July, 1994.
3. C. A. Russell, "Encouraging Complaints," *Target Marketing*, May 1987, p. 15.
4. "For Firms 800 Is a Hot Number," *The Wall Street Journal*, November 9, 1989, p. B 1.
5. Betsy Spethmann, "Crowning the New Brand Kings," *Superbrands '96* (supplement to *Brandweek*), October 9, 1995, p. 28.

11

CHAPTER

Make Integrated Marketing Data-Driven

Probably the single most important insight (and sound bite) that won Bill Clinton the presidency in 1992 was "It's the economy, stupid!" If he had been a marketing executive arguing for a customer focus rather than a sales focus he probably would have said, "It's the database, stupid!" This chapter is about how to set up and use databases as a strategic part of a relationship focused IM program.

Paine Webber learned the difference between focusing on sales versus focusing on customers when, with its advertising agency, Saatchi & Saatchi, it did an internal communication audit.[1] Although P-W knew how many accounts it had, it did not know how many actual customers it had, because it didn't know which customers had more than one account. It also didn't know the characteristics of customers who had multiple accounts. Consequently, it was not able to efficiently focus its efforts on increasing the value of its current customers.

Paine Webber, like many companies, was ignoring the fact that the data already in its possession could be extremely valuable in developing more profitable business strategies. It preferred to market each of its products to the "average customer," overlooking the fact that many of these people were already buying more than one product.

Saatchi's audit discovered that 1.8 million accounts were actually held by 717,000 individual customers. This revelation resulted in significant savings in P-W's marketing communications, not to mention the reduction in customer aggravation from continually receiving multiple mailings and being offered products which they already had purchased. The audit identified the penetration of the 22 products by each customer, making it possible to begin a customized cross-selling program. It also enabled P-W to identify its most profitable customers and their lifetime customer value. Finally, by combining databases the company was able to identify which of its products were most effective as "beachheads" for selling related products.

As a result of Saatchi's audit, Paine Webber's sales strategies were better focused and its targeting more precise. All of this analysis was undertaken on data that was already captured but not fully utilized by marketing. What will separate the more successful from the less successful companies in the coming years will not be the quantity of the data collected, but rather how this data is turned into actionable marketing strategies and programs.

> What will separate the more successful from the less successful companies in the coming years will not be the quantity of the data collected, but rather how this data is turned into actionable marketing strategies and programs.

Nearly every business has a database of some type, even if it's nothing more than a list of orders, inventory, and billing information. And as database management software becomes more developed, using databases to drive marketing is no longer the sole domain of large business-to-business companies. Brady's Clothing for Men in San Diego, for example, collects information on customers regarding their preferred colors, designers, styles, sizes, and garments. It also records customers' birthdays, their favorite radio stations and magazines, hobbies, occupations, and the names of family members. The database is then used to let customers know about new shipments and special sales based on their preferences.[2]

At the other consumer product extreme, some megacompanies are profiling millions of their customers and tracking their transactions.

For example, Kraft has demographic and product-buying information for customers from 30,000 food stores.[3] *Readers' Digest* has a mailing list of more than half the households in the United States—approximately 50 million, more than three times its magazine subscriber list. It uses this database to track not only its magazine subscribers, but also sales of its videotapes, music, books, specialty magazines, and other special offerings.[4] By profiling its customers it can determine the most likely prospects for other product categories.

The primary use of databases, however, is to identify your most profitable customers so you can make a special effort to retain them. This is because heavy users in many categories, especially consumer products, are heavy users of several different brands, which means your best customers are also the best customers of your competitors who value these customers just as much as you do.

SETTING UP DATABASES

Personalized, purposeful dialogue cannot occur without a database to track all interactions, not just transactions. Setting up an information system (IS) that tracks customer interactions and links customer databases that are already in existence (e.g., order entry, accounting, service and repair, customer service) can be costly. Therefore, its use must be clearly thought out ahead of time.

As many companies have learned, database management is a major breeding ground for ego and turf battles between IS, accounting, personnel, sales, marketing, production, distribution, and any other department that is using customer data. Up until now, it was not feasible to collect and store all the information all departments wanted, and a choice had to be made which configuration to use: One that was best for accounting, distribution, sales, or production?

Because most databases were originated to support accounting, production, or distribution rather than sales and marketing, marketing's needs are often difficult to satisfy. Because most databases weren't designed with marketing in mind, each marketing request often requires special handling. Thus, because marketing has low-priority access and requires more work, IS people are often unexcited about working with or for marketing.

To avoid the delays and frustrations of working with IS departments, some marketing departments have simply bought their own hardware and software. Needless to say, such moves have only intensified the ego battles with IS. It also means that marketing must train its own database experts. This reinvention of the wheel is avoided in IM. Through cross-functional management, the barriers between IS and marketing are removed. If not, integration does not exist.

Expanding current databases to capture and store details about customers' and prospects' preferences and needs still isn't an easy task, but getting it right has been shown to pay substantial dividends. IBM has embarked on several integrated, database-driven, pilot campaigns—one involving the medical field, another in manufacturing, and another with distributors. Using an IM approach, the company has generated three times as many qualified leads compared to previous campaigns. A key component of these IM programs is asking customers what they're looking for in products and service and how they like to be contacted by the company—by mail, phone, fax, brochures, salesperson's visit, or not at all.

To help alleviate the cost of setting up and managing customer databases, it is important to make sure they are of value to a variety of internal departments. This requires up-front planning by the cross-functional brand equity team to ensure all departments have input into what data to capture, what role they will play in capturing the data, and how the data will be configured for easiest use by all users. The larger the company and the more complex its sales transactions and aftermarket service, the more demanding the database needs and the more important it is to consider upfront questions such as the following:

1. *What and how much information needs to be saved? How much can you afford to collect? How much data can your system process and at what speed?* Data storage is conceptually similar to inventory storage. Both require a warehouse with a certain architecture that determines their efficiency for various functions such as receiving, assimilating, and keeping track of contents. The basic difference is that the database warehouse is electronic and exists inside a computer.

   In the case of database warehouses, their designs are heavily influenced by either financial needs, production needs, or sales needs. The more data has to be moved around and manipulated to satisfy each of these area's needs, the more costly and time consuming it is. Therefore, it is important that marketing be involved as much upfront as possible when these database warehouses are first set up. It should make sure that performing data analyses to determine lifetime customer value, customer profitability, extent of cross-category buying, profile heavy buyers, and track frequency of complaints, inquires, and compliments from profitable customers can all be done quickly and efficiently.

2. *What will be done with the database information? What kinds of analyses? What kinds of decisions will be based on it? Will you want to prepare reports directly from the database?* Levi Strauss & Co. has been building a database since 1990 of customers who wear its products. Through various direct-response techniques, such as 800-numbers and sweepstakes, the company has created customer profiles. According to P.J. Santoro, its database marketing specialist, "Everything we find out about customers is being put on the database. It helps us identify where our customers live, their spending habits throughout their life cycles, finances, the value of their home, and the kind of car they drive."[5] The information has generated 50 different psychographic profiles.

   Levi Strauss has used the list to do co-op promotions with retailers. The manufacturer combines its lists with retailers' to send special, direct-mail offers.

3. *Who will manage it? Will the marketing department or information systems management be in charge?* A survey of business-to-business marketers found that the marketing department handles the databases in 44 percent of companies, the information technology department in 15 percent, and both departments work together in 26 percent of companies.[6] Maintaining the accuracy of a database is not easy. In another survey it was found that 61 percent of the respondents said they had changed either their name, title, company affiliation, address, or phone number within the past year.[7]

4. *Who will have access to it? How easy does the system have to be?* Power used to mean that you controlled information. Now, power comes from providing great access to the information," says Robert M. Howe, head of IBM's consulting business.[8] Seagram has a database of about 10 million liquor buyers that it shares with retailers for special promotions. It has information

on at least 1,000 households in each of the 2,300 ZIP codes. Retailers can call a toll-free number to obtain information on the number of known customers in their areas and help in designing, printing, and mailing brochures or catalogs, but can't obtain the names themselves.[9] Seagram's research indicates that 75 percent of retailers like the program.[10]

5. *How secure does it have to be?* Because databases are becoming so valuable as corporate assets, security is now a major issue. Who has the right to change the data needs to be addressed and agreed upon. Who has the right to make copies of the database, and when and under what conditions are they sent to outside suppliers for application?

6. *How often will database users have access to it? Do they need it immediately, daily, weekly, monthly?* Access is an expensive item, because having all the information immediately at hand demands larger memory systems. If the data can be downloaded to long-term storage and only brought back on-line occasionally when needed, then the system can be smaller and more efficient.

7. *How accurate are the databases?* Another problem is the integrity of the data. Accuracy is critical. Some systems are more forgiving than others when it comes to how and when data is entered and accessed. Many systems do not allow someone in marketing to pull sales figures from the system at the same time someone in sales is entering an order. This means marketing may not get its numbers until after hours or on weekends when the system can be temporarily closed to new entries.

Resource Databases

It needs to be kept in mind that some databases should be designed for external customer use. Business-to-business companies who offer a broad range of products, such as electrical supply companies, find having an on-line database catalogue is of much greater value to customers than a traditional catalogue because it can be instantly updated as inventories and prices change. Critical to these resource databases, however, is providing methods for customers to ask questions and, in general, talk back to the company. When a customer takes time to interact with your information databases, your brand is top of mind and should facilitate whatever inquiries the customer has.

This type of database technology, whether on-line or in CD-ROMs sent to current customers, can also generate sales without personal handling. By enabling customers to manipulate the data and configure their own package—complete with pricing, delivery dates, and credit terms—cost per sale can be decreased.

In addition to providing better service, resource databases can provide the company valuable information if it tracks which customers are requesting which types of information. This is one way that customers self-select and categorize themselves. For example, sales data in a brokerage firm can identify customers who primarily buy bonds. However, by tracking inquires into the puts and calls database, the firm can identify which bond customers also have an interest in puts and calls and therefore have high potential for expanding their buying. And because this is behavior-based data, it has more validity than just asking customers what other products/services they are interested in.

When setting up databases, it is not necessary to invest in gathering all the desired customer profile information, especially for consumer packaged goods. Individual household data can be purchased from outside sources, such as Polk's Lifestyle Selector, and overlaid on your own databases.

It should also be kept in mind that databases are not just for recording orders, tracking inventories, names, and addresses, and other similar quantitative data. Special "notes" software is available to facilitate collecting and storing information from focus groups and other types of marketing research.

Database technology is not so advanced that it can fulfill every corporate need. There is no current system that is fast, inexpensive, easy-to-use, and capable of processing simultaneous transactions on large amounts of data. But the industry is moving in that direction with more sophisticated hardware and software, especially groupware systems and intranets.

IM DATABASE APPLICATIONS

Databases can be used in every type of business; however, for some it is easier than others. Those who should find it easiest are businesses that automatically maintain a history of transactions (e.g., financial companies; utilities; services that require customers to subscribe or sign-up, such as cable TV franchises and periodicals; those who sell industrial and business-to-business products; and those who sell on credit). All these already have accounting, distribution, and/or some other type of databases in existence. Harris Bank's emphasis on collecting customer information and using that information to provide more personalized communication and services has resulted in an average customer relationship of 20 years versus the banking industry average of four years.[10]

An interesting misperception is that mass marketers of packaged goods cannot use data-driven marketing because they don't know who their customers are. In fact, they know very well who their primary customers are—wholesalers, distributors, and/or retailers. Furthermore, with the availability of scanner data, they can now identify a sample of their end-users (not all stores use scanners, and in those that do, not all customers have or use ID cards). Such samples can provide excellent consumer profiles. Finally, mass marketers can use promotional campaigns designed to motivate heavy/loyal users to identify themselves. Lovers of Wheaties cereal, for example, can be offered a History of Wheaties Heroes book, the Breakfast of Champions (Wheaties' slogan) Cookbook, or a customized front panel of the Wheaties' package displaying the customer's own picture. All these offers can require customers to submit their names, addresses, and answers to product usage questions.

Having good customer data files and using them strategically are two different things, however. A survey of business marketers by Tucker Chicago and *Advertising Age's Business Marketing* found that 85 percent use their marketing databases only for building and using a mailing list.[11] Managers and their staffs now need to be trained to use these new capabilities. Although this will be a challenge for marketing people, not only will it enable them to plan more strategically and operate more cost effectively, but it's also another way they can re-integrate themselves into the total operations of the company and once again become key corporate players.

One of the biggest mistakes most companies make when using databases is focusing *only* on "How can we use databases to better target and send more brand messages?" This is a transactional rather than a relationship application of databases. As the foundation of purposeful interactivity, databases should be used not only to *push* more brand messages but also to enable customers to *pull* desired information from a company.

Focus should be on adding value to the total product offering, not just sharpening sales strategies. Although databases can be used to increase sales, as direct-response companies have proven time and time again, if that is the only use of databases their value is not being maximized.

For example, Figure 11–1 shows how a customer and prospect information database built by marketing, sales, and customer service inputs can be used. Note that the database captures all interactions, not just sales. A fairly simple software program can be designed to generate a "flag" report when a critical number of a certain kind of brand messages are received within a designated period of time. For example, a national car rental company may say it has a problem when it receives over 100 *complaints* within a month that its cars are too utilitarian—they offer few extras. Using this report, the brand equity team can decide if the cars needs to be upgraded or the planned messages need to be changed to lower expectations by explaining that economy cars mean economy rates (assuming that is true).

NEC corporation, a manufacturer of computers and peripherals, has a Technical Support Center staffed with 60 technicians and engi-

FIGURE 11–1

Building and Using Databases

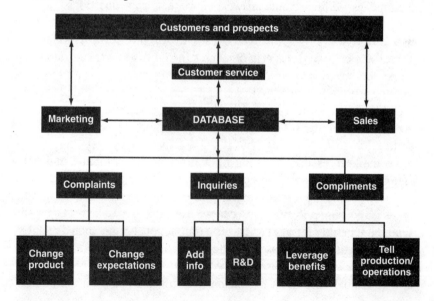

neers who not only respond to the nearly 50,000 questions they receive a month, but just as importantly they record these questions, comments and problems. In one particular month 1,500 of the calls were from customers who said they couldn't get a directory on their CD-ROM readers. In all these cases the problem turned out to be the customers didn't have a disk in their drives. Based on this information, the company modified the next version of their computers to include a LCD panel that indicated when a disk was not in the drive.[13]

Going back to Figure 11–1, when a company finds it is receiving a significant number of *inquiries* about a product or operation, it can make the decision to add more information in the packaging or give the information to R&D to see if the product should be changed to make its operation easier and more clear. Finally, when a significant number of *compliments* are received relating to a particular area, consideration should be given to how to leverage this particular product strength and at the same time those responsible for the design or service should be made aware of the compliments and possibly also given a special "compliment bonus."

As Figure 11–1 shows, there are many different ways databases can be used. In addition to those illustrated, some of the other more popular uses are generating leads, making customer service more personal, targeting planned messages, creating individualized messages, automating the sales force, and increasing retention.

Prospecting for Customers and Developing Leads

Just as the offers in direct-marketing need to be continually tested and refined, a company needs to continually prospect new customer segments. The database of current customers is still a good place to start because it provides a profile for those who have responded and become profitable customers. Once this profile is known, it can be used in the selection of databases from other sources which are then tested.

In developing a lead-generation program, the first step is agreeing on a definition of a "qualified" prospect. To what extent should they match the current customer profile? If a list can't be found that includes those characteristics, it may be necessary to merge several relevant lists. For instance, by combining a database of technical professionals with subscribers of a financial-services trade publication, a company could come up with a list of IS managers employed at companies with sales between $200 to $500 million who have an interest in financial planning.

For years the main criteria direct marketers have used in selecting prospects has been frequency, recency, and monetary (RFM). They have found that those customers who most frequently buy, who have most recently bought, and who have spent the most money, are the best prospects for future offers (within the same product category). Recency is also a good measure of a company's vitality. Although recency will differ for every product category, the important thing is its trend. If a smaller and smaller percent of customers have bought in the last month, for example, a company is soon going to have problems (unless the total number of customers is significantly increasing). Therefore, tracking recency is one of the ways to monitor a company's brand equity.

Smart direct marketers are now adding to RFM another criteria—relevance. The more relevant a product and offer is, the more likely a customer will respond. Relevance can be predicted on the basis of lifestyle and demographic profiles in addition to the types of products previously purchased.

Databases of leads and prospects can also be built by strategic interactivity. By tracking customer and prospect behavior—including what customers buy, what promotions they have responded to, and what they have complained about—companies can customize messages and responses to inquiries when talking to customers and prospects. This provides marketers a way to generate quality leads, as a person's request for information about a brand is a behavioral (rather than just an attitudinal) indication of interest.

Findings from traditional surveys that ask customers about their intent-to-buy have low validity. However, when a customer takes the initiative to request information about a product and is willing to provide information about him or herself in return, that behavior can be predictive of future buying. In addition to providing more qualified sales leads, this process can also be a valuable input when developing creative strategy. Finally, the types of information requested through these one-to-one interactions can provide creators of the brand's mass media messages with greater customer insight.

Making Customer Service More Personal

The use of customer databases should not be restricted to sales and direct marketing programs. All employees who have customer contact, regardless of department, should have access to customer databases. This improves service several ways. First, it allows the customer to be recognized as an individual. Second, by looking at the customer profile employees can be more relevant in their responses. Third, customers don't have to waste time telling the company once again their name, address, phone number, fax number, and so on.

But even this is not enough. Employees must also be given the authority to make decisions and respond as each situation requires. The added value of having access to individual customer records is that it enables a company to respond faster. Because there cannot be a rule or policy for every imaginable situation, employees must be trained and trusted to respond based on general, rather than specific, guidelines. Employees must be trusted to decide when taking a short-term loss will result in increasing and extending the lifetime value of a customer.

Targeting Customers

Using a database to find customers that match a need-specification profile is generally cost-efficient. For example, Meridian, a $100-million-a-year subsidiary of Northern Telecom, was able to pull from its files five customers for a software product. Each was invited to a one-on-one seminar that addressed its concerns. Four companies completed the seminar questionnaire, three attended a second sales presentation, and two bought the product. The payback was sales of more than $75,000.[14]

Retail stores with good customer databases are able to segment customers by their buying behavior, such as those that generally buy full-price merchandise, those that generally buy on the first mark-down (where there is still good selection), and those that generally buy only on second mark-downs and close-outs. Knowing this, stores can direct mail each group accordingly, and not offer discounts, or too much of a discount, to those who will buy at full price or when they receive a small discount. This also lets stores create strategies for moving the second mark-down buyers up to first mark-down buyers, and first mark-down buyers up to full-price buyers.

HOW TO BUILD A CONSUMER DATABASE

If a company decides to build a consumer database, the first problem is sourcing the data. There are a number of ways profile information can be collected:

1. *Surveys.* Our Own Hardware, a 1,200-store, 24-state chain, uses an electronic survey box in each of its stores. In return for sharing their names, addresses, and preferences, customers receive on-the-spot discounts and coupons.

2. *Coupons, Sweepstakes, and Promotional Offers.* These should be offers that generate potential customers, not just those interested in free offers. Edward Nash, author of *Database Marketing*, recommends offering information pamphlets on product-related subjects. Crayola generated names by running a sweepstakes in its first FSI. Parents could enter by filling in a coupon with their children's names, birth dates, addresses, and phone numbers. In return, each child received two free Crayola markers. Approximately 400,000 coupons were received.

3. *Warranty Cards.* When it was introducing its new rechargeable batteries, Gates Energy Products offered $20 rebate coupons to encourage consumers to return product registration cards. This information was used to market directly to customers, thus bypassing the retailer.

4. *Membership Clubs.* Mattel has been gathering names through its Magic Nursery line. After purchasing a doll, the child sends in the name she's giving it, and her address, age, and the store where it was purchased. In return, the child receives a Mother's Day card signed with the baby's name and a coupon. When another doll in the line was launched, those children in areas where the doll was available received an announcement. Mattel has also used the list, containing approximately 100,000 names, to mail out coupons for its Barbie line.

    Swatch started a collectors club in 1993, which is promoted in more than 500 designated "collector" stores in Europe. According to club manager Wolfram Ullman, "Our plan is to have at least one retailer catering to the Swatch collector in every city." Collectors pay approximately $80 a year for membership. In return, they receive a laundry list of special privileges: a Swatch watch produced exclusively for club members; a catalog of every Swatch watch ever produced; special offers on collectible watches and accessories like t-shirts and artwork; invitations to attend at least six special events a year, which include special travel and hotel arrangements; VIP seating at Swatch-sponsored music concerts, some of them held exclusively for members; and the quarterly *Swatch World Journal* with information on all new product launches and styles. There are more than 100,000 members in seven European countries and the United States. Ten thousand of them showed up for an exclusive rock concert in Italy.

5. *Point-of-Sale.* Information can be gathered right at retail. For many years, Radio Shack has asked customers for basic information—address and phone number—as the sale is made. Other techniques for gathering information as part of a transaction include:

- Proprietary credit cards. Many retailers offer their own credit cards, primarily to capture reliable information about customer purchasing patterns.

- Membership programs with ID cards. Egghead Software tracks sales through the use of a scanner card. Each time a customer uses it, he or she receives an automatic 5 percent discount on purchases. Over 1 million cards have been issued; to obtain one, a customer has to fill out an extensive questionnaire. This information, in turn, is used to develop customized quarterly newsletters.

- Phone numbers (which can be used to find out customers' names and addresses records). One good example involved a multibranch retailer in the do-it-yourself lumber/hardware industry. This organization captured all check, credit card, cash, and promotion data and tracked it back to a customer record, a practice called reverse-appending. All sale and product/department data were rolled up and recorded on a store-visit, current-year basis, with a summary detailing previous years' activity. Database output included targeted promotions, frequency usage programs, in-store promotions targeted to buying patterns, and regional and store-by-store activity reports.

How to Build a Customer Database Concluded

6. *Gift giving.* Special rates are offered to customers who sign up friends. MCI Friends and Family is a good example of this; two-for-one Christmas gift subscriptions are another.

7. *Catalogs.* Bloomingdale's offers approximately 300 different catalogs and promotional mailings per year. Customer purchases are tracked to determine who receives which offers. Someone who bought a men's suit would receive notice about a sale on men's accessories. Databases have revealed that 75 percent of its business comes from 25 percent of its customers.

   Little Tikes uses its mailing list to send catalogs twice a year, although parents cannot purchase directly but must go to retail stores. The catalog is sent out to more than 1 million customers who have called the company's 800 number (featured in all advertising and on all packaging) requesting to be on the mailing list. When they call, the company collects information on the ages of the children and whether the caller is a parent or grandparent. In addition, minicatalogs are placed in all toy packaging along with information on how to join the mailing list.

8. *800 numbers.* Health Valley Foods was able to move from health food stores to grocery stores by tracking consumers. Names were collected from letters and calls to an 800 number. Once a loyal customer base was established, the company was able to show supermarkets that the product would sell.

9. *E-mail and Web sites.* These new technologies can also be a source for database building. Many companies have created home pages, conferences, and Web sites for users of their products or people wanting information. These are excellent vehicles for collecting data as well as being interactive with customers.

Databases can also be used to direct customers to related product categories that they currently aren't buying. An electronics chain that had 16 product categories and 1,000,000 customers in its database found that 43 percent were buying only in one category. Since the average customer sale was over $200, it was worth developing special promotional offers to motivate current customers (the ones most easy to sell to) to buy in other categories.[15]

Canon Computer Systems, a subsidiary of Canon U.S.A., has a database containing information on 1.3 million customers. By using it strategically to target buyers of its color printer, the company had a 50 percent response rate in a direct-mail offer that asked owners of color printers if they wanted information on a new color scanner for desktop publishing. As a tie-in premium, owners of the color printer received four free ink cartridges for their printers if they bought the color scanner.

Another way databases can be used to segment customers is according to where they are in the relationship-building process. This is most relevant for considered purchases such as cars or insurance polices, or selecting a bank or stockbroker, as well as major business-to-business purchases. By asking the right questions (either through direct personal contact or other planned messages), you can determine if people/companies are potential customers or qualify as customers and whether they have tried your product but not yet bought again, have made repeated purchases, are profitable, or are recommending your products to others. Each of these stages in the brand relationship call for a different set of brand messages because the more a message can speak directly to an individual's situation (relative to buying) the more relevant the message will be and thus the more likely it will generate a response.

Database analysis is also useful in determining when segmenting is not necessary. Blockbuster Video, which has nearly 70 million households in its database, analyzed a sample from this database to determine video rental patterns. It wanted to find out how subject-specific a household was and whether households could then be targeted in terms of types of movies (e.g., comedies, westerns, dramas, science fiction, murder mysteries). For example, did certain households skew high on comedies or adventure movies? The number one finding was that nearly all households skewed high in renting new releases. Another finding was that when Disney movies were rented, there were generally children in the household. And that was about it. The study did not find that households fell into movie-type segments other than for short periods of time. In other words, Blockbuster determined, contrary to what it had hypothesized, it wasn't possible to segment households by movie category.

Another strategic use of databases is to remove unprofitable customers. Some are unprofitable because they are more demanding and high-maintenance; some just buy on price; and some are just low-volume, and the amount of hand-holding for the sales realized is not cost-effective. This is where the lifetime customer value equation mentioned in Chapter 3 comes into play; it lets you figure out which customer relationships are worth nurturing for the long run. However, this can't be done without a database that has sufficient customer tracking data to allow these analyses to be performed.

Retaining Profitable Customers

A company needs to have the same sort of institutional memory about its dealings with a customer as the customer has. An example comes from Washington D.C., where Mary Naylor, president of Capitol Concierge, operates a personal and business service that runs errands—everything from picking up dry cleaning to waiting for the repairman—for employees in certain commercial buildings. She had been experiencing some success with her new business, but quickly ran up against a wall. Naylor was unable to tap into sources of potential customers. "It takes a lot of trust for someone to hand over their to-do list," she admits.[16]

Naylor and her team concluded that what was lacking was a consistent system for developing ongoing relationships with individual customers. Now Naylor and her staff make note of "every transaction, every time [customers] call to ask a question or make a complaint." It's not as expensive or time-consuming as it sounds considering how much more profitable it is to win repeat business than to chase new prospects, according to Naylor.

Naylor uses database marketing techniques in an exemplary manner: she doesn't just send out personalized messages as a facade for "knowing" her customers. She uses it to truly develop relationships, which includes responding to complaints and altering her services to better meet the needs of her clients. These adjustments benefit both parties.

Automating the Sales Force

Providing salespeople with easier access to more relevant databases and the laptops and modems to use them (known as sales force automation or SFA) can make a sales force more productive. For example, a salesperson can sit in a customer's office, input that customer's needs, and using a software program and a modem access the corporate databases to determine product design alternatives, product availability, prices based on this customer's past volume, profitability, the customer's line of credit, and delivery schedules. Before leaving the customer's office the salesperson is able to configure a customized product offering. Being able to do this quickly and accurately is also an added value to customers. Such automation will become even more necessary as companies downsize their sales forces and require each salesperson to be more productive.

Unfortunately, according to Computerworld magazine, 79 percent of sales organizations are dissatisfied with their SFA systems and nearly two-thirds of the companies that have adopted them have failed to see any measurable benefits. The reason for these disappointing numbers is not because SFA is not conceptually sound, but because of inadequate planning, application, and training on the systems.

Most of these disappointed companies failed to set realistic and practical SFA objectives. For example, was the system designed to shorten the sales cycle? Does it have value at point of sale—does it allow a salesperson to configure an offering on the spot? Was it designed to increase sales close rate? Another problem is that each company feels it is totally unique in its sales needs and therefore needs to completely customize its own SFA system. The downside to this has been a limited industry learning curve.

What we are slowly learning is that SFA should really be thought of as S/MA—sales/marketing automation. This is because the more functionally specific IT solutions are, generally the more tactical they are. The more they are cross-functional, however, the more strategic (as well as tactical) they can be.

Data Mining

Soon brand managers will be talking about data mining and geographical information systems with the same ease they now talk about test marketing and concept testing. Database mining is simply the act of using software programs to analyze the customer databases to look for such things as trends and buying patterns and to determine customer segments that are only buying a small portion of your product offerings.

For example, when KeyCorp analyzed its banking customer databases, it learned that 850,000 of its loan customers were not using its checking and savings account or its credit card services. With a targeted mailing to a test group of these loan customers, the bank was able to motivate 11 percent to sign up for a credit card. Another example of mining is for a local branch bank to be told when one of its customer's certificates of deposit is coming due or when a customer will soon pay off a mortgage, both of which will generate cash that could be used to buy another investment product. In the more sophisticated marketing setups, the corporate marketing department will send the customer some ideas for re-investing, but the real payoff is when this mailing is followed up by a personal call from the customer's local branch bank.

Creating GISs

Geographical information systems (GIS) are software programs that analyze sales and other transactional data based on geography. They are used primarily by companies to determine geographic sources of sales and profitability, to help in site selection of plants and retail stores, and to demonstrate compliance with local and national regulations (this applies especially to heavily regulated industries such as banks, utilities, and government agencies who must show they are providing equal-opportunity service to all geographical areas regardless of income or ethnicity).

They also include such things as traffic patterns and traffic density by day and even times of day. By combining such information with customer data, retailers can determine which geographical areas produce what percentage of their sales. Banks, for example, can determine the impact of business on their branch units when ATMs are installed or removed from various locations.

An ongoing challenge to companies using mass media advertising is to determine to what extent its geographical coverage is consistent with the brand's distribution. GIS can help answer this question by overlaying the reach of the various media used with a map of its distribution points. It can also show how far away customers will travel in response to certain promotions and from which specific areas they come.

DATABASE APPLICATION CHECKLIST

A sad story about failing to understand the evolution of databases comes from book publisher Commerce Clearing House, which in the late 1980s was a top-10 Fortune 500 performer in earnings and return on equity. But its management failed to foresee that the accounting and law firms making up the bulk of its customers would turn to electronic databases for much of the information CCH had been providing. Says an executive vice president, "It's like we were sitting there with our feet stuck in concrete."

Frequently data that could guide better communication decisions and that already exist within the company are not recognized for their value. For example, completed warranty cards are often filed away and not used as a source of vital data for consumer profiling which can facilitate cross-selling, product performance follow-ups and evaluations, identifying which retail chains are doing the best jobs, and so on. Rebate offers are often fulfilled, then the forms destroyed, with no hard data captured. Likewise, mass media advertising (other than straight image advertising) that is tightly targeted but has no response device isn't working as hard as it could to provide important customer information.

To help clients increase the efficiency of their communication, Saatchi & Saatchi asks them the following questions to see to what extent they are maximizing the use of their databases, especially in strategic planning:[17]

- ◆ Do you know how much promotional money you can afford to spend to attract a new customer?
- ◆ When you undertake sales promotion or other direct-response activities, do you keep in contact with the respondents?
- ◆ What resources does your company have at present to capture data on your customers and prospects?
- ◆ Do you know what proportion of your sales comes from what proportion of your customers?
- ◆ Can you identify existing customers of one brand who might be receptive to promotion and cross-selling of another?
- ◆ Do you know if your number of accounts is the same as your number of customers?
- ◆ Can you determine the lifestyles of your customers?
- ◆ Can you quickly and inexpensively identify actual customers of your product for inclusion in focus panels or other research purposes?
- ◆ Do your sales representatives visit all your potential customers?

- ◆ If you could differentiate between your high-, medium-, and low-value customers, would you spend your marketing money the way you do today?
- ◆ Have you monitored the relationship between various schedules of media activity with brand awareness and sales across countries?
- ◆ Do you regularly test different uses of media across brands and countries?

PRIVACY ISSUES

Databases, direct marketing, and telemarketing all must win customer approval because of increasing privacy concerns and issues. People are suspicious of companies that have gathered information about them and their lives. Some customers are more comfortable when they can determine the information that goes into the database. Outside the United States, direct mail is often difficult to use because data protection laws do not allow selling or renting marketing information on individuals.

Customers become most concerned when they are asked for personal information which they feel is not relevant to the product being purchased. On the other hand, when it is explained how having certain information will help a company better service a customer, the privacy objections often decrease.

Certain intrinsic contact points, such as when customers are waiting in lines, requesting more information, or arranging for a repair, are generally more acceptable for collecting customer profile data than intrusive contacts. The same is true for created contact points, such as sweepstakes entries, rebates, and warranty cards, where consumers have chosen to be involved and respond. As kiosks, the Internet, and electronic yellow pages become more widely used, companies will be able to use these less intrusive communication systems to collect customer data making privacy more top-of-mind with customers.

Companies are becoming more sensitive, as they should, about customer privacy. For example, TRW's credit bureau, which maintains credit records on some 180 million Americans, has spent over $30 million in the last few years updating its computer network and launching programs to soothe customer concerns. One program provides customers with a free, annual credit report to help take the mystery out of what the company knows and is saying about them. TRW's efforts have led to an 80 percent reduction in mix-ups on financial data from people with similar names. "Consumers have interests in economic choices and privacy," says Martin E. Abrams, director of TRW's privacy and consumer policy. "Our job is to find an equilibrium between the two."

A more direct approach to generating customer preference is used on the All Conditions Gear survey cards given to purchasers of this line of Nike products. The headline, in large, bold print, asks, "Would you like to receive Nike publications?" Then several descriptions with "yes" or "no" replies are listed; for instance, "If Nike makes its mailing list available to other companies, do you wish to be included?" The options are immediately visible and well explained, giving the consumer the feeling that it's his or her own choice.

THE DATA FUTURE

Having a data-driven customer focus is no longer an option if a company wants to stay competitive. First, customers have more brand options, and this will only increase as globalization and deregulation continues. Second, your competitors are, or will soon be, offering better service. Third, even if a customer focus isn't currently widespread in your industry or product category, it is in many others. As customers experience better service from other business interactions, regardless of product category, they will expect the same from you.

Data-driven marketing is a far more sophisticated strategy than direct marketing. It means capturing information and utilizing it to develop relationship strategies, open up two-way communication, and personalize messages. Databases are tools to prospect for new business by predicting what type of people are most likely to be interested in your brand. Databases are useful in developing more effective targeting and retention strategies. When the appropriate information is captured and fed back into the system, databases also help monitor programs and provide a knowledge base for sharpening strategies.

ENDNOTES

1. Saatchi & Saatchi, *The Total Communications Audit.* (London: Saatchi & Saatchi, pp. 6-7).

2. Karen Marchetti, "Customer Information Should Drive Retail Direct Mail," *Marketing News*, February 28, 1994, p. 7.
3. Michael Treacy and Fred Wiersema, "Customer Intimacy and Other Value Disciplines," *Harvard Business Review*, January–February 1993, p. 89.
4. James Brian Quinn. *Intelligent Enterprise*. (New York: The Free Press, 1992), p. 247.
5. Jim Emerson, "Levi Strauss In The Early Stages Of Shift To Database Marketing," *DM News*, December 7, 1992, p. 1.
6. "DMA: Over 90% of BTBers Use Databases; majority of survey respondents house them internally, more than half build them," *DM News*, January 31, 1994, p. 10.
7. John Coe, "The Decay Rate of Business Databases—A Surprise," *DM News*, February 14, 1994, p. 25.
8. Ira Sager, "The Great Equalizer," in Business Week, *The Information Revolution* (New York: Business Week, 1994), p. 104.
9. Gary Levin, "Seagram Offers Database to Retailers," *Advertising Age*, October 19, 1992, p. 34.
10. Toni Apgar, "The Fast Trackers," *Direct*, 5:4 (April 1993), p. 24.
11. Brent Keltner and David Finegold, "Adding Value in Banking: Human Resource Innovations for Service Firms," *Sloan Management Review*, Fall, 1996, p. 63.
12. Kim Cleland, "Few Wed Marketing, Communications," February 27, 1995, p. 10.
13. Jennifer Dejong, "Smart Marketing," *Computerworld*, February 7, 1994, p. 118.
14. Diane Luckow, "Better Selling Through Technology: Companies of All Sizes Are Using Database Marketing to Boost Sales Through Old-Fashioned Personal Service," *PROFIT*, 13:4 (January 1995), Sec. 1, p. 43.
15. Fred Newell, presentation to National Direct Marketing Institute for Professors, Sponsored by the DMEF, San Francisco, March 20, 1996.
16. Susan Greco, "The Road to One-to-One Marketing," *Inc. Magazine*, October 1995, America Online.
17. Saatchi & Saatchi, *The Total Communications Audit*, p. 6-7.

12 CHAPTER

Create a Partnership with an Integrated Communication Agency

All advertising and other communication agencies want to be business partners with their clients. Most feel it is demeaning when clients refer to them as a supplier or vendor. The problem is that it is difficult for a client to consider an agency a communications partner when all the agency wants and can offer is a small part of the relationship-building process. As we have said throughout this book, relationship building and nourishing requires managing a wide array of communication messages. The more agencies want to provide only one of the communication elements that drives these relationships, the more they are positioning themselves to be mere suppliers or vendors.

In a speech to the IAA World Congress of Advertising in 1996, Martin Sorrell CEO of WPP, said western-based advertising agencies were extremely conservative with old-fashioned management structures that were inflexible and slow to respond to client demands. If agencies wanted to keep their clients in this new age of marketing, he said they will have to do "strategic thinking" rather than just great creative.

According to John Fitzgerald, former vice chairman of McCann Erickson, "the reality of business today is that all clients are doing integration; it's a fundamental part of their business to have integrated marketing programs, or at least multidimensional marketing programs . . . Every agency has observed this trend and is well aware of it. The truth is, however, very few agencies of any size are truly an integrated marketing communication company, yet we're all trying to claim that turf."[1]

When Mitch Engels, Managing Director of FCB in Chicago, was asked about FCB's efforts to offer its clients more integrated marketing services, he explained that there was a lengthy learning curve:

> We tried the hard way, like everyone else back in the 1980s, to jam all these other services down the throats of our clients—Impact [sales promotion], Direct, Medical, Hispanic, PR—we had them all. When we did occasionally get a taker we then proceeded to piss all over our shoes because we really weren't one agency, we were just one agency that owned a lot of different services. Then the light finally went on and we realized we couldn't just serve it up on *our* terms. We realized we had to serve it up on their terms, what they needed. When we started looking at it from their standpoint rather than the typical agency greedy standpoint, we started making headway.[2]

Full-service in the 21st Century will be significantly different from full-service today. As Guy Geertz, managing partner at Moors•Bloomsbury in Brussels, tells his agency managers, "You must take responsibility for the brand, not just the campaign." The new meaning of full service will not only include the use of marketing communication tools other than advertising, but also involve managing or advising on product, service, and unplanned messages for all stakeholders and developing two-way message strategies that create and nourish brand relationships for the long term. An advertising agency that focuses only on creating brilliant advertising is still needed, of course, as there will always be a need for creative campaigns. But that type of agency, if that is all it can do, will be seen as a creative boutique, not a full-service agency.

Full-service in the 21st Century will be significantly different from full-service today.

A good example of an agency recognizing there are more impactful messages than media advertising is Allen Brady & Marsh when it pitched the British Railway account several years ago. Its research prior to the pitch found that the operations of British Railway were very poor—few on-schedule departures and arrivals, dirty coach cars and offices, and employees who had never heard of customer service. Needless to say, passengers had many complaints.

For AB&M's final pitch, the potential client was asked to come to AB&M's offices. When the Railway group arrived, they found the reception area quite depressing with old furniture and dim lighting, not to mention the candy wrappers and cigarette butts on the floor. In addition, the receptionist paid no attention to them even when they approached her. When they finally got her to look up and acknowledge them, she asked three times why they were there. She claimed she knew nothing about any meeting and then proceeded to complain how no one ever told her anything.

When the Railway group was finally taken to a conference room, the presentation began with the agency saying what the visitors had just experienced was what each of their passengers experienced every time they had contact with BR. And unless BR was willing to make significant changes in how it performed its service, the agency was not interested in its business because no amount of marketing communications could overcome these strong product messages. The Railway folks got the message and Allen Brady & Marsh got the account.

FEW AGENCIES UNDERSTAND AND PRACTICE INTEGRATION

According to Leslie Winthrop, who helps clients find agencies, there has been an increase in the number of clients looking for agencies who understand integration and can help clients talk with a consistent voice to the trade, their customers, and other important stakeholders.

Nearly every MC agency will tell clients and potential clients that it can provide integrated services. But beware: Most of these agencies, and especially ad agencies, have little expertise in integrating marketing communications and designing consistent messages that create purposeful dialogue, move customers through the buying process, and speak to all key stakeholders.

Joe Plummer, who has been a key strategist for Leo Burnett, Young & Rubicam, DMB&B, and is now vice-chairman of Audit & Surveys, explains what agencies must begin to do:

> Advertising agencies have always been sitting down with the client at
> the brand manager level and selling a single product. But I believe
> there is an opportunity for agencies to become more like management
> consultants, to sit down with the chief executive and help him solve his
> problem, help him build the equity of the company and its brands with
> all his stakeholders. That's a whole new level. We're not ad guys any
> more, we're strategic planners.

But clients must be willing to pay to get this new kind of thinking and communication leadership. Because most advertising agencies have done strategic planning as part of their traditional full service, clients expect that thinking to continue to be free even though media commissions have been reduced and the communication challenge is much greater and demands higher levels of agency expertise.

The flip side of this situation is that ad agencies (or any MC communication agency) promising integrated strategic thinking—and the expertise and facilities to plan and execute an IMC campaign—must deliver on this promise. To date, very few have. When it comes to IM or even IMC, agencies often promise more than they can deliver.

20 QUESTIONS FOR DOING AN ICA AGENCY SEARCH AND REVIEW

Clients typically have a vertical view of their business which is right and proper for them. Agencies should complement this with a more horizontal view of all the marketing communication functions and how they add value to the product and drive brand value. An integrated agency should know better than its clients what communication tools and programs work best to ensure that customer and other stakeholder relationships are healthy (that is, long-term and profitable).

For clients who want to find an agency that understands and practices integration, the following questions can be used to separate true integration agencies from the wannabees and those that will promise anything to get the business. Although these questions were designed to help clients in the agency selection process, they should also be used by clients who already have an agency but would like to see that agency think and act in a more integrated way. (And for agencies that want to become more integrated, but are not sure what they need to do, this list is a place to start.)

Understanding Integration

1. *What strategies does the agency recommend for creating and nourishing customer relationships versus those used to generate transactions?*

   One ad agency we talked to said it should control integration because it "understands what buttons to push to get the consumer to respond, and in what sequence to push those buttons." Although a customer must respond behaviorally to MC programs (e.g., buying, trying, recommending the product), a manipulative approach to create this behavior can backfire if it is short term or turns off more customers than it delights. This manipulative mind-set has also been responsible for many product categories spending the majority of their dollars in sales promotion. And as companies have sadly learned, when customers are conditioned to respond to the best deal, that's exactly what they will do—forgetting all about brand loyalty.

The purpose of this question is to see if the agency understands how integrated marketing differs from traditional mass media advertising in both concept and practice and if it understands that to build and grow relationships requires position consistency, purposeful dialogue, and a mission beyond increasing shareholder value. Most of all, this question seeks to determine if the agency has made any effort to master the communication dimensions of relationship marketing.

2. *What level of IMC responsibility does the agency believe it should have in order to maximize a client's MC synergy?*

An agency that truly believes in integration will want to make sure that there is a structure in place, both at the client and the agency, that ensures positioning consistency, purposeful dialogue, and marketing of the client's mission.

In other words, the agency should be willing to take leadership responsibility if the client so desires and be able to explain how it would do so.

We are often asked to what extent an agency should push their clients toward integration. Although there is no one answer, the agencies that are doing so, such as Hal Riney, Fallon McElligott, and Price/McNabb are getting the new business and plenty of publicity for their integration expertise.

Practicing Integration

3. *What are recent examples of integrated strategic planning where a client's MC investment had a synergistic effect as a*

direct result of the agency's integrated planning and creativity?

An integrated agency will have examples of both IMC and IM planning. In other words, is the agency capable of diagnosing problems in product, service, and unplanned messages, as well as in the planned marketing communication areas? These will show that it has worked with a client on product and service messages and helped integrate communication with other stakeholder groups besides customer segments. Most of all, these examples should demonstrate the positive value of synergy in increasing message effectiveness.

4. *To what extent has the agency worked with other MC agencies in planning and executing an integrated campaign?*

What kinds of working relationships does its staff have with people in these other companies? Who manages the effort? What has the agency learned about more effective management of cross-functional efforts when more than one agency has been involved?

5. *What campaigns has the agency created where the big idea and lead MC tool was not mass media advertising? Has it ever taken a good idea from another MC agency working on the same brand and executed it as part of the client's integrated campaign?*

This is an ego-detector question. A good integration agency will have a process for working with other MC specialty agencies, both those inside and outside its family of agencies. This organizational approach should be clearly articulated and include a process for the cross-functional planning, monitoring, and evaluation of the planned messages.

6. *What method does it use for analyzing and prioritizing brand contact points?*

As we have been discussing, customers and other stakeholders receive brand messages from many different sources and in many different places. These need to be identified and prioritized in order to make brand building most cost-effective.

7. *How knowledgeable is the agency in motivating and using databases and customer feedback?*

Agencies are generally engaged in one-way communication based on copy tests, attitude and usage studies, tracking studies, and sales and share reports. Although some clients are beginning to build customer databases, agencies are making little use of this resource. Even the majority of direct-response campaigns which use addressable media are using these databases only to target, not to personalize messages. With only an average 2 to 3 percent response for direct-mail efforts, even the use of these databases for targeting seems limited.

An integrated agency knows how to use databases, affinity groups, customer service programs, and new media to facilitate customer initiated communication. Furthermore, it will know how to use those interactive opportunities to capture feedback that will further enrich the databases and keep them current.

8. *What are the agency's best practices regarding strategically combining a mix of mass and one-to-one media?*

Mass media are important tools for delivering certain kinds of messages; one-to-one media have other uses. It isn't a question of whether or not mass media is dead, but rather how the two can be integrated to take advantage of the strengths of both. An integrated agency will be able to show how it has used mass media to motivate customers to self-select themselves and then followed up by targeting these prospects with more personalized messages.

9. *Has the agency ever reduced a client's MC budget while continuing to grow the brand?*

In the early 1990s, Continental bank in Chicago went through reorganization and repositioned itself as a commercial bank, terminating its consumer accounts. During this transition it also decided to use integrated marketing communication to help create and manage its new relationships with commercial customers. Working with Fallon McElligott in Minneapolis, the bank was able to significantly increase both the number of business accounts and average business per account and at the same time reduce its marketing communications budget 20 percent.

When asked what the agency's reaction was to this reduction in spending, the bank's marketing director said, "It was a little upset, to say the least." On the surface this seems a natural, and predictable reaction; however, it's the wrong way to think about agency profit. Rather than thinking of this as a loss in billings, the agency should have used it as a testimony to its ability to help its clients increase profits while at the same time making their marketing communications more efficient. Such an achievement would ensure that the agency receives new business assignments from this client; it would also create a new business pitch that is hard to match!

10. *How much and on what basis does the agency bill for its integrated thinking?*

If an agency says IM strategic thinking is free, unless you are a mega spending client, beware. Good strategic thinking is time consuming and requires input from senior agency executives. If it's free, the agency probably uses a standard, cookie-cutter formula and/or junior people.

Preparation and Learning

11. *What kind of ongoing, cross-functional training program does the agency have?*

In many ad agencies the training in other MC areas and integration is serendipitous. What people know depends on the accounts they have worked on. As one agency executive told us, "Our people's knowledge is very client-driven." Needless to say, this type of internal training produces a follower, not a leader who is going to be on the cutting edge of new thinking and strategies.

Integrated agencies approach training in different ways, from rotating assignments to formal training sessions. Some have senior managers attend integration workshops and then go back and train their respective departments. The important thing is that managers and aspiring managers must go through some process to develop their core competencies in marketing communication (which includes more than mass media advertising). This includes senior executives.

12. *To what extent does the agency have organizational memory? Does it share its learning internally, with synergistic results?*

Unless a company is as big and diverse as P&G it doesn't have the luxury of seeing results of numerous MC campaigns and programs used in a wide range of product categories. But every marketing communication agency has this luxury, they just seldom take advantage of it. This is because they fail to integrate the results so their people and, more importantly, their clients can benefit from all this learning. (Admittedly there are client confidentiality considerations that must be realized and protected).

When an agency has organizational memory, such collective learning will be more widespread than among the agency's executive committee or creative review committee. Organizational memory, when properly captured and used, is a competitive advantage and a major reason an ICA can justify charging for strategic, integrated thinking. It simply has a much greater basis on which to build its clients' plans and recommendations.

13. *Is the agency a learning organization? Does it have a systematic way of capturing campaign results and making a cumulative analysis available to each account planning team?*

Most agencies have a variety of advertising solutions on their agency reels, but actual case history results are in the heads of managers. Few agencies systematically analyze campaigns in terms of what has been learned that can be shared with other clients. An agency that is a learning organization will compile results as a bank of experiences that can be used to analyze solutions that worked and didn't work. As an integrated agency expands its stakeholder management services to more and more clients, it gains a broader, deeper perspective of integration and relationship building than most individual clients can acquire.

Infrastructure for Supporting Integration

14. *Is each MC functional area a separate profit center? If so, is there any way one area is compensated for working with another?*

If each MC function is a separate profit center, a client should be concerned. Separate profit centers are fertile breeding grounds for turf battles, in which the client pays the price. The only way such a structure is justified is if there is a significant, companywide bonus system or some other method to reward the various areas for cooperation and a willingness to see billings move to another area when it is best for the client.

> **Separate profit centers are fertile breeding grounds for turf battles, in which the client pays the price.**

15. *Does the agency have an internal communication system that shows planning calendars, tracks production of messages and media plans, and provides easy access to agency databases?*

An integrated agency will have groupware in place that connects its own staff, as well as key staff in related agencies and client headquarters. Agencies, however, have been slow to get into systems for managing both their own client contacts and internal communication.

16. *With how many clients is the agency on-line?*

Because of the efficiency of being on-line with clients, and the fact that electronic communication is a way to keep many different departments informed, an on-line link is a basic characteristic of a close client-agency relationship. As explained in Chapter 8, if a client is not internally integrated (and its communication agencies must be considered part of its internal communication system), it will never be able to achieve integration synergy externally. Ad agency Messner Vetere Berger McNamee Schmetterer/Euro RSCG attributes much of its success to not only being internally networked but on-line with each of its clients.

17. *Does the agency have an ongoing system for making sure each client's planned messages are strategically consistent?*

Most agencies have a good track record of coordinating one-voice mass media messages. Some have also done a good job integrating the big idea into collateral materials for which they are responsible. Few, however, have taken the initiative to motivate clients to integrate the big idea into other types of brand messages (product and service) being sent by clients.

Integrated agencies use either a formal or informal audit to analyze all brand messages for consistency. An integrated agency will also strongly urge that every client department that communicates with customers be involved in communication planning. Integration agencies recognize that the more consistent product and service messages are, the more impact and cost effective planned messages will be.

Beyond IMC

18. *What are recent examples of how intrinsic brand contact points were included in a recommended brand media strategy?*

This question will help determine to what extent the agency has been involved in advising on product and service messages and helping a client influence unplanned messages.

19. *What has the agency done to guide its clients in developing relationships with stakeholders other than customers?*

Marketing communication practices are being used for internal marketing, proving they can be as effective with employees as with customers. But companies need help in transferring and using MC skills to other stakeholders besides customers. One agency that is doing this is Ogilvy & Mather with its "brand stewardship" program which can be applied to all stakeholders. Its brand audit, for example, is done among all stakeholders, not just customers.

20. *How has the agency worked with clients in marketing their missions?*

As explained in Chapter 7, most clients don't understand the potential value of integrating a real mission into operations and communications. Because few clients have made this a part of their communication program, few agencies have experience in this area. But some have taken leadership in building strategies based on a client's mission. A good integrated agency knows a respected mission can help drive stakeholder allegiance by creating deeper levels of respect for the company and its brands. If there is an opportunity to develop a socially responsible dimension, an integrated agency recognizes the power and impact of that mission to drive stronger relationships with all key stakeholders.

WORKING WITH AGENCY NETWORKS

Many agencies feel they are already providing integration by having a network of affiliated agencies. But as we know from the early attempts at integration, merely having a network doesn't guarantee integration at the strategic level.

Some client and agency executives say IMC was tried by agencies but didn't work. They are generally referring to the late 1970s and 1980s, when advertising agencies bought a stable of other MC agencies and began offering what they thought was integrated marketing communications. Leaders in this effort were Ogilvy & Mather, with its "Orchestration," and Young & Rubicam with its "Whole Egg" concept. Most of the acquired agencies, however, remained in their old headquarters, continued to serve their old clients (some of whom were competitors to clients in their new mother agency), and remained separate profit centers—all of which were barriers to providing the benefits of integration.

According to former Y&R president, Peter Georgescu, Y&R's Whole Egg project focused on cross-selling services that benefited the agency rather than on strategic planning that focused on its clients' needs. Georgescu said the agency failed to develop a "process of looking at the brand and letting the market dictate the optimum role for, and the allocation of resources to, various marketing disciplines."[3]

Driving the creation of these agency conglomerates was the need for ad agencies to find a way to retain the MC billings that were flowing to other communication areas. Ad agencies, especially those with consumer goods and services, have watched clients move mass media advertising dollars into trade and consumer promotions while at the same time refusing to pay the traditional 15 percent commission.

According to DDB Needham's Mike White: "In the 1980s integration was merely a concept that people talked about but didn't practice at any level . . . agencies didn't have the ability to deliver on it, clients didn't have people trained in it, and most clients had structures that actually fought against it." Clients and potential clients, however, soon learned there was no reason for them to terminate the relationships they had built up over the years with their "other" agencies just so their ad agency's new conglomerate would be more profitable.[4]

Just as a new product that has no added value fails, "integration" fails when there is little or no added value for clients. These families or networks of MC agencies have rarely provided clients with strategic integrated thinking, have rarely done cross-functional planning, and have rarely shown clients how to get a synergistic effect from using the agency's stable of communication services. Such agencies have focused internally rather than externally. They have been more interested in creating one invoice than one voice.

> Just as a new product that has no added value fails, "integration" fails when there is little or no added value for clients.

THE INTEGRATED COMMUNICATION AGENCY MODEL

The 21st century full service agency will be an integrated communication agency (ICA). It will be conceptually similar to a primary care physician. Just as this type of doctor is responsible for taking care of a patient's basic health care needs, an ICA will be responsible for a client's basic marketing communication needs plus advising clients on their other communication practices (think of this as advising the client on its communication nutrition). This does not mean that an ICA will exclusively plan and perform every marketing communication program for clients, just as a family doctor doesn't perform every kind of medical procedure. When a patient has a medical problem that is beyond the expertise of the primary care physician, he or she brings in the necessary specialist. The primary care physician doesn't hand the patient off, however, but continues to be involved in that patient's treatment by working as a liaison between the patient and the specialist.

It is critical to the organization of the ICA to avoid having separate profit centers. By eliminating profit accountability for each MC area, the ICA takes a big step in eliminating turf and ego battles which are the number one barrier to integration. Leo Burnett, an agency that emphasizes integrating the various MC tools, has only one profit center—the agency. FCB operates the same way although it has distinct divisions for sales promotion (the Impact group), direct response (FCB Direct), and mass media advertising.

> An ICA must be able to show clients how to not only generate, but also handle and process purposeful dialogue with customers and other stakeholders.

An ICA must be able to show clients how to not only generate, but also handle and process purposeful dialogue with customers and other stakeholders. The ICA model means the lead agency must be prepared to advise on, and often execute, stakeholder relationship-building and nourishing programs, because, as explained in Chapter 3, stakeholders are increasingly overlapping. Also, if the ICA is an expert in communication and relationship building, there is no reason these skills and principles should not be used with all stakeholder groups.

Just as the primary care physician is responsible for helping monitor a patient's ongoing health, the ICA should share the responsibility for monitoring the key stakeholders' perceptions (e.g., brand equity) of the brand and company and for working directly with the client's cross-functional brand equity management team. It also must understand the critical role stakeholder database-tracking and continuous feedback loops have in determining communication strategy.

The ICA approach is similar to the model that has been championed by GM's marketing manager, Phil Guarscio—what he calls the general contractor model. He is pushing GM's advertising agencies to become "general contractors" who will manage GM brands while turning to external boutiques and other specialists to help execute creative and below-the-line efforts. In this model the advertising agency is responsible for the big idea, placing the mass media messages, and then acts as a communication services broker by finding the best communication specialists to execute other MC programs besides advertising.

The danger of the general contractor model is that the ad agency remains king of the communication mountain and the other MC areas continue to be treated as supporting functions. This model also doesn't deter the other specialty agencies from competing with each other and with the ad agency. With the ICA model, however, it is recognized that the specialist agencies have skills that don't exist inside the ICA (just as the heart surgeon has skills beyond those of the primary care physician). The respect for the specialists' skills minimizes the competition between the CIA and specialists.

The ICA model, which is founded on a partnership philosophy (which agencies always claim they have with good clients), is the best approach for an agency with clients interested in integrated marketing and IMC. Regardless of whether integration is managed internally by the client or externally by the agency, there should be a designated lead communication agency. The lead agency (e.g., ICA) should be able to package campaigns and present these as "turnkey" operations to the client. Les Margulis, international media director at BBDO New York, explains how BBDO has done this in the media and promotional areas:

> We put these packages together to help keep our clients from going outside. Having a turnkey, prepackaged promotion is the secret. In effect, the agency is dealing with one main supplier who has put many other suppliers together to form this turnkey marketing communication program. The client will never hear about the lower level of suppliers, just the main one.

Although the ICA must have an MC core competency, the client should select an ICA that specializes in the area in which the client is spending the largest portion of its MC budget. In packaged goods, this will most likely be the advertising agency; for a business-to-business company this may be a direct-response agency, a sales promotion agency, or even a PR agency (especially in the case of highly regulated product categories such as chemicals or drugs).

In IMC, the ICA's primary strength is not in doing ads (or press releases or direct-mail pieces), but in strategic integrated planning and coordinating a complex communication program involving a variety of messages being delivered *and received* by a variety of media used by a variety of stakeholders. In other words, its strength lies in its ability to coordinate all the client's brand messages to create and build long-term relationships with strategic consistency.

HOW PRICE/MCNABB MANAGES ICA PROGRAMS

One U.S. agency that has organized itself to operate using the ICA strategy is Charlotte, N.C. based Price/McNabb. According to its president, Thomas Eppes, this model will become the full-service agency of the future:[5]

> I think the change is going to be so dramatic that in the future there won't be any such thing as an advertising agency.. . . We have begun to refer to ourselves as a communications company, and that might change because we are getting involved with our clients' business in ways that go beyond communications.

It took Price/McNabb over three years to make the transition from a traditional full service advertising agency to an integrated communications agency whose primary business is "creating and managing relationships." The transition, which was done with the help of outside consultants, required a complete overhaul of the agency's structure, compensation, planning processes, training, and new business strategy. It maintains a core competency in IMC strategic thinking, mass media advertising and public relations. Following are some of the specific changes that the agency has made in its effort to be an integrated agency.

- ◆ Developed strategic alliances with agencies specializing in product design, packaging, and sales promotion
- ◆ Consolidated the P&Ls of its three regional offices (so they wouldn't compete with each other)
- ◆ Eliminated incentive bonuses that were disincentive to doing integrated marketing communications; they are no longer based on functional area performances
- ◆ Eliminated media commissions and the standard 17.65% mark-up on non-media placement tasks
- ◆ Added database marketing capabilities
- ◆ Made personnel changes where necessary and recruited top national talent that understood and believed in the integrated approach
- ◆ Changed name from Price/McNabb Advertising Inc. to Price/McNabb, Inc.

Concluded

♦ Designed office interiors to make employees more accessible to each other as well as dispersed specialists such as PR people, around the agency

♦ Developed its own proprietary step-by-step planning process (e.g., "Focused Communications") based on IMC theory

♦ Installed a local area communication network

♦ Wrote a focusing mission/vision statement and lived by it: "Our team mission is to set the standard for understanding and building relationships with the individual customer and prospects of our clients, and to use that knowledge to create communications that are recognized for extraordinary business results." Note the statement says nothing about doing "break-through creative" as it assumes that creativity is inherent in marketing communications.

The transition was completed in 1996 and is now attracting larger and more national accounts.

The internal organization of an ICA is a challenge. One study of seven agencies that have positioned themselves as integrated agencies found few organizational commonalties.[6] Several of these agencies had separate creative and account groups assigned to do "integrated programs"—a rather ironical organizational structure, although it has proven somewhat successful for them. The majority of people interviewed in these agencies, however, admitted that the separate "integration" groups had less prestige internally than did the "advertising" people.

This type of agency organization may be more practical for packaged-goods brands that are heavily dependent on brand image. When it becomes profitable for a client to have one-to-one dialogue, or when the agency is given responsibility for developing and growing relationships with the trade and other stakeholders (other than end users), an agency with a separate integration group should be approached with caution, as it has obviously been conditioned to think mass media advertising first.

The Hal Riney agency and its work on the Saturn launch has proven that the ICA model can work. Riney began working with Saturn several years before the first car came off the assembly line. The agency was involved in planning every message opportunity from the hang tags on the rear view mirrors to the sales associates' training programs, the union relations program, and the community relations connections with the town of Spring Hill, Tennessee, where Saturn cars are made. Riney also has a group of networked agencies, such as its freestanding design studio, which it uses for specialist work. Riney's plan for Saturn reaches all stakeholders with a message of respect and trust supported by business practices that deliver on these values and a communication program that maximizes two-way communication. For its integration work on the Saturn account it was named *Advertising Age* agency of the year in 1992.

Hal Riney also has used an integrated approach with many of its other clients, and this involves managing a variety of nontraditional promotional activities.[7] For Stroh's Old Milwaukee Genuine Draft beer, for example, the agency designed a repositioning campaign led by a new package design. For Mirage Resorts in Las Vegas, the agency managed a multitude of other communication assignments such as its annual report, the chairman's parties, the guests' in-room videos, the logo design for the company's new Treasure Island hotel/casino, and a film intended to persuade Connecticut residents to allow gaming.

Routine Versus Specialist Tasks

One thing that makes the ICA model different from the general contractor model is the agency's ability to do routine work across all marketing communication functions. In marketing communication, just as in health care, there are certain routine tasks (e.g., PR releases, print ads, media planning and buying, packaging revisions, local adoptions of planned messages) that do not demand the services of a specialist. In other words, the ICA would handle all the routine planned message needs, regardless of the MC tool involved. This obviously requires, as stated above, that the ICA have a core competency in all the MC functions and internal specialists in each of these areas. Having one or two specialists in each MC area, however, does not mean the ICA can or should do major projects in these areas.

When the client opportunity or problem moves beyond the scope of the ICA, such as a global sales promotion program tied into the

Olympics, an initial public offering (IPO), a major packaging redesign, or a situation such as the Exxon or Tylenol crises, the ICA would bring in an agency that specializes in the appropriate area but remain in the loop to ensure strategic consistency. The ICA would also manage the evaluation of the special effort as well as any necessary follow-up, such as taking advantage of an expanded customer database or leading a brand repositioning if the situation required it.

One of the ICA's assets should be ongoing relationships with, and knowledge of, specialized communication agencies, many of which may be in its own corporate network. Note that the ICA concept is based on team management. It claims that the relationship between the lead agency and the specialized agencies is more critical than the relationship between the specialized agencies and the client. Patients, for example, seldom have an ongoing relationship with a specialist, but their primary care doctors do, and it is these professional relationships that are of value when a patient needs the help of a specialist.

Interestingly, clients will entrust the spending of millions of dollars to their ad agency, and yet question the agency's judgment when it comes to recommending a specialist agency. The shortsightedness of this is evident if we return to our health care metaphor. Rarely does a patient turn down the specialist recommended by his or her primary care doctor, because the patient respects the primary care doctor's advice, otherwise he or she wouldn't be using that doctor. In addition, the patient realizes the relationship between the primary doctor and the specialist is to his or her advantage in that these two know how to work together and have a system for keeping each other informed.

Mega-agencies with a network of specialty agencies can provide a real added value to clients if the specialty agencies are oriented towards working as a team. Such tangible things as a communication network linking all the family agencies together is one measure of just how close these agencies work. Personal relationships between members of these agencies are important. Issuing a single invoice with a single contact and offering access to centralized media databases can provide an added value to clients of an agency network. Periodic cross-functional training workshops designed to increase the staff's core competencies in integration should also exist.

For large clients that use a number of different communication agencies, one of the simplest ways to move toward integration is to provide a way for all the various agencies to get together and talk. Tony

Lavely, who has been director of marketing for several large packaged goods companies, explains how rewarding such an integrated experience can be:

> While at Burger King, I was put in charge of a new subsidiary—Easy Wok—which had been struggling. It was using kid agencies, black, Hispanic, white agencies, sales promotion agencies, a couple of packaging design firms, a merchandising firm . . . 18 different agencies in all. One of the first things I did was to bring a couple of representatives from each of these together at one time in one room. It was electric. They said things like "I never understood that before, but now I see what you are trying to do." "I understand now what we're doing and where we fit in." It made all of them feel good; they called for months and talked about it. I did it again when I went to Long Johns . . . brought in our three ad agencies, the design firm, and sales promotion agency plus all related internal departments including purchasing. We distributed a list of names and phone numbers of everyone there, and they all began calling each other to come up with ideas and work things out before presenting them to me. The quality of the ideas improved and the logistics were significantly simplified.

Core Competencies: Generalists Versus Specialists

Having a broader vision has always been a prerequisite for people moving into positions of greater responsibility. What keeps some very bright people from advancing is that they enter a field as a specialist and are never able or willing to move beyond that narrow focus. According to Steve Davis, former general manager of JWT's Chicago office, the rising stars in his agency are those who have broadened themselves:

> The new heroes of our culture are really the multi-talented people who can operate in the different sectors—client service, media, creative—of our business rather than being the specialists who have departmentalized. I have creative people right now performing traditional functions of account management such as anticipating needs, building client relationships, talking to clients.

Unfortunately, few agencies do a good job of helping employees acquire this broader focus. A generalist brings a neutral vision to the planning table. People who specialize in and know only their own area of mass media advertising, direct mail, public relations, or any of the other MC tools believe in their functional area, as they should. But when they lobby for their own function to the extent they fail to recognize that different situations call for different MC tools and that good ideas can come from *any* MC area, they become counter-productive to the IM process. A good communication manager is a generalist who has the ability to make informed decisions about the best use of the entire spectrum of communication tools as well as how to evaluate their effectiveness.

> A good communication manager is a generalist who has the ability to make informed decisions about the best use of the entire spectrum of communication tools as well as how to evaluate their effectiveness.

For an ICA agency to have a core competency in MC does not mean that everyone in the agency must become a generalist. If there was ever a time that MC specialists are needed it is now, as communication alternatives and their complexities increase and customers and other stakeholders become more skilled at avoiding commercial messages. However, having a core competency in integrated communications requires both a breadth and depth of MC. A person has integration *breadth* when he or she:

- ◆ Understands the strengths and weaknesses of each major MC function, what they can and can't do in a cost-effective way.
- ◆ Has a rough idea of the cost of using each of these tools.
- ◆ Knows how long it takes to plan and execute each tool.
- ◆ Knows who are the experts who can best execute each tool.

For a person to also have IM *depth*, he or she must understand:

- ◆ The meaning of strategic consistency and how it is created and maintained.
- ◆ Interactivity and what it takes to generate purposeful dialogue.
- ◆ The benefits and criteria for mission marketing.

According to FCB's Mitch Engels: "Learning has accelerated in the last several years. Our people recognize that if they don't have a working knowledge of sales promotion, database marketing, and PR, it's going to be a deficiency in their ability to help their clients. We all have to be broader generalists." A similar recognition comes from Saatchi & Saatchi in NYC, according to one of its executives, Tom Burke:

> A few years ago getting our people to pay attention to nonadvertising services was like pulling teeth. Now there is a sense that advertising is changing, the clients want to approach things differently, they want new ideas, and account people are seeking out things to bring to their clients before being asked. This is very encouraging. The calls are coming from upper management as well as junior people.

The quickest, easiest way for an agency to *begin* motivating people to understand and think beyond their own areas of specialization is to use cross-functional account teams. This means that representatives from account service, media, creative, sales promotion, and any of the other specialty areas involved meet regularly. Some agencies that have worked with cross-functional teams have found that by combining better training with a multidisciplinary approach, they can reduce the number of management levels.

Some agencies move people around when they join the agency—two to four weeks in each area—to familiarize them with these areas. An advantage of a rotating program is that it enables employees to build personal relationships.

Retraining current staff is also necessary. For example, we have conducted conduct seminars and workshops for BBDO agencies throughout Europe and in North America. Leo Burnett and Lintas have done similar retraining using other IMC consultants. These workshops begin to build the depth of integration that agency staff have little opportunity to develop on their own.

Leadership

A question we are frequently asked is, "Who should lead the integration process—client or agency?" The answer is, both. On the one hand, no major client is going to abdicate strategic planning to an outside agency. On the other hand, few clients are capable of keeping up with all the changes and opportunities that the new media and marketplace offers, tasks that a good communication agency can do successfully.

The larger the client organization (in terms of sales, number of customers, and extent of distribution—local, national, and global) the more challenging and important it is to practice integration (because disintegration has been caused, in large part, by the specialization and isolation that comes with growth). An ICA can provide integrated solutions to marketing and identify other communication problems and opportunities.

COMPENSATING THE ICA

Agencies that offer integrated communications face three basic dilemmas regarding billing: a) how to bill for strategic planning (which the 15 percent commission used to cover), b) how to make money from non-mass media projects, and c) how to bill for big ideas that are not primarily for mass media, such as coming up with the Nike Town concept and name, developing a unique and engaging Web site, or designing an internal marketing program for a client who wants to increase employee motivation.

According to many agencies, clients resist paying for strategic thinking and big ideas. Clients tell a different story. They say they will pay for strategic thinking if it is truly cross-functional, not self-serving, and either saves money and/or increases the impact of current spending. FCB has found that working on a fee basis is the best compensation system for doing integrated work. According to Engels:

> Any ongoing integrated account that we have had success with has been successful because we have worked on a fee. This ensures that the agency isn't motivated to use consumer mass media because it is commissionable. We like to get to a fee that is cost plus. Profit isn't necessarily a plus factor. Sometimes profit might be tied to a different system. We love this, if we can cover our cost through a cost-plus ongoing fee arrangement then tie our profits to marketplace performance, or consumer research such as ongoing tracking. This is a great approach for us because clients know that we're motivated to grow their business in the marketplace and our profit isn't tied to generating more hours. If we can keep our cost down and covered, we can make a huge amount of profit and the client never questions our motivation.[8]

As compensation moves from being commission-based to fee-based, the danger is that each project suddenly has a price tag on it. Not only can a fee-based system encourage clients to look at MC on a project-by-project basis rather than as an integrated process, it also calls attention to the price of each project, making clients more price sensitive than process sensitive. The result can be more price shopping, which in turn leads to communication disintegration since elements of the communication process each end up being handled by a different agency, which is the low-price supplier.

Another downside to fee-based pricing is the effect it has on the already strained relationship between most clients and agencies. As one agency executive explained: "It used to be you would only discuss money once a year, now it's all the time because 75 percent of what you are doing (looking at the whole family of agencies) is not commissionable; therefore there is a wide variety of fees, not just a retainer and cost-plus. You're constantly going to clients not only with ideas, but with a price list—if you buy it, here's how much it will cost."

Below-the-line projects can be profitable, although not all ad agencies have been able to accomplish this. The two determining factors are the degree of overhead applied to each job and the client's willingness and financial ability to pay a premium for these services when integrated strategic thinking is a part of the package.

Ad agency overheads are generally higher than in other MC agencies for several reasons: average salaries are higher and offices are generally located in premium locations. Location can be a killer when it comes to overhead. According to Joe Cappo, *Advertising Age* has found that the cost to maintain its employees (e.g., rent, office equipment, maintenance, utilities, mailroom expenses, but *not* salaries) in New York is twice what it is in Chicago. In Detroit and Cleveland the cost is even less than in Chicago. Often sales promotion, direct response, packaging, and merchandising firms are located in more affordable sites than ad agencies. Because of the overhead and salary differentials, below-the-line agencies' generally charge less than ad agencies for the same services.

Ironically, one reason some agencies are finding these below-the-line services more profitable today than several years ago is that they have been forced to accept smaller margins from their primary revenue stream, mass media advertising. This has forced them to lower their overheads. As one agency executive explained to the authors:

> Most of these other [MC] areas are probably more profitable than advertising because the agency business isn't what it used to be because of the squeeze on compensation. This squeeze is for several reasons—we made too much money in the past and media inflation was so much ahead of CPI for so long that advertisers finally said this is out of line.

One global agency has found that its below-the-line agencies' gross margins vary between break-even and 40 percent. The gross margin an individual agency is able to produce depends on two things: how good the agency is at planning and executing successful programs and how good it is at selling its clients on paying a premium for these programs. FCB has an overall operating margin objective of 20 percent pretax. Its Impact (sales promotion) and Direct (direct-response) operations have been at or above that for the last several years.

One major barrier related to compensation arises when the lead agency recommends an external specialty agency. For example, when credibility is a major problem on a brand and PR is needed, an ad agency will be reluctant to tell the client to take money out of the media budget and spend it on developing a PR program with another agency. There are two ways to handle this. One is to bill the client for the planning, selection of the PR agency, and directing the work of the PR agency. The other is to receive a finder's fee from the PR agency that will also compensate the ad agency for staying involved and consulting with the PR agency on the project.

BENEFITS AND CONCERNS OF USING AN ICA

The ICA model provides the client with consistent strategic thinking and production convenience for the majority of its planned messages without sacrificing the expertise of specialists when it is really needed. Specific characteristics of the ICA model that result in better work at lower cost to clients are:

- *Consistent strategic planning.* By having one agency working with the client to develop and manage planned messages, strategic positioning consistency is easier to monitor.
- *Minimal support of multiple agency overheads.* Since all planned messages would be handled by one agency and the specialist agencies would only be used on an as-needed basis, the client will not be paying the overhead of many different agencies on an ongoing basis. It is true that it will be expected to pay a larger share of the lead agency's overhead, but this increase should be far less than the net sum of the many smaller shares formerly being covered.
- *Controlled confidentiality.* By dealing primarily with one agency group a client will have to distribute less of its

confidential information and therefore has more control over who sees what. When there is a leak, it should be easier to determine its source. Also, because confidential information can be controlled, the client should be willing to share more information with the agency and therefore increase the input for even better thinking and planning by the agency.

◆ *Meeting efficiency.* By working with fewer agencies there should be fewer meetings. But more importantly, the meetings should focus on the relationship-building process, not on MC tools. Turf wars over which MC tool is better or which should be used will be minimized.

◆ *More accountability.* By having one agency responsible for the majority of work, there will be more accountability and less finger pointing.

◆ *Performance-based compensation system.* By having fewer agencies responsible for the brand's or company's overall performance, responsibility for results will be easier to determine and therefore should reduce the debate over which agency was responsible for what results.

Some clients are concerned about using specialist agencies owned by its lead agency because these agencies aren't the best in their category. This is generally a weak excuse for several reasons. In most cases, the agencies that have been brought together under one financial umbrella generally have the same level of expertise and reputation. Secondly, the idea of only working with the best sales promotion agency, best direct response agency, and best PR agency is a hunt for the holy grail.

Although we agree there are different levels of ability among agencies (although this varies depending on who is working on what account this month), a company must ask itself what is the trade-off between going to an agency with a slightly better track record and giving up the strategic consistency that can be obtained by staying within a family of agencies. Again, this assumes the family of agencies is organized and managed in a way that produces integrated thinking and synergy among its members.

There is also concern that a network specialist agency may not be the least expensive. However, if the ICA is doing its job to ensure that integration saves the client money in the long term, it's up to the ICA to ensure that the partner agency's billing is competitive with others of similar quality. This financial control is part of the lead agency's strategic integration work.

These are legitimate client concerns because few of today's agencies with MC subsidiaries provide cross-functional strategic planning and evaluation processes (although many say they do). Consequently, using a family of agencies that merely has a financial relationship offers no significant benefit for clients. When a family of agencies offers true cross-functional integration, however, the added value will more than outweigh the difference in expertise that may be found outside the network, not to mention the cost of finding these other agencies and bringing them up to speed on your business.

Agencies are not yet aggressively pursuing the idea that a client has a total communication budget and the agency can help that client maximize the return on that total investment This is because many ad agencies have lost their commitment to leading clients into new ways of thinking, and many clients are not open to this type of thinking from their agencies. Because of financial pressures, agencies are scared to do anything other than exactly what clients ask them to do.

Bob Lamons, in a column in *Marketing News*, lays the blame for this situation on clients.[9] He reported on a Business Marketing Association study that found many business-to-business advertisers reluctant to form partnering relationships with their agencies. He says the study is proof that clients are only seeking buyer/vendor relationships. The study also found a serious perception gap between agencies and clients. Of 17 possible services, two-thirds or more of the agency respondents listed 12 as being provided to current clients. The client sample, however, identified the agency as the preferred provider for only 2 of the 17 services (advertising production and media planning/buying). Only 19 percent said they used their primary agency for marketing communication strategic planning.

Lamons' conclusion is that agencies should quit trying to sell clients some vague concept of partnering. Our conclusion, however, is that vendor relationships signal the end of the full-service agency concept, and that's probably not a desirable outcome for either agency or client. If advertising agencies are to have a competitive advantage in this new communication environment, they need to redefine the business they are in and what it really means to be a full-service agency. With the encouragement of their clients, they need to take charge of their future as communication managers. According to an *Advertising Age* editorial:

> It's no longer enough to own companies offering advertising, direct response, sales promotion, event sponsorship, and/or public relations. Tomorrow's agency must combine all those disciplines not merely under a single corporate roof but into a single marketing strategy tailored to an individual client. The program—often using a client's database—then must be implemented by a small team of agency execs working together hand-in-glove.[10]

"Agencies are trapped in a box," Tom Burke of Saatchi & Saatchi has observed. "They are too often too narrow about what business they think they are in. Only by restructuring and retraining can agencies get account service right so clients rely on us for broad thinking and not just great ads."

Organizing to deliver an integrated communication strategy is difficult for most agencies, but the kind of strategic planning needed to guide an integrated program is even more of a challenge.

ENDNOTES

1. John Fitzgerald, "Reinventing Advertising," *Reputation Management,* March/April, 1995, p. 46.
2. Mitch Engels, Personal Interview, Chicago, 1994.
3. "Best Alone, Better Together," *PROMO*, June. 1991, p. 7.
4. "Agencies Have Poor Track Record, Says Lintas Executive," *PROMO*, April 1991, p. 7.
5. From a presentation by Tom Eppes at the IIR Integrated Marketing workshop, Sept. 10-11, Chicago.
6. Manjot Kochar, "A Study of Advertising Agencies Providing Integrated Marketing Communication," *IMC Research Journal*, 1:1 (Spring 1995), pp. 16-22.
7. Alice Z. Cuneo and Raymond Serafin, "With Saturn, Riney Rings Up a Winner," *Advertising Age*, April 14, 1993, p. 2-3.
8. Steve Engel, personal interview, January, 1994, Chicago.
9. Bob Lamons, "It's Always Wise to Sell What Your Customers Are Buying," *Marketing News*, October 25, 1993, pp. 13, 19.
10. "The New Agency" *Advertising Age*, (February 2, 1993), p. 44.

PART FIVE

IM VALUE AND AUDIT

13

CHAPTER

Evaluate Using Relationship Metrics and the IM Audit

There are two primary ways to evaluate to what extent a company is practicing integrated marketing. One is output controls and the second is process controls. Both measures are needed if a company wants to maximize its brand equity.

OUTPUT AND PROCESS CONTROLS

Output controls are *external* measures of IM results such as awareness studies, tracking studies, and customer satisfaction surveys (as well as sales results). One area of output controls that has not been monitored effectively, however, is relationship building. In this chapter we will explain a set of relationship metrics that can be used to better conduct this critical evaluation.

Process controls are *internal* measures of how a company is doing IM; they evaluate how programs operate and function and the attitudes and knowledge of those responsible for these programs. Financial audits, time and motion studies, and corporate communication audits are examples of process controls. Up to now, process controls have seldom been used in managing stakeholder relationships. Although some companies do track awareness and trial, which are output controls, few take advantage of process controls to examine the procedures used to improve their marketing communications programs and make them more integrated.

The importance of process management has been heighten by TQM and the need of many companies, especially manufacturers selling internationally, to meet the ISO 9000 standards. Both TQM and ISO 9000 standards require companies to continuously monitor *all* their processes and procedures, continuously looking for ways to improve them. One of the primary messages from the quality experts is that process is the key to the productivity of any operation. In the case of marketing, therefore, it follows that the overall process being used to create and nourish customer relationships which produce brand equity should be periodically evaluated.

DuPont evaluated its process management when it had Saatchi and Saatchi conduct an audit of how DuPont handled inquiries. DuPont has a wide range of technical products and receives frequent requests for information. Saatchi's findings demonstrated how a centralized inquiry handling system could shorten the response time as well as provide management with better information (e.g., nature and number of inquires by type) on which they could take action. The audit found that many routine inquiries were being handled as special cases, requiring significant staff time. By setting up a system for separating routine requests from the truly special inquiries, DuPont was able to significantly reduce customer service costs. Systems were also set up to handle the needs of advertising managers, sales managers, and the field sales force.

If the production process used for producing relationships and eventually brand equity is not managed and executed by people who are in constant touch with each other, the process can produce confusion rather than communication. But unlike the car industry, which can announce a recall when it discovers it has installed defective parts, it is virtually impossible to recall 1,000,000 brand messages to replace a broken promise or align inconsistent messages after they have already been sent.

Integrated marketing needs new tools to better assess the IM process. The IM audit developed in the IMC graduate program at the University of Colorado is one such tool. We are not suggesting, however, that the IM audit replace marketing communication output controls such as tracking studies, because results are the bottom line. Companies should use *both* types of evaluation methods.

RELATIONSHIPS METRICS—OUTPUT CONTROLS

Relationship metrics help explain sales and share trends and provide a basis for more accurate forecasting. The six metrics that we have found companies using most successfully are customer profitability, LTCV quintile analysis, recency index, referral index, and share of customer.

- *Customer profitability:* As we have emphasized throughout this book, in most cases it only makes sense to invest in relationship building with profitable customers or those who will soon become profitable. (The same is true for building relationships with other stakeholders: Invest in those who can most impact cost or revenue.) Once individual customer profitability can be determined, it becomes simple to determine average customer profitability. If it begins to go down, this is a red flag (unless there has been an unusually high influx of new customers that could temporarily dilute the average profitability). By tracking the profitability-to-customer ratio, a company can determine if customers are in fact buying more and/or demanding less.

- *LTCV quintile analysis:* A more sophisticated analysis of customer profitability is dividing customers into five equal groups based on their LTCV. In the top group would be those 20 percent with the highest LTCV and in the bottom group, the 20 percent with the lowest LTCV. Tracking the average profitability of each quintile with their corresponding LTCV will provide a more in-depth analysis of the sources of revenue. For example, assume last year the top quintile's average profitability was $75 and the average number of customer "life years" was 4.3. If this year's average customer profitability is $80 and the average "life years" has increased to 5.5, this shows IM is working as it should—higher retention and profitability per long-term customer is growing.

   Ideally the averages in all five groups will continue to increase. A red flag could be an increase in the top group and decrease in all the others, indicating your basis of support is shrinking even though total revenue may be unchanged or even slightly increasing.

- *Recency index:* One of the things the direct response industry has proven is that the more often people buy, the more likely they are to buy in the future. Tracking the average purchase frequency—the percent of customers who purchased within the last 30 days (the period will vary depending on product category)—indicates to what extent acquired customers are becoming more loyal.

♦ *Referral index:* This tracks the percent of new business resulting from a customer or other stakeholder recommending the brand. It applies more to large ticket and service products where it is possible to ask new customers what motivated them to choose your brand. Referrals are confirmation that you are doing what you are saying you will do for customers (remember the say-do-confirm triangle discussed in the chapter on strategic consistency?). Because referrals are one of the key behaviors of brand advocates (the highest level of brand relationships), a higher referral index score indicates an increase in the number of brand advocates, a good indication your relationship-building practices are working.

♦ *Share of customer:* Because the most profitable customers, especially in packaged goods categories, buy multiple brands, one brand objective is to get an increasing percent of these customers' category purchases. Scanner data is helpful in determining this share trend.

When any of the above metrics show a negative trend, a company needs to find out why: What areas of the company are sending messages causing the negative trend? What needs to be done to reverse the trend? The same diagnostic approach should be used when a trend makes a significant increase. Determining why it increased may enable a company to leverage still further certain brand communications.

> **Although the IM audit is basically an evaluation tool, it is also a way to custom design a road map for an organization to reach a fully integrated program.**

THE IM AUDIT—A PROCESS CONTROL

The IM audit is a unique tool we developed for the University of Colorado's IMC graduate program as a way to expose our students to the corporate mechanics of producing brand messaging. Over the years as it has been applied we have continually refined and improved its sensitivity and specificity. Although the IM audit is basically an evaluation tool, it is also a way to custom design a road map for an organization to reach a fully integrated program. It provides an objective, well-documented list of what must be changed in order for a company to maximize the benefits of integration.

The "production" of brand equity is like the production of a car. Just as a car is the end result of the process of coordinating different groups of people as they plan, develop, buy, and produce the pieces and parts that are ultimately combined into a single product, the same is true for relationships. They are the result of a process that involves different groups of people who plan, send, and receive a variety of messages. How well customer and other stakeholder relationships are built depends upon the effectiveness of this complex process. To evaluate this effort takes a complex measurement tool, similar in philosophy to the new multivariable testing being used to evaluate quality programs. As managers of quality programs have found out, "If you test factors one at a time, there's a very low probability that you're going to hit the right one . . . ."[1] The IM audit is both a quantitative and qualitative evaluation. It involves analysis of all the multiple relationship-producing efforts and strategies and the processes that produce them.

Marketing audits and communication audits have been used by organizations for years.[2] Saatchi and Saatchi developed its Total Communications Audit tool in the early 1990s to guide its clients' decisions on how to spend communication investments more efficiently. The IM audit, however, is the first management tool of its kind that enables an organization to determine to what extent its current marketing communication process is integrated and identify what it needs to do in order to become more integrated.

FOCUS OF AN IM AUDIT

Although it incorporates elements of traditional communication audits, the IM audit differs in focus because the basic tenet of IM is that all elements of marketing and communication must be integrated and work toward common goals. The IM audit, therefore, focuses specifically on such things as the core competency of the people managing marketing communication, the amount and nature of internal communication, the consistency of the MC messages that have been produced, and whether or not they were on strategy. The following examples of findings illustrate the types of information an IM audit can produce.

- ◆ *Confusion about objectives.* In one company, managers gave 9 different responses when asked what the corporate marketing communication objectives were, and 10 different responses for the brand marketing communication objectives. Obviously, when people are working against different message objectives, it is impossible to have message consistency, which was subsequently proven by a content analyses undertaken as part of the audit.

- ◆ *Lack of agreement on message themes.* In a retail chain that had begun advertising "Low Prices Every Day," there was no agreement on the definition of what this meant or should mean regarding the chain's pricing strategy. Out of seven different explanations of what this new strategy meant, none was given by more than 15 percent of the organization's managers.

  In a national consumer goods company, one message theme was used in 100 percent of television advertising, but only 22 percent of other advertising; another theme was used in 80 percent of television advertising, but only 20 percent of sales promotion materials.

- ◆ *Lack of agreement on primary stakeholders.* In a health care facility, patients/families received the third highest importance rating when all responses were averaged, but the group was ranked eighth by senior management. Political leaders were ninth on the list when all responses were averaged, but ranked third by public affairs/public relations. We were not investigating specific stakeholders to whom specific types of messages are addressed by specific departments, but rather the overall importance to the organization.

- ◆ *Messages not targeted to primary stakeholder groups.* In one company it was found that 24 percent of all printed messages were not targeted to any of the high-priority stakeholder groups identified by management, and only 1 percent was specifically directed to the target audience rated most important.

- *Not enough information available.* Most marketing managers say that they receive enough information from other departments to do their jobs effectively only about half of the time. In some cases the desired information did not exist, however, many times it did, and these managers were unaware of it or how to access it. The types of information frequently mentioned as difficult to get were sales results, research results, and promotional and other special marketing plans for specific events and programs.

- *Limited use of research results.* In one packaged goods company, which was spending approximately $150 million on marketing communication, 37 percent of the managers said they did not know of any market analysis being done by the company, 33 percent said some was being done but didn't know if it was being used, and 15 percent said very little was used.

- *Little knowledge of annual planning.* In one company, 60 percent of the managers did not know how the budget was allocated among departments, and half of the managers did not know to what extent each year's communication plan compared to the previous one.

- *Little understanding of evaluation.* In a high-tech company selling computer components to other manufacturers, 35 percent did not know if or how the company evaluated its marketing communication programs. Of those who said the company did evaluate these programs, half did not know what was evaluated, and over a third did not know how the results of those evaluations were used in marketing communication planning.

- *Limited use of computers for networking and consumer databases.* In one company, which had a relatively small number of industrial customers, customer buying behavior was not captured although there were many opportunities for doing so.

An audit can identify problems a company doesn't even know it has. For example, in one audit for a high-tech manufacturer (annual sales over $300 million) we were told that the company was working hard to apply for the Baldridge Award and also was getting ready for its ISO 9000 evaluation. Consequently, it had really maximized the quality and efficiency of its processes and, according to its director of marketing services, was doing everything it could to integrate its marketing communication programs. The audit discovered, however, that the marketing communication department had little knowledge of, and made little use of, the company's databases, even though the company had less than 200 customers.

HOW TO CONDUCT AN IM AUDIT

To improve an IM process, or any process, requires an understanding of how and why it works, and when and where it works and doesn't work. As Gregory Watson has found in his work in benchmarking, "identifying the specific key aspects of a process that lead to increased performance is tantamount to trying to understand how a whole process fits together."[3] The IM audit closely examines the *elements* and *structure* of the integration process.

Characteristics of a good audit procedure, besides being objective, are that it be systematic, unbiased, and comprehensive. Therefore, the IM audit includes:

- An analysis of the communication network (internal and external) used to develop marketing communication programs.
- Knowledge and awareness of and agreement with marketing and marketing communication objectives.
- Identification and prioritization of key stakeholder groups.
- Evaluation of the company's customer databases.
- A content analysis of all messages (ads, PR releases, packaging, video news releases, signage, sale promotion pieces, direct response mailings, etc.) used within the last year.
- An assessment of what marketing managers, top management, and key agency managers know of IM and their attitude toward it.

Who Does the Audit?

Performing an IM audit requires a thorough understanding of integration strategies and practices. To properly administer audit surveys, measure responses, and evaluate results the audit team should understand not only the philosophy of integration, but also the more traditional disciplines of marketing, marketing communication, marketing research, information systems, organizational management, and change management. The more familiar they are with integration, the more effectively they can probe and interpret results, thus providing clients with better recommendations.

Therefore, an IM audit, just like a financial audit, should be done by an outside team both to assess the integration competency but also to ensure objectivity. Because the main barriers to IM are egos and turf battles, it is difficult for an internal team to do an objective audit. Another benefit to using an outside group is that it can more accurately see things as they really are. In *The Fifth Discipline* a story is told by Bill O'Brien, CEO of Hanover Insurance, that clearly demonstrates the need for this fresh, unconditioned point of view. According to O'Brien, early in his career he moved to a town dominated by a paper making plant. He says the odor was so bad his family nearly left immediately; however, after two weeks they had all gotten used to the smell and seldom even mentioned it. The same thing, he points out, can happen within an organization. "Organizational politics is such a perversion of truth and honesty that most organizations reek with its odor. Yet, most of us so take it for granted that we don't even notice it."[4]

While it is possible, and often much less expensive, for an organization to do an IM audit with its own people, this generally only works when the organization is large enough to have a special, trained audit team that is from another office where the team members have no personal relationships with the business unit being audited.

Who Is Included?

The audit is based on a census, not a sample, of people responsible for an organization's marketing communications. Since everyone interviewed plays a role in the MC process, all responses are considered significant. Everyone who has direct input into the planning, approving, and executing of marketing programs, therefore, should be included. Internally this includes top management (because they are approving budgets and plans), marketing and marketing communication managers, brand or product managers, customer service managers, and division managers. In the case of service industries, a sample of those delivering the service such as retail clerks should also be included.

Externally, beside customers, marketing communication agency managers (with those agencies with which the company has an ongoing relationship) are surveyed, as well as representative vendors and resellers. Other stakeholders that may or may not be interviewed include media representatives, investors, members of the financial community, and government representatives, depending upon the relative importance of each of these groups to the company's operations. The reason for including outside stakeholders is to determine their perceptions of the brand/company in relation to key competitors.

In the service industry, customer handling may be audited by using mystery shoppers to visit stores and make trial calls to customer service. The audit team should also undertake a contact-point analysis to determine key sources of product and service messages that are being sent in addition to planned messages.

Where To Begin

Use as benchmarks the marketing and marketing communication plans as well as any other formal memos describing the company's marketing and marketing communication objectives. The purpose of analyzing these documents is to identify the formally stated objectives and strategies, as well as the targeted audiences. The reason we consider this information to be a benchmark is because it provides a way to measure both the process and the produced materials in terms of their contributions to the accomplishment of these objectives.

These materials are obtained in an *orientation meeting* with top management and marketing managers. Specific corporate objectives for the audit are also identified. At this meeting an audit administrator (to work as a liaison between the audit team and the company) should be appointed. Next, a list of people to be interviewed is also agreed upon, and a timetable for interviews is determined. In addition to the planning documents, the audit administrator provides the audit team with an overview of the company's marketing and communication programs. Finally, arrangements are made with all departments to gather samples of the planned messages they have produced over the last 12 months for the content analysis.

What Tools Are Used?

The audit employs several primary tools and a variety of optional tools depending on the type of business being audited and how in-depth the organization wants the audit to be.

1. *Knowledge, Attitude, and Practice Questionnaires.* The purpose of these instruments is to evaluate the following areas:

   ◆ Corporate vision and/or mission. How well does the company communicate a central vision or mission?

   ◆ Awareness of corporate marketing and marketing communication objectives. Are there measurable marketing communication objectives? Is the marketing communication objective-setting process inclusive of all groups/departments/functions that create messages? How much awareness of and agreement on communication objectives exists within the various marketing groups/departments/ functions? What are respondents' perceptions of their responsibilities in helping meet these objectives? Does the organization use zero-based planning, especially for annual and short-term programs? To what extent are objectives based on some kind of prioritized SWOT analysis?

   ◆ Knowledge of the company's or brand's positioning, key themes, and image. What are the key messages to priority stakeholder audiences? How well does the company communicate a coherent brand/corporate image?

   ◆ Familiarity with strengths of the various marketing communication tools and how they are used by the company/brand. How much do communication staff and management know about the strengths of the various marketing communication functions/tools? How much agreement is there among and within the groups on the responsibilities of the various marketing communication departments/functions? How is coordination managed? Who is responsible for coordinating communication efforts?

◆ Perception of target/stakeholder priorities. Which
   stakeholders are most important? Which ones should be?
   How well does the company communicate with each of
   these key groups?

◆ Perception of key messages by target audiences. How well
   does the company/brand communicate its key messages to
   priority stakeholder groups?

◆ Perception of marketing communication database use in
   the company. How much sharing of market research
   findings and other types of planning information exists
   among internal groups? To what extent are databases
   accessible and utilized?

◆ Perception of contact points. Who controls them? What
   kind of influence do they have? How well does the
   company recognize and take advantage of all its brand
   contact points? What physical structures and resources
   facilitate or inhibit internal communications?

◆ Perception of the brand's current level of integration,
   advantages/disadvantages of integrating marketing
   communication, barriers to MC integration. How much
   agreement exists among and within the groups on the
   responsibilities of the various marketing communication
   departments/functions? How is coordination managed?
   Who is responsible for coordinating communication
   efforts? To what extent is marketing communication a
   cross-function?

◆ What is the understanding of, and attitude toward,
   integrating the organization's communication efforts?
   What are the perceived advantages/disadvantages and
   barriers to more integrative planning and execution? How
   much integration does the company perceive there to be in
   its current MC activities? To what extent are client's
   marketing communication agencies involved in strategic
   planning? How much communication/sharing of ideas is
   there among clients' agencies? How far has it moved into
   interactive, two-way communication?

◆ Awareness of evaluation programs. How much agreement exists among and within the groups on the evaluation of the various MC objectives and tools? What testing methods are used? How effective are they? To whom are testing results distributed, and to what extent are they used in planning?

There are usually two versions of the knowledge, attitude, and practice assessment questionnaire: a long version for the majority of respondents who are knowledgeable of the marketing communication programs, and a shorter one for top management and people who are less involved in marketing communication planning and execution, such as sales clerks.

2. *Communication Network Interviews.* This is a matrix of closed-ended questions to pinpoint the following information:

◆ Who talks to whom, how often, and about what? Who drives planning and decisions? Who influences them? How often are respondents involved in MC planning (formal/informal)? What information sources do they read? How much and what kind of information sharing is there (research, other information)?

◆ What is the infrastructure for recording and handling customer responses and dialogue? What are the patterns of internal communication among departments?

◆ Internal communication system? The last thing that marketing departments need is more memos, reports, and paper flow. The need to know increases directly with number of messages received. The availability of truly helpful information seems to decrease proportionally to the increase in paper flow. How much MC information is circulating to whom, and how?

3. *Content Analysis.* All messages sent out by the company over a 12-month period are systematically analyzed to determine the amount of creative strategy and execution consistency and whether they are consistent with marketing communication objectives; whether key messages are

appropriate for key audiences; and whether there is consistent portrayal of company/brand positioning and image. The audit team uses content analysis to look for gaps in performance.[5]

The analysis looks at the following elements: the objective of the piece; the audience; key themes; the tone; brand/corporate image/position cues; use of response devices (active and passive); and mission/vision cues.

Content analysis findings are then compared with interview findings to determine the organization's level of strategic integration as demonstrated by these materials. This documents how well the company is doing what it says it wants to do.

4. *Vendor/Supplier and Other Stakeholder Interviews.* This tool is used with some, but not all, IM audits. Its purpose is to analyze the relationship between the organization and its suppliers: communication systems; research and other data sharing; incentives and rewards; business management (e.g., ordering, paying on time); and supplier perceptions of the organization's strengths, mission, and positioning.

Findings are compared with internal interviews to determine the gap between the company's and suppliers' perceptions of their relationships.

5. *Mystery Shopper/Phantom Caller.* This tool is used when retail operations are audited. All store-based customer contact points are analyzed to determine what messages are being sent during the shopping experience (including outside appearance of the store; parking and other details of the approach; the experience of entering the store (signs, staff, counters); store navigation; initial encounter with store representative; appearance of sales clerk (uniform dress, name badge); ease with which sales clerks can be distinguished from customers; knowledge processed by sales clerks (merchandise, store policies); clerks' efforts to up-sell (professional or pushy demeanor); relationship overtures (card, "ask for me," individual sales clerk, customer list); facilities (dressing rooms, space and opportunity for testing or trying products); store policies (returns, guarantees—and how they are communicated through signage and store

personnel); other store information (posters, newsletters, flyers); feedback and response devices such as comment cards; any unpleasant experiences (rude sales clerks, long waits—and how frequently these occurred?).

Phone calls to the store are also analyzed. How long before the phone is answered? How many transfers before a question is answered and how long a wait each time? What is the knowledge level of the final contact, in terms of merchandise and store policies? Are there any relationship overtures—e.g., "Ask for me?" How are unanswered questions dealt with—will staff find out, call back, and so on? Were there any unpleasant experiences (e.g., put on hold forever)—and how frequently did they occur?

6. *Contact Point Analysis.* Analyzing product and service messages is a priority of the research team that has the greatest understanding of the communication dimensions of these unplanned messages. A store's or plant's appearance, for example, says a lot about the company. In order to get a better reading on these messages, the research team needs to develop a list of all the ways a stakeholder comes in contact with the company and then analyze the communication effectiveness of that experience. What happens at that point of contact? What messages are being sent? Are they consistent? Are they on strategy? The research team may need to interview company representatives about their practices in order to develop a comprehensive contact point list and understand the nature of the interactions. Compilation of the list itself, however, and its analysis is an important responsibility of researchers trained in integration analysis.

How Audit is Done

After a memo from a member of top management has been sent to the staff notifying them of the audit and asking for their cooperation, personal interviews by trained interviewers are conducted onsite. Personal interviews take about 90 minutes, although the executive version is usually shorter as is the questionnaire for outside stakeholders.

Other research programs are conducted as needed, such as vendor interviews, mystery shopping, and so on. Some of these will need to be arranged through the company's executives either by phone or memo, so there is a scheduling dimension to these external contacts.

The content analysis begins as soon as samples of all planned marketing communication messages (advertising, PR releases, packaging, product instructions, etc.) used within the last 12 months are collected. These need to be identified by date used and audience targeted.

The researchers individually begin the development of their contact point lists as they move around the company and interview people. Much of this is observational.

Entering, coding, and tabulating the data from the interviews and content analysis can take two to three weeks depending upon staffing.

A top-line presentation of the data may be made to senior marketing managers. The objective is to determine if there are any inaccuracies in the way the data were gathered, summarized, and interpreted. Once the data has been confirmed, the audit team determines the recommendations that will move the company toward a more strategic and integrated marketing effort. These recommendations are then tied back to key findings, which help prove the recommendations are valid.

In the final report the strengths and weaknesses of the organization's communication processes are identified and recommendations are made as to how the strengths can be leveraged and the weaknesses addressed. This report may be presented first as a top-line report to marketing managers or as a more formal report to top management and everyone else involved in marketing planning. The final report and presentation should focus on the recommendations rather than on the findings themselves.

The IM Audit Follow-Up

Once the audit is completed, its findings should be compared to tracking study results on key measures such as awareness and trial. Audit findings can be used to help better understand the cause of problems uncovered by more traditional research. Three to four months following the audit, the audit recommendations should be reviewed to determine progress and barriers to the organization's adoption of the recommendations.

BENEFITS OF DOING AN IM AUDIT

Companies that have done IM audits have realized benefits that far out-weigh the time and cost involved to conduct the audit. As stated earlier, the main purpose of the audit is to identify process gaps and barriers— those procedures and departments that are obstructing or slowing down the development of strategically consistent messages, the inadequacies in properly handling purposeful dialogues, and the unrealized potential of merchandising the corporate mission. Specifically, an IM audit has many benefits.

- It identifies areas in which managers are working toward different MC objectives and where they have different understandings about the brand's strengths and weaknesses, targets, positioning, and competitive advantages.
- It provides marketing managers a confidential channel for conveying ideas and opinions about the organization's communication process.
- It identifies the level of coordination (or lack thereof) between communication units, both internally and externally.
- It indicates which units/people need to increase their core competency of marketing communication tools in order to have a basic understanding of, and appreciation for, the strengths and weakness of each MC tool. (A basic understanding of all the major communication functions is a prerequisite for strategic use of IM.)
- Merely by participating in the audit, MC managers are motivated to think about what they are doing and why they are doing it from a broader communication perspective.
- Doing the audit sends a message not only to the marketing communications staff and outside communication agencies that their jobs are important, but also sends the message throughout the organization that management believes in, and endorses, the IM concept.
- The audit objectively shows to what extent planned messages contain a consistent strategy.
- The audit provides a basis for refocusing and re-allocating resources against the primary marketing and MC objectives.

◆ Findings provide top management with an objective basis on which to build more effective leadership in marketing and relationship-building, and makes top management aware that building and nourishing relationships is a cross-functional challenge and responsibility.

Findings of IM audits clearly show that before a company can benefit from an IM program, it must have an integrated *process* for developing its marketing communications—in other words, a marketing infrastructure that encourages and facilitates communication between functional areas. Just as important, it must have people managing these areas who have a basic understanding of, and respect for, the strengths of each of the major marketing communication functions. This level of integration knowledge and attitude is an indication of the company's core competency in the management of relationships.

The fact that a company has invested in an IM audit sends the message that the company believes in, and wants, an integrated marketing communications process for building stronger brands and customer relationships.

INTEGRATING THE AUDIT

The IM Audit is the last topic in this book, but it is the first place to start in the development of an integrated marketing or IMC program. As in all planning, it helps to know where we are before setting our course in a new direction. The Audit provides baseline information, not only about what has been done in the past, but more importantly, about the overall level of an organization's integration.

In particular, it answers critical questions about the focus of the organization: is the corporation focused on relationships rather than transactions? Are other stakeholders addressed as well as customers? Is an integrated approach being used to manage all the stakeholders or is it still being done department by department?

In addition, the insights gained from the Audit will help analyze and refine both *the processes* being used to create and manage relationships, as well as *the infrastructure* which can either support or impede these processes.

Finally, it will uncover the level of strategic consistency in all the organization's messages, the amount of interactivity being used to manage the stakeholder relationships, and the extent to which the organization's mission anchors the relationship commitments.

Integrated marketing is not only about relationship building programs, it is the ultimate team effort. It demands cross-functional teamwork within the organization to manage the strategy behind the messages, and it works best when there is teamwork between the organization and the outside agency (or agencies) that are involved in the marketing communication program.

Companies that are truly learning organizations are well on the road to becoming more integrated because they can accumulate a wealth of insight about how best to manage the communication (both one- and two-way) that creates, retains, and nourishes the stakeholder relationships that drive brand value.

ENDNOTES

1. Rita Koselka, "The New Mantra: MVT," *Forbes*, March 11, 1996, pp. 114-117.
2. Cal W. Downs, *Communication Audits*—(Glenview, IL: Scott, Foresman and Company, 1988); Philip Kotler, William Gregor, and William Rodgers, "The Marketing Audit Comes of Age," *Sloan Management Review*, Winter 1977, pp. 25-43.
3. Gregory H. Watson, *Strategic Benchmarking* (New York: John Wiley & Sons, 1993), p. 48.
4. Peter M. Senge, *The Fifth Discipline* (New York: Doubleday Currency, 1990), p. 271.
5. Audrey Ward and Jeremy Hebert, "Content Analysis: A Tool for Evaluating Perception Against Reality," *IMC Research Journal*, 2:1 (Spring 1996), pp. 28-31.

Index

A.B. Dick, 79-80
Aaker, D.A., 21
Abrams, M.E., 229
accessibility of brand, 47
Acuvue contact lenses, interactive
    campaign, 162-164, **163**
addressable media, 110-111, 160
advertising (*see* consistency of message;
    media/media mix)
Advertising Age magazine, xiv, 7, 215,
    248, 254, 258
All Conditions Gear, 229
Allen Brady & Marsh, 232-233
American Association of Advertising
    Agencies, xiv
American Association of Retired People
    (AARP), 105
American Express, 138, 143-144
Apgar, T., 230
Apple Computer, 64, 133, 141, 142
Arco, 144
Arm & Hammer, 142
AT&T, 4-5, 7, 180
Audit & Surveys, 233
auditing IM, xvi-xvii, 26, **27-28**, 208-
    209, 259-279
    analyzing the information gathered,
        275-276
    beginning the audit, 270
    benchmark data, 270
    benefits of audit, 277-278
    communication audit, 273
    conducting the audit, 268-276
    consistency of message audit, 273-274
    contact point analysis, 275
    customer relationships audit, 274-275
    focus of the audit, 265-268
    follow-up to audit, 276
    integrating the audit, 278-279
    lifetime customer value (LTCV), 263
    mini-audit form, **27-28**
    mystery shopper/phantom caller to
        audit, 274-275
    orientation meetings, 270
    output controls, 261-262, 262-264
    process controls, 261-262, 264-265
    profitability, 263
    quality control, 262
    questionnaires for audit, 271-273
    recency indexes, 263-264
    referral indexes, 264
    relationship metrics, 262-264
    stakeholder relationships audit, 274
    team selected to conduct audit, 268-269
    tools used, 271-275
    Total Communications Audit tool, 265
    tracking brand loyalty, 42-45, **44**, 48-
        50, 263-264
    who and what is included, 269-270
automation of sales force, 187, 224-225
Avon, 45, 134

Bain and Co., 42
Banyan Software, 188
Barron's magazine, 4
Barry Blau & Co., 44
Bavelas, J.B., 22
Baxter International, 41-42
BBDO, 185, 245, 252
Beatrice Foods, 87
Ben & Jerry's, 133, 135, 142
Berkshire Hathaway Investment Co., 63
Bickert, J., 53
Biel, A., 21
Binney & Smith, 142
Black & Co., 134
Black Gold, 157
Blockbuster Video, 223
Bloomingdales, 82

Body Shop, The, 133, 134-135, 142
Boise Cascade, 98-99
Bonary, G., 147
bonding levels between customer and
    brand, 48, 152
Brady's Clothing for Men, 209
Brady, J., xvii
brand equity/loyalty, xii-xiv, 4-5, 3-21, 9,
    12, 14
    consistency of message vs., 70
    cross-functional planning, 170-189
    drivers of brand value, 15-21, **16**
    equation of brand equity, 10, **10**
    stakeholder relationships, 65
brand identity (*see* also logos—tracking
    brand loyalty—trademarks), 9, 72-73
    integration triangle to create image,
        90-91, **91**
brand positioning (*see* positioning the
    brand)
brand relationships (*see also* customer
    relationships), 3-21, 41-54, 266-267
    accessibility of brand, 47
    affinity or identification with brand,
        48, 152
    bonding levels between customer and
        brand, 48, 152
    committment of company to
        customers, 48
    competition, 42-43
    consistency of brand's quality, 47
    cost of first vs. repeat sales, 43
    cost-per-sale (CPS) measurement, 43
    definition, xi-xvi
    financial links of customer to brand, 47
    getting new customers, 43, 51-52
    keeping old customers, 43
    learning through interactive
        communications, 120-123
    leveraging brand relationships, 43-45, **44**
    lifetime customer value (LTCV), 42,
        50-51
    liking the company, 48, 128, 152
    losing customers, 43
    mass customization of brand
        messages, 112-113
    monitoring relationships, 174-177
    psychological links of customer to
        brand, 47, 103-104
    recognition of customers and
        stakeholders, 115-116
    recourse when needing help, 114-115
    reinforcement of customer/brand
        relationship, 119-120
    reminding customers of benefits, 52-53
    repeat sales, 43
    respect for customers, 117-119
    responsiveness to customer problems,
        47, 116-117, 122-123
    shareholder relationships, 45-48
    social links of customer to brand, 46-47
    structural links of customer to brand, 47
    tracking brand loyalty, 42-45, **44**, 48-
        50, 152, 209-210, 263-264
    trust of customer in brand, 47
    value-added products/services, 42, 52-
        53
breadth of integration, 251
British Railways, 232-233
budget reallocation, 36-37, 178, 237-238
Buffet, W., 63
Bulkeley, W., 124
Burger King, 250
Burke, T., 252, 258
Business Ethics magazine, 131, 135
Business Marketing Association, 257
Byrne, J.A., 66, 191

cable TV as marketing tool, 33-34

Canon, 141, 194-195, 223
Capitol Concierge, 224
Cappo, J., 254
Carl Byoir, 130
Carlzon, J., 98, 124
Carringer, P., 147
Caterpillar, 141
cause marketing, xvi, 17,130-137, 141-144
    limitations, 137-139
    mission vs. cause marketing, 139, **140**
    relevance of the mission, 142-144
    sponsorship/events, 203
Cespedes, F., 38, 174, 190
Champy, J., 190
charitable works (*see* cause marketing)
Charles Schwab Corp., 106
Chrysler Corp., 205
Church & Dwight Co., 142
Citibank, 119
Cleland, K., 42, 230
CNN, 107
Coca-Cola, 34, 56, 73, 81-82, 101-102,
    158
Coe, J., 230
Colgate, 111
Collins, J., 132, 147
Colorado Public Utilities Commission, 6
Commerce Clearing House, 226-227
communications (*see also* media/media
    mix), 9-19, 267
    auditing IM, 273
    "big creative idea" concept, 25-26, 80-
        82, 156-158
    communications system for internal
        use, 186-189
    cross-functional planning, 183-186
    groupware, 186-189
    integrated communications agencies
        (ICAs), 231-258, 240-241
    interactive communication, key
        points, 96-97, 99-104, 114-120
    Internet, 189
    intranets, 186-189
    learning through interactive
        communications, 120-123
    local area networks (LAN), 186-189
    making knowledge available, 25, 36
    one-voice, one-look marketing
        strategy, 25, 80-82,
    online, 186-189
    stakeholder relationships, 57, 64-66
    strengths/weaknesses, 196-206, **198-199**
    zero-based planning, 165, **165**
compensation programs, 36-37, 181-182
competition, 3, 8, 12, 32-33, 42-43, 58,
    60-63, **60**, 72
CompuServe, 109
Computerworld magazine, 225
ConAgra, 130-131
Cone Communications, 137, 138
Cone, C., 138-139
conflict resolution, 179-180
Conrades, G., 32
consistency of message, 15, 17, 47, 69-
    94, 158-161, **159**, 266-267
    auditing, 273-274
    "big creative idea" concept, 80-82,
        156-158
    brand equity, 70
    brand identity, 72-73
    competition, 72
    confusing messages, 75-77
    customer perceptions of
        message/image, 72, 196
    distribution point consistency, 82-83
    employee relationships' importance,
        75-76
    factors affecting consistency, 70-74, **73**

impact of message vs. source, 91-93, **92**
infrastructure: corporate core
    values/mission, **71**, 71-72
integrating stakeholders to achieve
    consistency, 77, 90-91, **91**
logos, trademarks, names, 72-73
maintaining consistency, 70, 75-77, 93
one-voice, one-look marketing
    strategy, 74, 80-82
planned messages, 78-82, 158-161, **159**
planning for strategic consistency, 93
positioning the brand, 73-74
price vs. brand loyalty, 83
product messages, 82-83
quality control, 70, 73
responsiveness to customer problems,
    84-86
service messages, 84-86
sources of brand messages, 77-90
unplanned messages, 86-90, 107
contact points, 33-34, 96-97, 161, **161**,
    236, 241, 275
Continental Bank of Chicago, 237-238
Continental Cablevision, 7
Cooper & Lybrand, xi, 5
Coors Brewing Co., 131
Coors, P., 131
core competencies,190, 192-207
    benefits of core competencies, 206-207
    communication tool
        strengths/weaknesses, 196-206, **198-
        199**
    creating core competencies, 194-206
    customer service, 204-206
    defining core competencies, 192-194
    direct mail marketing, 202-203
    integrated communications agencies
        (ICAs), 250-252
    levels of, 192-193
    mass media advertising, 200-201
    packaging, 203-204
    personal sales, 196-200
    product publicity, 201-202
    sales promotions, 202
    specialists vs. generalists, 206-207
    sponsorship/events, 203
    understanding customer behavior, 195-
        196
Corporate Citizen, 136
corporate structures (see infrastructure)
Corvette, 73
cost cutting vs. brand equity, xiii, 10, 31,
    83
cost per thousand (CPM), 101, 200
Cowles, D., 22
Cranfield School of Management, xiv
Crayola Crayons, 142
Creative Artists Associates, 81
Crest toothpaste, 83
crises management (see media/media
    mix, negative)
Cross, R., 48, 54, 152
cross-functional planning, 18, 169-191,
    267
    brand equity teams, 170-189
    budget reallocations, 178
    charting cross-functional, **171**
    communications system for internal
        use, 186-189
    communications team, 183-186
    compensation programs, 181-182
    conflict resolution, 179-180
    integrated communications agencies
        (ICAs), 238-239
    monitoring relationships, 174-177
    opening corporate culture to change, 180
    organizational dimensions of integrated
        marketing (IM), 189-190
    planning across divisions, 176-179
    responsibilities of brand equity team,
        174-180

support for cross-function teams, 179-
    189
top-down integration movement, 182-
    183
Cuneo, A.Z., 258
customer relationships (see also brand
    relationships & stakeholder
    relationships), xii-xv, 3-21, 204-206, 26
    accessibility of brand, 47
    affinity or identification with brand, 48,
        152
    automation of sales force, 187, 224-225
    bonding levels between customer and
        brand, 48, 152
    commerical message "overload," 34
    committment of company to customers,
        48, 152
    consistency of message, 47, 72, 196
    contact points, finding new outlets, 33-
        34, 96-99
    database marketing, customer-accessed,
        213-214
    financial links of customer to brand, 47
    geographical information systems
        (GIS), 226
    getting new customers, 43, 51-52, 102,
        217-219, 223-224
    interactivity, 95-125
    keeping old customers, 43, 102, 224
    learning through interactive
        communications, 120-123
    lifetime customer value (LTCV), 50-51,
        263
    liking the company, 48, 128, 152
    losing customers, 43
    mass customization of brand messages,
        112-113
    monitoring relationships, 174-177, 274-
        275
    negative news stories, minimizing
        damage, 33, 86-90, 107
    overlap of stakeholder influence, 60-63,
        60
    perception of product/message, 72, 196
    personalizing the advertising message, 31
    price vs. brand loyalty, 31, 83
    profile of modern consumer, 126-127
    psychological links of customer to
        brand, 47, 103-104
    re-integrating the customer, 25
    recognition of customers and
        stakeholders, 115-116
    reinforcement of customer/brand
        relationship, 119-120
    reminding customers of benefits, 52-53
    repeat sales, 43
    resistance to commercial message,
        breaking barriers, 34-35
    respect for customers, 117-119
    responsiveness to customer problems,
        47, 84-86, 96-97, 114-115, 116-117,
        122-123, 204-206, 219
    social links of customer to brand, 46-47
    structural links of customer to brand, 47
    switching brands, decreasing the risk, 33
    SWOT analysis, 151-152, **151**
    targeting customers, 223-224, 226
    too many products, too many brands,
        32-33
    tracking brand loyalty, 42-45, **44**, 48-
        50, 162, 209-210, 263-264
    trust of customer in brand, 47
    understanding customer behavior, 195-
        196
    value-added products/services, 52-53

Dalton Books, 142
data mining, 225-226
database marketing, xiv-xv, 19, 110-111,
    118, 120-121, 160, 208-230, 267
    access to the database, 212-213

accuracy of information, 213
analyzing the data, 212, 223-224, 225-
    226, 227-228
applications for databases, 214-228
auditing performance, 208
automation of sales force, 224-225
building and using databases, 216-
    217, **216**, 220-222
checklist of database applications,
    226-228
collecting data, 211-212, 220-222
continuous feedback loop, 113
customer database building, 220-222
customer service improvements, 219
customer-access databases, 213-214
data mining, 225-226
geographical information systems
    (GIS), 226
getting new customers, 219, 223-224
information systems (IS) and
    databases, 210-211
integrated communications agencies
    (ICAs), 237
keeping old customers, 224
learning through interactive
    communications, 120-123
managing the database, 212
mass customization of brand
    messages, 112-113
privacy of data, 228-229
prospecting for new customers, 217-
    218
resource databases, 213-214
security, 213, 228-229
setting up the database, 210-214
storing the data, 211-212,
targeting customers, 219, 223-224, 226
tracking brand loyalty, 209-210
transactional vs. relationship
    applications, 215-216
uses of database information, 212
what information is needed?, 211-212
Davidow, W., 54
Davis, I., xvii
Davis, S., 98, 250
DDB Needham, 243
Deighton, J., 166
Dejong, J., 230
Dentsu, 194
depth of integration, 251
Desert Rose Foods, 106
DiMaggio, Joe, 80
Direct Line Insurance Co., 45
DIRECT magazine, 51
direct mail marketing (see also
    addressable media— database
    marketing), 110-111, 117-118, 160,
    202-203
Direct Marketing Research Associates,
    117
dis-integrated marketing, 29-30, 35-36
Disney Co., 71, 141, 142, 174
Disney, W., 145
distribution points, consistency, 82-83
DMB&B, 233
Domino's Pizza, 112-113
Donna Karan International, 4
Donnelley Marketing, 111
Downs, C.W., 279
downsizing (see cost cutting)
drivers of brand value, 15-21, **16**
Drucker, P., 8
DuPont, 179, 262

Earl, M., xvii
Eastman Kodak, 133
Eckrich & Sons, 204
Edward D. Jones Brokerage Co., 45-46
Eichenwalk, K., 54
Eisner, M., 141, 174
Emerson, J., 230

employees (*see also* stakeholder
    relationships)
  auditing performance, 274-275
  consistency of message important,
      75-76
  disgruntled employees, whistle-
      blowers, 86-90
  disregarding stakeholder
      relationships, Ford example, 61-62
  integrating employees, 24-25, 45-46
  morale building, 45-46
  overlap of stakeholder influence, 60-
      63, **60**
  perceptions of employees, 64-66
  responsiveness to customer problems,
      84-86
  sales personnel, 196-200
  stakeholder role, 58
Engel, S., 258
Engels, M., 232, 258, 251-252
Engels, T., 253
Ennis, T., 179
Eppes, T., 258
everyday low price (EDLP) strategy, 83
Express, 139
Exxon, 144, 249

Fallon McElligott, 100, 237-238
FCB, 232, 244, 251-252, 253,
    255
FedEx, 113, 189
feedback loop, database marketing, 113
financial analysts/financial press as
    stakeholders, 57
financial links of customer to brand, 47
Finegold, D., 230
Fitzgerald, J., 231, 258
Fizdale, R., 124
Food Lion, 8
Ford Motor Co., 61-62, 73, 109, 132, 248
Ford, H., 145
Forrester Research, 189
Fortini-Campbell, L., 66
Fortune magazine, 128, 175, 180
Frank, R., 66
Freedom Forum, 87

Gaines, S., 147
Gates, B., 145, 174
Geertz, Guy, 232
General Electric, 173, 206
General Motors, 20, 171, 173, 180, 183,
    244-245
geographical information systems
    (GIS), 226
Georgescu, P., 242
Gillette, 185
Gimini Consultants, 176
global marketplace, 3
Goizueta, Roberto, 56
Gold, Christina, 45
Goldstein, M., 100
Gordon, V., 191
Gore, B., 179
Gore-tex, 179
Gouillart, F., 176
government regulators as stakeholders, 58
Greco, S., 230
Green Giant, 80
Green, M., 54, 117
Greising, D., 124
Gronstedt, A., 38, 190, 191
groupware, 186-189
Groves, J., 134
GTE, 109-110
Guarscio, P., 244
Gummesson, E., 12, 22

Habitat for Humanity, 143
Haggerty, M., 87, 94
Hal Riney Agency, 248
Hallberg, G., 42, 53
Hallmark Cards, 132, 170
Hamel, G., 191, 192
Hammer, M., 190
Hannah Andersson, 133

Hanover Insurance, 269
Harper, M., 130-131
Harrah's Entertainment, 172
Harvard Business Review, 72
Harvard University, 174
Haskett, J., 66
Healthy Choice dinners, 131
Hebert, J., 279
Heinz, 143
Hertz, 116
Hesket, 56
Hewlett-Packard, 71, 74, 132, 142
Hill & Knowlton, 130
Homan, G.R., 190
Howe, R.M., 212
Hughes, A.M., 54
Hunter, V., 124
Hwang, S., 54

IAA World Congress of Advertising, 231
IBM, 20, 32, 51, 64, 89, 114, 141, 174,
    184, 190, 212
image as product, 4-5, 130-133, 157
  consistency of message, 69-94
  image linked by association, 35
  integration triangle to create image, 90-
      91, **91**
  integrity of product/services, 37
  mass media advertising, 35
Incredible Universe, The, 75
information systems (IS) and databases,
    210-211
infrastructure, xvi, 15
  budget reallocation, 36-37, 178
  communications teams, 183-186
  compensation programs, 36-37, 181-182
  conflict resolution, 179-180
  consistency of message and
      infrastructure, **71**, 71-72
  core competencies, 71-72, 190, 192-207
  cross-functional planning/monitoring,
      18, 169-191
  database marketing, 208-230
  integrated communications agencies
      (ICAs), 238-239
  knowledge availability, 25, 36
  leadership of integration process, 252-
      253
  media mix, 18
  mission marketing, 26, 130-133
  opening corporate culture to change, 180
  planning across divisions, 176-179
  support systems, 179-189
  top-down integration movement, 182-
      183
integrated communications agencies
    (ICAs), 231-258
  agency networks, 242-243
  benefits of using ICA, 255-258
  budget reallocation, 237-238
  communications systems, 240-241
  contact points analysis, 236, 241
  core competencies, 250-252
  cross-functional planning, 238-239
  database marketing, 238-239
  drawbacks of using ICA, 255-258
  fees and compensation for ICA, 238,
      253-255
  finding the right agency, 233-243
  infrastructure of agency, 238-239
  integration strategies of agency, 234-235
  leadership of integration process, 252-
      253
  media/media mix, 237
  mission marketing, 241-242
  model for ICA performance, 243-253
  practicing integration, 235-238
  Price/McNabb model for ICA, 246-247
  responsibility of agency for client, 235
  routine vs. specialist tasks, 248-250
  support systems, 240-241
  training programs, 238-239
integration triangle to create image, 90-
    91, **91**

integrity of product/services, 37
Intel, 107
interactive media, 15, 17, 95-125
  addressable media, 110-111
  barriers to interactivity, 96
  communications, 114-120
  contact points, finding new outlets,
      96-99
  customer-access databases, 213-214
  database marketing, 110-111, 120-
      121, 160
  direct mail advertising, 110-111, 160
  interactive media, 104-110, 160
  Internet as marketing tool, 100, 104-
      110, 160
  Johnson & Johnson Acuvue
      campaign, 162-164, **163**
  learning through interactive
      communications, 120-123
  mass customization of brand
      messages, 112-113
  media mix, 102-104, **103**
  negative news stories, minimizing
      damage, 107
  purposeful interactivity, 123-124
  quality control of interactive media, 110
  recognition of customers and
      stakeholders, 115-116
  recourse when needing help, 114-115
  reinforcement of customer/brand
      relationship, 119-120
  respect for customers, 117-119
  responsiveness to customer problems,
      96-97, 116-117, 122-123
  toll free telephone numbers, 104-105
  value-added interactivity, 99-104
Interbrand, 130
International Events Group Sponsorship
    Report, 138-139
Internet as marketing tool, 33-34, 89,
    100, 104-110, 160
Internet communications, 189
intranets, 186-189
investors as stakeholders, 57, 60-63, **60**
ISO 9000 audits, 262
Isuzu, 79

J. Walter Thompson, 98, 130
Jackson, D., 22
Jackson, P., 146
Jacob, R., 53, 124, 190
Jaguar, 20
Jane's Cosmetics Co., 106
Jobs, S., 141
Johnson & Johnson, 162-164, **163**
Johnson, B., 22
Jordan, M., 153
just-in-time delivery, 5
JWT, 250

K-Mart, 83
Kano, N., 123
keiretsu relationship of
    suppliers/producers, 57
Kelleher, H., 133, 141, 145
Kellogg, 81, 171
Keltner, B., 230
Ketchum Interactive, 106, 155
KeyCorp, 226
Khermouch, G., 166
Kim, B.O., 22
Kimberly-Clark, 171
King, J., 21
Kirk, D., 124
Knight, P., 141, 174
Kochar, M., 258
Komatsu Co., 141
Koprowski, G., 124
Koselka, R., 279
Kotter, J., 56, 66
Kraft, 4, 171, 172, 210
Kurschner, D., 147
Kuttner, R., 147

L.L. Bean, 202
Labich, K., 191

Lamons, B., 257, 258
Lands End, 202
Lauterborn, R., 151, 166
Lavely, T., 249-250
leads to new customers, 217-218
Leo Burnett, 233, 244, 252
Lettuce Entertain You Restaurants, 75
Levi Strauss & Co., 212
Levin, G., 230
lifetime customer value (LTCV), 42, 50-51, 263
Limited, Inc., 139
Lintas, 252
local area networks (LAN), 186-189
logos, 9, 72-73
long-term planning, 142
Lotus/Lotus Notes, 187, 188-189
loyalty of customer (*see* brand equity)
Lucas, R., 129
Luckow, D., 230

Magrath, A.J., 124, 166
Malone, J., 99-100
Malone, M., 54
Marchetti, K., 230
Margulis, L., 245
Market Research Corporation of America (MRCA), 42, 44
marketing departments, traditional, xi-xv, 5-9, 18-21, **19**, 33, 35, 78
Marketing News magazine, 257
Marlboro, 53, 73, 80-81, 177
Marriott, 141
mass customization of brand messages, 112-113
Maxwell, H., 4
McCann Erikson, 231
McCaw Cellular Communications, 4-5
McDonald's, 71, 74, 105, 131, 136
MCI, 7, 148
McKenna, R., 53, 54, 191
McKinsey report, xi
McManus, J., 191
measuring performance (*see* auditing IM)
Media Research Center, Freedom Forum, 87
media/media mix, xvi, 18, 99-104, 161-165, **161**, 196-206
addressable media, 110-111, 160
"big creative idea" concept, 25-26, 80-82, 156-158
commerical message "overload," 34
confusing messages, 75-77
consistency of message, 15, 69-94
contact points, finding new outlets, 33-34, 96-99
cost per thousand (CPM), 101, 200
database marketing, 110-111, 160
determining the mix, 102-104, **103**
direct mail advertising, 110-111, 160, 202-203
dis-integrated message problems, 29-30
image linked by association, 35
impact of message vs. source, 91-93, **92**
integrated communications agencies (ICAs), 237
interactive media, 104-110, 160
Internet as marketing tool, 33-34, 89, 100, 104-110, 160
mass customization of brand messages, 112-113
mass media advertising, 35, 200-201
negative news stories, minimizing damage, 33, 86-90, 107
niche media, 200
one-voice, one-look marketing strategy, xiii-xiv, 25, 74, 80-82
overlap of stakeholder influence, 60-63, **60**
packaging, 203-204
personal sales, 196-200
personalizing the advertising message, 31
planned message consistency, 78-82, 158-161, **159**

PR events, 157
price vs. brand loyalty, 31, 83
product message consistency, 82-83
product publicity, 201-202
resistance to commercial message, breaking barriers, 34-35
sales promotions, 202
service message consistency, 84-86
sponsorship/events, 203
stakeholder role of media, 58, 86-90
strengths/weaknesses, relative, 196-206, **198-199**
switching brands, decreasing the risk, 33
toll free telephone numbers, 104-105, 160
too many products, too many brands, 32-33
Merck, 37, 135, 142
Meredith Direct, 23
Meridian, 219
Mervyn's Department Stores, 122
Metropolitan Life Insurance Co., 169-170
Microsoft, 14, 109, 174
Miller Brewing Co., 139
Mirage Resorts, 248
mission marketing, xvi, 15, 17, 26, 126-147
benefits of mission marketing, 128-130
cause marketing, 130-137, 139, **140**
communicating the mission, 144-145
corporate mission's role in IM, 130-133
criteria of mission marketing, 140-145
defining mission marketing, 127
establishing mission marketing, 145-146
executive committees, 146
focusing the mission, 140-141
institutionalization and staffing, 145
integrated communications agencies (ICAs), 241-242
limits of cause marketing, 137-139
long-term planning, 142
management involvement, 146
managing mission marketing, 145-146
measuring mission contribution, 145-146
pervasiveness of mission, 141-142, 146
relevance of the mission, 142-144
Mitchel, Helen, xiv
Montblanc, 36, 73, 83
Moore, J., 12
Moore, R.J., 124
Moors/Bloomsbury, 232
Morgan, B., 172, 190
Motorola Co., 64
Mottram, S., 130
Mr. Coffee, 80
multi-tiered branding, 20
Murphy, Bill, 23

Naylor, M., 224
NEC Corporation, 184, 216-217
Newell, F., 124, 230
niche media, 200
Nieman Marcus, 82, 116
Nike, 71, 132, 153, 174, 185, 229, 253
Normann, R., 12, 22
Norris, F., 21
Northern Telecom, 219
Northwestern University, xiv

O'Brien, B., 269
Odwalla, 83
Ogilvy & Mather, xiv, 130, 184, 241, 242
Old Milwaukee Beer, 248
Oldsmobile, 78-79
Olympics promotions, 249
Omnicom, 185
one-voice, one-look marketing strategy, xiii-xiv, 25-26, 74, 80-82
online communications (*see* Internet as marketing tool)
opportunities, SWOT analysis, 149

Orchestration project, Ogilvy & Mather, 242
organizational structures (*see* infrastructure)
Owens Corning, 143

Pacheco, A.M., 191
packaging, 203-204
Paine Webber, 208-209
Paradyne, 180
Parker-Pope, T., 66
pay scales (*see* compensation programs)
PepsiCo., 69-70, 80, 92
personal sales, 196-200
personalizing the advertising message, 31
Peters, T., 30, 38
Petersen, D., 132
Petsmart, 143
philanthropic activities (*see* charitable work)
Philip Morris, 4
Pillsbury, 171
planning (*see* cross-functional planning; zero-based planning)
Plummer, J., 233
Poe, S., 134, 141
Polk's Lifestyle Selector, 214
Porras, J., 132, 147
Porter Novelli, 185
positioning the brand, 25, 73-74
Power Express, 106
Prahalad, C.K., 191, 192, 207
Preston, J., 134
price vs. brand loyalty, 31, 83
Price/McNabb model for ICA, 246-247
prioritized SWOTs, 148, 153-155, **154**, 155-158, **156**, 165
privacy issues in database marketing, 228-229
Procter & Gamble, 102-103
Prodigy, 109
productivity, xiii, 5, 6, 30-31
profitability, 55-56, 57-60, 65-66, 263
Promo magazine, 137
promotional events, 202
Prudential Securities, 46
psychological links of customer to brand, 47, 103-104
publicity, product publicity, 201-202

Quaker Oats, 171
quality control, 5, 23-24, 36, 70, 73, 110, 171-172, 190, 262
questionnaires for audit, 271-273
Quinn, J.B., 230

Radio Shack, 85
Ramirez, R., 12, 22
Rapp and Collins, 185
Rasmussen, W., 87, 94
re-integration of marketing function, 8-10, 20-21, 23-28
Avon example, 45
barriers to integrated marketing (IM), 26, 29-30
"big creative idea" concept, 25-26
brand positioning, 25
commerical message "overload," 34
competition, 32-33
consistency of message and stakeholder integration, 77
contact points, finding new outlets, 33-34, 96-99
corporate mission, 26
customer integration, 25
Edward D. Jones Brokerage Co. example, 45-46
employee integration, 24-25
examples of dis-integrated marketing, 29-30, 35-36
integration triangle to create image, 90-91, **91**
integrity of product/services, 37
interactivity, 96-97
knowledge availability, 25, 36
linking other departments to marketing, 33

re-integration of marketing function (continued)
 local and global brands, 37
 mass media appeal decline, 35
 negative news stories, minimizing damage, 33
 one-voice, one-look marketing strategy, 25
 personalizing the advertising message, 31
 price vs. brand loyalty, 31
 resistance to commercial message, breaking barriers, 34-35
 shareholder relationships, 25, 45-48, 63-65
 suboptimization problems, 35-36
 switching brands, decreasing the risk, 33
 too many products, too many brands, 32-33
Readers' Digest, 210
recency indexes, 263-264
Recreation Equipment Inc. (REI), 141-142
reengineering, 23-24
referral indexes, 264
Reich, R., 134
Reichheld, F., 53, 54
Reichheld, R., 44
relationship analysis, 148, 152-158, 174-177, 262-264
resistance to commercial message, 34-35
respect for customers, 117-119
responsiveness to customer problems, 47, 84-86, 96-97, 114-115, 116-117, 122-123, 204-206, 219
rewards (see compensation programs)
Rielly, J., 191
Rigdon, J.E., 124
right-sizing (see cost cutting)
Robert Mondavi Winery, 155
Robert, M., 66
Rockhart, J., xvii
Roddick, A., 134-135, 141
Rogaine, 201
Rolex, 83
Ronald McDonald House, 131, 136
Roper Starch Worldwide, 126, 137, 138
ROSE Foundation, 134
Ross, J., xvii
Royal, W., 190
Russell, C.A., 207
Ryka Inc., 134

Saatchi & Saatchi, 208-209, 227, 229, 230, 252, 258, 262, 265
Sagan, C., 126
Sager, I., 230
Saks, 82
Sales and Marketing Strategy News, 130
sales personnel, 196-200
sales promotions, 202
San Diego Padres, 112
San Jose Mercury News, 205
Santoro, P.J., 212
Saturn Car Company, 13-14, 42, 248
Scandinavian Airlines, 98
Schultz, D., 166
Seagram, 212-213
Sealey, P., 34, 81, 94
Sears, 20, 116
security in database marketing, 228-229
Senge, P.M., 36, 38, 141, 191, 279
Senior Network, 98
Serafin, R., 258
service vs. product, 3
Seth, J., 21
Seven-Eleven stores, 98
Shannon, D., 147
Sharp-Paine, L., 94
Singer, I., 38
Sisodia, R., 21
situational analysis (see SWOT)
SMH Inc., 73

Smith, C., 136, 147
Smith, G., 147
Smith, R., 180
social causes (see cause marketing)
Social Investment Forum, 128
social links of customer to brand, 46-47
Sorrell, M., 130, 231
Southern California Edison, 173
Southwest Airlines, 90-91, 133, 141
Spark, B., 170
Special Olympics, 139
specialists vs. generalists, 206-207
Spethmann, B., 207
Spiegel, 202
sponsorship/events, 203
Sridhar, R., xiv
stakeholder relationships, xi-xv, 3-21, 45-48, 55-60, 266-267
 benefits of good stakeholder relationships, 56
 building the relationship, 62-63
 communications' importance, 57, 64-66
 competitors as stakeholders, 58
 consistency of message, integration, 77
 customers as stakeholders, 58
 disregarding stakeholder relationships, Ford example, 61
 employees as stakeholders, 58
 financial analysts/financial press as stakeholders, 57
 franchise of stakeholders, 55
 government regulators as stakeholders, 58
 investors as stakeholders, 57
 keiretsu relationship of suppliers/producers, 57
 media as stakeholders, 58, 86-90
 monitoring relationships, 174-177, 274
 overlap of stakeholder influence, 60-63, 60
 perceptions of stakeholders, 64-66
 profitability vs., 55-56, 57-60, 65-66
 re-integrating the stakeholder, 25
 recognition of customers and stakeholders, 115-116
 relative importance of different stakeholders, 59-60, 63
 Standard & Poors index as stakeholder, 57
 suppliers as stakeholders, 57
 value field integration, 63-64
Standard & Poors index as stakeholder, 57
standardization of product/services, 42
Stanford University, 10
Stodghill, R., 147
strategic planning (see cross-functional planning)
strengths, SWOT analysis, 150
Stroh's Brewing Co., 248
structural links of customer to brand, 47
suboptimization problems, 35-36
Suchecki, M., 191
suppliers as stakeholders, 57, 60-63, 60
support systems, 240-241
Swatch watches example of consistency of message, 73
Swift, 204
switching brands, decreasing the risk, 33
SWOT analysis, xvi, 18, 148, 149-152
 customer-focused SWOT analysis, 151-152, 151
 external factors, 149-150
 internal factors, 150-152
 opportunities, 149
 prioritized SWOTs, 153-155, 154, 155-158, 156, 165
 strengths, 150
 threats, 150
 weaknesses, 150
2 Market Corp., 111
3M Corporation, 98-99
Tandy, 20

Tannenbaum, S., 166
Target, 83
targeting customers, 219, 223-224, 226
Taylor, W., 94
TCI, 99-100
Thorson, E., 38, 191
threats, SWOT analysis, 150
Toffler, A., 3, 21
toll free telephone numbers, 104-105, 160
Tom's of Maine, 133
Total Communications Audit tool, 265
total quality management (TQM), 5, 23-24, 36, 70, 73, 110, 190, 262
Toyota, 205
tracking brand loyalty, 42-45, 44, 48-50, 72-73, 152, 209-210, 263-264
traditional marketing (see marketing departments, traditional)
training programs, 8, 238-239
Treacy, M., 230
trust of customer in brand, 47
TRW, 228-229
Tucker Chicago, 215
Tylenol, 249

Ukman, L., 138-139
Ukrop Food Stores Co., 6-8, 84, 155
United Airlines, 80
University of Colorado, xiv, 264-265
Upshaw, L., 106
US West, 6-8, 97, 155

value field vs. value chain, xi, 11-15, 11, 13, 63-64
value-added products/services, 12, 42, 52-53, 99-104
Wacker, W., 38, 126, 146, 207
wages (see compensation programs)
Wal-Mart, 83, 92
Wall Street Journal, 205
Ward, A., 279
Watson, G.H., 125, 279
Watson, T., 145, 174
Watzlawick, P., 10, 22
weaknesses, SWOT analysis, 150
Web sites (see Internet as marketing tool)
Webster, F.E., 38, 125
Weyerhaeuser, 175
Wheaties cereal, 215
White, Mike, 243
Whole Egg project, Young & Rubicam, 242
Wiersema, F., 230
Williams, T., 21
Windows 95 marketing example, 14
Winfrey, O., 134
Winthrop, L., 233
Women in Community Service, 139
World Congress of Advertising, 231
World Wide Web (see Internet as marketing tool)
WPP Co., 130, 231
Wylie, K., 54

Xerox, 141, 194

Yafie, R.C., 147
Yankelovich Partners, 93, 126, 128
Young & Rubicam, 85, 233, 242
Young, J., 132

zero-based planning, xvi, 15, 18, 148-166
 communication planning, 165, 165
 complexity management, 165-166
 consistency of message, 158-161, 159
 contact points, 161, 161
 integrating messages, 149, 158-161, 159
 Johnson & Johnson Acuvue campaign, 162-164, 163
 media/media mix integration, 161-165, 161
 prioritized SWOTs, 153-155, 154, 155-158, 156, 165
 relationship analysis, 148, 152-158
 SWOT analysis, 148, 149-152, 165